Graphis Titles

Poster Annual 2010

Advertising Annual 2010

New Talent Annual 2010

Annual Reports 2010

Promotion Design 2

Brochures 6

12 Japanese Masters

Logo 7

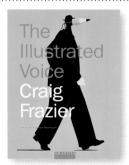
The Illustrated Voice

Letterhead 7

Nudes 4

Nudes 3

Photography Annual 2010

Dana Buckley: Fifty

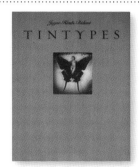
Tintypes

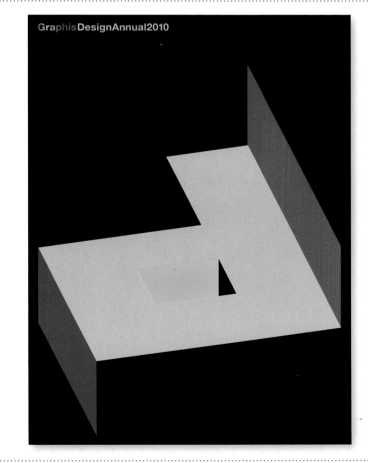

It's green!

It does 0-60 mph
in 3.7 seconds!

No gas, no oil,
& it's beautiful!

Michael Deas: The man behind the Columbia Lady

Michael Deas is a tiger at pursuing
whatever is required to breathe life into
his assignments.

Michael works harder at his art now
than he did when I first met him 20 years
ago... He has always been generous
with his praise for colleagues and stingy
with criticism.

GRAPHIS DESIGN JOURNAL: THE AMERICAS

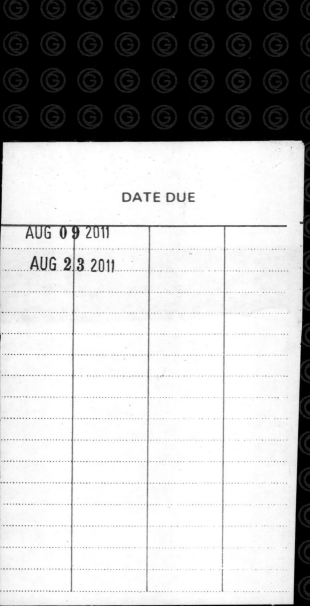

DATE DUE

AUG 09 2011		
AUG 23 2011		

Graphis Inc. is committed to presenting exceptional work in international Design, Advertising, Illustration & Photography.

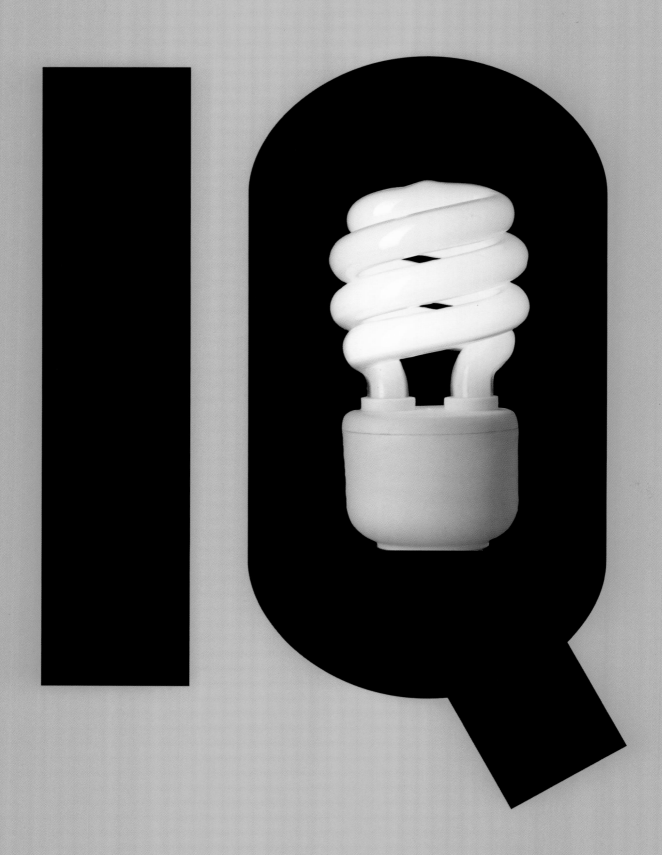

Published by **Graphis** | Publisher & Creative Director: **B. Martin Pedersen** | Design: **Yon Joo Choi and Gregory Michael Cerrato** | Editorial: **Abigail Lapp and Leah Michele Hansen** | Production: **Jennifer R. Berlingeri and Abigail Lapp** | Webmaster: **Abigail Lapp** | Support Staff: **Rita Jones** | Editorial Intern: **Amy L. Bergen** | Design & Production Interns: **Dana Davis, Diana Lau, Gloria Pak, Elisa Penello and Mariana Uchoa Santa Cruz**

Remarks: We extend our heartfelt thanks to contributors throughout the world who have made it possible to publish a wide and international spectrum of the best work in this field. Entry instructions for all Graphis Books may be requested from: Graphis Inc., 307 Fifth Avenue, Tenth Floor, New York, New York 10016, or visit our web site at www.graphis.com.

Anmerkungen: Unser Dank gilt den Einsendern aus aller Welt, die es uns ermöglicht haben, ein breites, internationales Spektrum der besten Arbeiten zu veröffentlichen. Teilnahmebedingungen für die Graphis-Bücher sind erhältlich bei: Graphis, Inc., 307 Fifth Avenue, Tenth Floor, New York, New York 10016. Besuchen Sie uns im World Wide Web, www.graphis.com.

Remerciements: Nous remercions les participants du monde entier qui ont rendu possible la publication de cet ouvrage offrant un panorama complet des meilleurs travaux. Les modalités d'inscription peuvent être obtenues auprès de: Graphis, Inc., 307 Fifth Avenue, Tenth Floor, New York, New York 10016. Rendez-nous visite sur notre site web: www.graphis.com.

Times
ARE Tough.

Prices
ARE Rising.

Values
ARE Falling.

Contents

Graphis Platinum, Gold & Silver Award Winners by Location

Pages 7, 23, 73, 159, 232: Award photograph by Henry Leutwyler

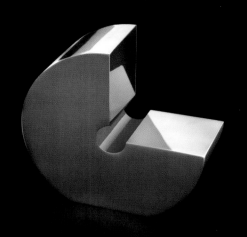

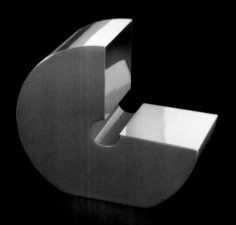

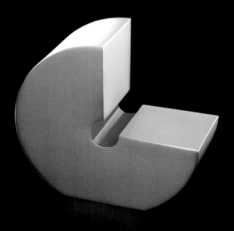

Publisher'sLetter

Dear Reader,

With the world economy still staggering, the design, advertising and photography professions have been the first to be affected. Clients are unable to, or don't want to be seen, spending a lot of money. Thus, for designers, producing a good product and maintaining your competitive edge within the industry have become more difficult.

One opportunity that allows design firms to earn more money while keeping a client's costs down is AR2.0, or digital/online Annual Reports. You can gain additional income by adding this service to the printed version of a Report, while still saving the client money on the overall project because the print run can possibly be significantly reduced. If you have not ventured into this technology, I have presented two firms, INC Design and Savage, which have successfully executed this platform for their clients, and I hope there are some helpful revelations to assist you. Next year, Graphis will be accepting this version online in our CFE's.

We're also featuring design legend Michael Weymouth on the state of Annual Reports today, and why they're necessary even during a down economy. To demonstrate that the competitive spirit is alive and well in Annual Report design, this edition of the Annual presents the 100 best Reports of the past year. Ten Reports were selected to receive the Graphis Platinum Award, 18 were awarded a Gold Award and a Silver Award was granted to 72 winners, a Graphis first. The Silver Award will now repeat each year. Q&A's and detailed descriptions are partnered with each winning entry, to really get at the heart of how the winners have achieved their successes.

B. Martin Pedersen
Graphis CEO & Creative Director

Commonly referred to as the "father" of the modern corporate annual report, Robert Miles Runyan forever changed the face of annual report design with his 1971 assignment for defense contractor Litton Industries. This was the first report to break away from the dry and formulaic financial documents that had until then been the norm. Runyan passed away in August 2001, but his legacy lives on in every Annual Report designed since. He is, in every sense of the word, a Legend. The following article and biography originally appeared in Graphis International Journal issue 236, 1985.

Robert Miles Runyan navigates the challenging, sometimes frustrating world of graphic communications with the skill and tenacity of a Formula One driver. And after thirty-three years at the wheel of his internationally acclaimed Los Angeles-based design organization, he is racing full-throttle in what he calls his 'flat-out pursuit of excellence.' Fuelled by a fiercely competitive spirit and conviction that even the most mundane setting can be powerfully portrayed through photography, type and dramatic design, Runyan continues to triumph in judgings by his peers. At the latest Mead Annual Report Show, Robert Miles Runyan & Associates dominated with four winners.

Yet Runyan—who specializes in corporate identification programmes—believes his highest achievement is now recognizable worldwide. In the early 1980s he was commissioned to design what would become the 'logo' for the 1984 Olympic Games in Los Angeles. After 2000 to 2500 sketches he responded with the action graphic 'Stars in Motion'—the official symbol of the XXIII Olympiad. Runyan terms the Olypmic commission the 'greatest assignment any designer in the world can have.' Another graphic, designed for the 17th International Design Conference in Aspen, now hangs in the permanent poster collection of the Museum of Modern Art in New York.

A rugged, rangy 60-year-old who wears tailored Western clothes, cowboy boots and barks orders to a staff of fourteen, Runyan, nevertheless, is not an egotist running wild. He does not grab the spotlight; he shines it on his staff. 'We stay on top, but I'm not saying it's my genius or creativity that does it,' he says. "I give my guys most of the credit. I give myself the credit for picking, almost flawlessly, very strong graphics people who also understand marketing. We have drawers full of awards, but the real reward is the ability to create graphic communications that help our clients achieve their marketing objectives.'

Runyan refers to his 55000 square-fooot office in and adobe-styled sixty-year-old building, a block from the Playa del Rey beach, as 'the university'. He is also quite proud of the 'thirty-five or so competitors we've spawned over the years.' All the graduates, he says, have been subjected to the same philosophy. 'I try to give a guy his head and let him think out the solution. I encourage him, but I put no time limit on a job and I don't let up until the job is answered. 'He serves as the firm's creative director; Jim Berte functions as the design director.

Bob Runyan's work-style and life-style seemed merged. His office resembles a museum of European and American antiques. Two gasoline pumps, circa 1930, tower opposite the sofa and glass coffee-table that functions as his desk. A vintage gold-finished cash register sits on the floor. Scattered about are hundreds of miniature automobiles, a set of timbales, Mucha enamels, Altoons, Ellwoods and Gallos. A hearty 'meal' of sculptured steak, potatoes, pie a la mode, and a glass of wine have been on the same table for years.

His home mirrors his office. He took a boring one-storey stucco bungalow, a block off the sand at Manhattan Beach, and redesigned it to an ornately detailed two-storey Victoria home—with a rooftop deck for entertaining. It houses sixteen more gleaming gas-pumps and is full of artistic and architectural antiques accumulated in a lifetime of searching. The intertwining of his life and work produces unforgettable dividends, he insists. A retrospective of his work at the Axis gallery in Tokyo led to guest lecturing in Japan and a hard-cover book entitled State of the Art of Robert Miles Runyan. A corporate identity assignment for Universal Oil Product's Shadow Formula One racing team whisked him around the global racing circuit. For the self-described 'racing freak' and exotic car collector, 'it was a hellluva thrill.' Yet Robert Miles Runyan maintains his exhiliration isn't foud in an automobile's performance or the cheque that comes after a job is shipped. 'The pay-off in this business isn't the money. In the fifth dimension—the world of the creative, the choreographesrs, writers, painters, sculptors—the pay-off is aesthetic excellence. Sounds corny, but I do it for the sheer love of it.'

Robert Miles Runyan was born in Nebraska in 1925 and studied at the Art Center College of Design. His career really began with the design of annual reports (see Graphis Annual Reports, a book published in 1971). Through his innovative use of photography and strong visuals he found a new approach to annual reporting and ever more companies were motivated to turn to him with their design problems. Now, with a large prestigious clientele, his California-based design group covers annual reports, logos, sales brochures and corporate identity programmes. The group achieved the ultimate when it had its design 'Stars in Motion' chosen as the official emblem for the 1984 Olympics. For the designer's recent Japanese exhibition—a twenty-five year retrospective of his creations—a book entitled State of the Art of Robert Miles Runyan was published by the Obunsha Company of Tokyo. Our text is authored by Chris Barnett, one of the leading journalists on the West Coast, and who is familiar with the work of Robert Miles Runyan.

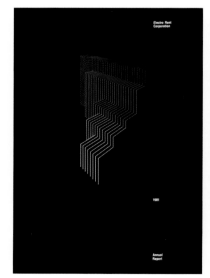
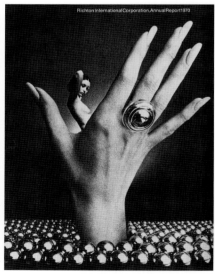

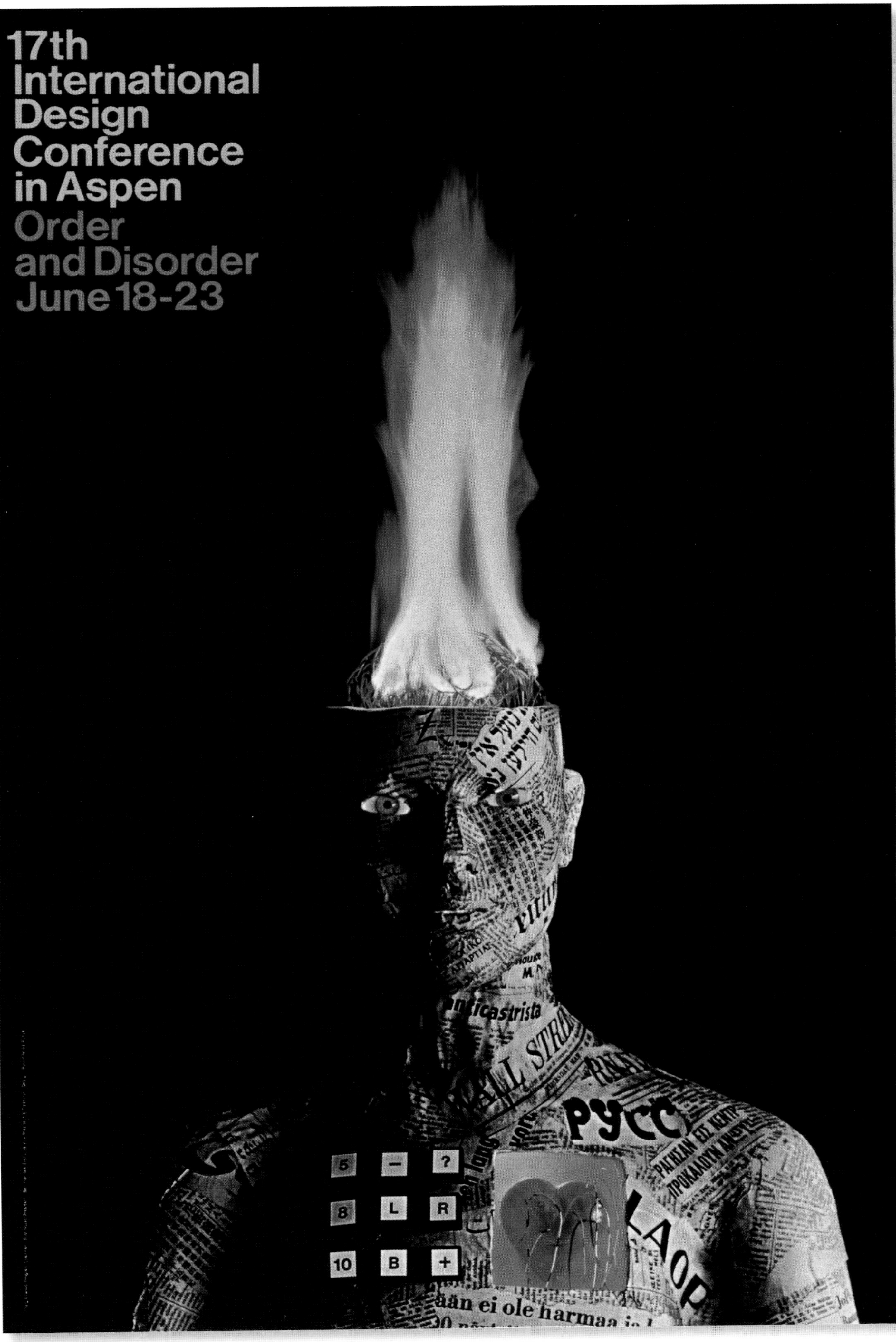

17th
International
Design
Conference
in Aspen
Order
and Disorder
June 18-23

At the 2008 NIRI conference in San Diego, a suggestion was made in one of the meetings that graphs and diagrams be added to the Management Discussion section of the Form 10K in order for the information to be more easily understood. It was a sign of the times that the suggestion was made by a person who was new to investor relations and had only known the state of the annual report/Form 10K business as it had existed for the past few years. What the person was asking for was exactly the purpose of the traditional corporate annual report: to distill information from the SEC-required jargon in the Form 10K and make it more accessible to the shareholder. Only those of us who have participated in the evolution of the contemporary annual report could appreciate the irony. It may come as a surprise to most people in our business, that the annual report, as we have known it all these years, has never been a required document by the SEC. Even though it undergoes extreme scrutiny by the company financial and legal departments, it is merely an attempt to create a more accessible snapshot of the year that the lengthy Form 10K does not provide. Granted, that snapshot conveys a number of subtle messages the Form 10 K is unable to convey: a former savvy client once pointed out that the annual report message begins the moment the recipient hefts the envelope in which it comes. And, while the language is carefully vetted to avoid forecasts, the reader can hardly avoid inferring certain things, most notably in the context of "past as prologue:" recounting a company's past successes portends future successes.

This larger context in which to view a business is fair game, and shareholders are better informed as a result. Perhaps most importantly, shareholders gain a sense of continuity about the company they have invested in and how its business is tied to the economy as a whole, and what its long term goals are, which is critical since business decisions often have life cycles that span many years.

Segue to the state of the printed annual report business today, where the number of pages in many reports has been so reduced that this type of contextual positioning is seen less and less. Instead many companies have pulled back to a report consisting of an executive letter wrapped around the Form 10K. This trend began with the fall of Enron in December 2001 and continues today in the midst of the greatest economic meltdown since the Great Depression.

ONLINE RISING

There are also those who would say that the diminishing of the printed annual report for many companies during this period was due to the growth of the web as a powerful "and competitive" form of communication. But it is highly unlikely the demise would have ever taken place had it not been for the scandal-motivated broken trust that occurred between the investor, the investment community and the companies they invested in. Had the scandals never happened and the economy continued its bullish ways, the relationship between the web and printed reports would have evolved in a much more natural and mutually beneficial way.

What that natural relationship might have been like is represented by those companies that never broke stride in their IR outreach through the corporate scandals and economic downturn, companies whose print and web annual report efforts remained in perfect harmony through it all. One company that seems to have this relationship well in hand is General Electric with a Form 10K fronted by a 16-page operations review that mirrors the content of a very robust online report.

At the heart of the GE online version are four video case studies. The two-plus minute videos include interviews with numerous layers of management and convey the sense of community and commitment any company would be proud of.

"With video, we complemented the annual report by bringing GE stories to life in multiple dimensions." Says Russell Wilkerson, Director of Financial Communications for GE, "To see our products, such as aircraft engines, hear from our global partners and view the world through the eyes of our employees is a compelling experience. A static chart of numbers can be informative, but when it is brought to life with an actual story with human beings showing the "how and why" behind the numbers it is far more engaging."

Photographs courtesy of Michael Weymouth.

A different, but no less impactful online report, was done by California-based Life Technologies. Only in this case, it replaced the print report entirely, according to Amanda Clardy, Vice President of Investor relations.

"What the online approach enables that the printed report cannot," says Clardy, "is an ongoing conversation. "We think the concept of an annual report, whether it's online or printed is pretty much passé. Just thinking that you only need to communicate to your constituents once a year has gone by the board. We believe it's better to have an ongoing dialogue with your stakeholders, via videos or podcasts, or whatever you post - a more continuous conversation.

"This is the second year we have taken this approach," continues Clardy. "The goal this year was to bring management much closer to our shareholders, through a series of interviews interspersed with B-roll illustrating the company's commitment to innovation and customer service. One important feature of the Life Technologies "news gallery" from which the annual report can be viewed is the ability to provide updates throughout the year, so shareholders can view additional content, including new videos. The current content is then archived so it remains available to the viewer."

This ability for shareholders to hear management firsthand is one of the most compelling aspects of the online report, insofar as it provides a fluid and intuitive human interface that is engaging and interactive, a goal that would be impossible to achieve with a printed annual report.

"In addition," says Clardy, "employees loved it, because it was so innovative, and new employees being interviewed loved the fact that they could go to the annual report and see the CEO, and felt like he really conveyed what he was about and what the company was about. And customers appreciated that we recognized they are a key constituent."

ORIGINS

It helps to look back over the past several years at the converging forces that have led to the emergence of the robust, interactive online format, in order to understand what these forces are. And as economist Steven Levitt, in the bestselling book Freakonomics points out, we need to be able to shed preconceptions and look at real cause and effect, i.e. things are not always what they appear to be.

For example, the emergence of the online report did not happen overnight, and it was not willed into existence by any one omnipotent force. While it may have been an idea waiting to happen, it took major strides in video and web technology to give it wings.

One of these changes was simply the web's ability to play video, which in and of itself was no big deal. It was the resulting emergence of Youtube, with its low-grade, amateurish, home-grown style that began to reshape the way we see and appreciate video. Viewers have come to respond just as viscerally to its gritty format as they do to the much higher quality video they see in TV commercials, a video style that requires a large production crew and the costs that go with it. In many respects they have come to trust the Youtube look and feel even more than the more polished commercial style.

Marketers quickly latched onto this dynamic, lending further credence to the medium, and it was only a matter of time before corporate communicators were on board.

At the same time, digital camera technology improved to the point where small, hand-held cameras can now shoot HD video directly to a hard drive, thus eliminating the need for videotape and vastly compacting equipment requirements. And, even though larger format cameras are still used, video shot with a hand-held HD camera for use on the web looks just as sharp at 72 dpi as that shot with a broadcast-quality HD camera. Virtually anyone with a computer and a video camera can make a fairly competent video these days using simple programs such as Imovie and the more professional level Final Cut programs. Even the new Iphones can shoot video, and the time will most assuredly come when an employee, caught up in a significant corporate event, will whip out his Iphone and shoot a video that will appear on the company website moments later.

SMALL FOOTPRINT VIDEO:
A STEP IN THE RIGHT DIRECTION

One of the video-related challenges many companies have always had to face is the intrusion factor: it's not easy to set up a company-wide video shoot with all the crews and their equipment continually shutting down operations. But all the aforementioned technology shifts are changing that precept. More and more companies are subscribing to the so-called "small footprint" video crew, a result in part from the downsizing of the equipment. Cameras, lights, sound are all still present albeit occupying a much smaller footprint with a much smaller crew, in some cases no more than a videographer and an assistant, who also handle sound and lighting. Most importantly, they have an acute understanding of how to visualize the corporate message.

THE ANNUAL REPORT DESIGNER AND PHOTOGRAPHER:
R.I.P. OR PHOENIX RISING FROM THE ASHES?

If the AR 2.0 concept has been driven by advances in web and video technology, it doesn't mean that the print designer is out and the web designer is in and that the annual report photographer will be replaced by a video crew.

Far from it. As Mark Twain famously said, "The reports of my death have been greatly exaggerated."

Doug Oliver, of Douglas Oliver Design Office in Los Angeles, is quick to remind his clients that the only thing that has changed here is the delivery system. Well beyond being a designer, Oliver is an annual report consultant with years of experience and finely honed instincts for helping his clients shape their shareholder message and this skill far outweighs changes in the way that message is delivered.

"An annual report designer sees the big picture," says Oliver, "and that's vitally important when it comes to successful messaging, regardless of whether or not it plays in print or on the web."

When it comes to coordinating print and web, Oliver sees the role of web developer as just another team member, albeit a very smart and important one. "The goal is not to simply maintain consistency within the team," says Oliver, "it is to keep the storytelling aspect rolling and that is the annual report designer's stock-in-trade. No amount of technology will change that."

Jeff Corwin, one of the country's leading annual report photographers, has long addressed the technology issue by going on photo shoots with a still camera in one hand and a video camera in the other, whenever the situation calls for it.

Corwin says, "it makes perfect sense, both aesthetically and financially, to have the video and the stills shot in concert by the same shooter."

"This year," reflects Corwin, " I shot an annual for a California client. At the same time, they hired a crew to do the video: double the fees, double the expenses, two different looks, no consistency."

Corwin also reinforces the small footprint concept: "The equipment needed to shoot an effective video is perfect for the web and can fit in one additional case. It's not like I'm shooting Gone With the Wind and Michael Bay I'm not."

And when asked about where creativity fits into all this, he responded with a story about a recent shoot for a Starbucks web project. "I was hired to shoot stills and video," says Corwin. "The idea was to show all the activity that goes into the process, from harvesting and roasting the beans to the cup of coffee being served at the store. I used a Canon XH-G1 on location and shot everything in motion: hands sifting through beans in roasters, beans being turned by huge blades, bags being filled, people moving on forklifts, anything that moved was fair game. In the end, we melded the video with black and white still photos and created A Day in the Life of Starbucks.

The big picture extolled by Doug Oliver is also part of Corwin's gestalt: "At the end of the day, it is my ability to see the entire story and maintain continuity throughout that story that is important, regardless of how it is shot. That is what I'm really selling. And if it means a less expensive bottom line for the client, then all the better."

THE EDITOR

Anyone who has ever made a video will tell you that the best material in the world can be turned into mediocre pabulum by a bad editor and conversely the worst footage can be spun into gold by a great editor.

Both the General Electric and Life Technologies online videos are beautifully edited and yet quite different. Each reflects the type of company for which they were made. General Electric, with its diverse product lines, suffers no shortage of material and its global reach is second to none. Life Technologies, on the other hand, is a fraction of the size of GE and like many life science companies, has a product line that is much more difficult to visualize.

"They are in the same boat as are many of our life science companies," says Bob Kellerman, head of Weymouth Design's San Francisco office. "Their physical product may be a tiny vial of liquid, but what goes into that vial, the years of research, the knowledge and the desire to seek cures, is not easy to show. And when you look at most life science publications and web sites, it's even more difficult to differentiate one company from another. Their employees all wear white coats and work in labs." Part of creating a different and distinctive look and feel is through video editing claims Kellerman. "The Life Technologies project was somewhat unique for us, because we were working with our own shooter as well as another hired by the company. In our case, our shooter was also our editor, which is the magic formula for us"

His ability to bring this together is evident in the six senior management videos, highlighting the accomplishments in each of their respective businesses. The intent was to shoot the interviews and b-roll in two locations as part of the same trip. Last minute script changes combined with management's availability meant that a couple of interviews would be re-shot by another videographer. It also meant that we'd be working with b-roll from past shoots. Through it all, I worked closely with our editor from the initial rough cuts through the final edit, keeping an eye on the storyline, as well as the editing style and pacing. Just like working on a printed report. Same type of thinking, just different medium."

Continuity and a fully aligned story are also at the forefront of the General Electric online annual. "We are fully integrated in our strategic content development process," says Russell Wilkerson," with the writer, photographer and video producer all at the table in the beginning of the process. This also creates a more efficient use of resources and ultimately a better communications platform."

How this relationship between the printed and online annual report and the Form 10K evolves in the future is anyone's guess. According to Jeff Corwin, who has spent his professional career visualizing corporate success stories, "…these three mediums working together make for amazing possibilities for corporate communicators."

Doug Oliver also makes a strong case for the three-way relationship. "Our entire business culture is rooted in accountability," says Oliver. "The Form 10K is the deep dive into the numbers while the online report is a flowing series of vignettes that represent a manifestation of those numbers. The printed annual report provides a pause in that rapid flow of online information in order for a shareholder to gain perspective. It is like a bridge between the continually accumulating information on the web and the cast-in-stone financial data in the Form 10K. And at the end of the day, it is in a corporation's best interest to make sure shareholders are able to gain this perspective."

Having an IR plan that enables a greater degree of perspective is vitally important for corporations in these times of economic turmoil. And as opportunities present themselves, the operative term is to be proactive and not reactive, to play a leadership role and seize the moment rather than lose the moment: carpe diem not carpe diem cras. And when you add up the components of this new paradigm, one thing is for sure: the stage is being set for a major shift in the way corporations communicate with their shareholders. We will all be affected by it one way or another, but as the old sage once said, "change brings disaster for some and opportunity for others."
Carpe diem.

The online report was not willed into existence by some omnipotent force…it took major strides in video and web technology to give it wings.

DUPLICITY
MARCH 20

What is "AR 2.0"? In truth, the term is a buzzword that describes the presentation of Annual Reports using digital mediums, such as online, e-books or cell phone applications. Of course, e-books, cell phone applications and the like are rarely used for such a purpose at this point; but Annual Reports are increasingly migrating from the printed page to a computer screen in the form of "digital Annual Reports."

The 10-K form and the Annual Report that public companies must distribute per SEC guidelines long ago morphed from dry financial statements into straightforward, thoughtful and impeccably designed pieces of work. These Reports still include the financial data, but they also explore the human side of a company: its goals, its ethics, its employees and its mission. Annual Reports serve as marketing and fundraising tools; they are designed to be engaging, informative and perhaps even a good read. Some are so eye-catching that we wouldn't hesitate to call them works of art, a testament to the designers who create them. So with all the creativity being applied to Reports, it was inevitable that the printed page would one day be too limited. Thus, Annual Reports are going digital: "AR 2.0" is born.

With the page counts for some Annual Reports increasing in order to communicate all that companies want to share, presenting a Report online makes more sense. Many companies have been taking advantage of the internet for years. Houston-based design firm Savage Brands created its first online Annual Reports way back in 1999, for Kodak and General Motors, though at that point the online and printed portions were treated very differently than today. "The '99 [Reports] were definitely very separated processes," says Robin Tooms, Principal & Brand/Web Strategist at Savage in Houston. "Even when the decision was made to go online, the online was more an interpretation of the print… They weren't planned [together] as much as they are now."

It's rare to find an online report that isn't partnered with a printed original. Traditionalists still hold on to the printed Annual Report, and with good reason. Consider this: No matter how advanced or interactive or fun an online Report may be, if an investor doesn't have a computer or internet access, he can't view it. With all the flash animation and streaming video included in these websites, even an investor who does have access to a computer may have trouble with an online Report if he isn't tech-savvy or uses an outdated machine.

Additionally, a printed document possesses portability. You can pick it up, carry it around or read it in transit. Yes, laptops do afford portability to a certain degree, but only if you have wireless internet and a charged battery. There's also the sheer enjoyment of holding a paper document, which is often said of newspapers and magazines. Says Bill Ferguson, Managing Partner at New York's INC Design, "There's a certain permanence when something's in print that just makes the experience a little bit more enjoyable."

There's also the fact that extensive numbers (as in the financial section of a Report) and long stretches of text tend to be easier to read on paper as opposed to a glaring screen. Additionally, one can flip from page to page and take notes on paper, not so on a computer. However, there are design solutions that can ameliorate some of these issues. If empty space on a page is kept to a maximum and font size remains relatively large, reading text online can be quite easy on the eyes. Financial data can be exported to an Excel spreadsheet or a graph, making it simpler to organize the data to the reader's choosing than it would be even on paper.

Even in spite of that fact that not everyone owns a computer or is tech-savvy, the internet is still a more democratic medium that print. It allows for much wider distribution. "On the digital side, one of the biggest advantages is reach," says Tooms. "In the past, annual reports, even when printed, were really only mailed out to shareholders. Now it's so much easier for anyone, whether you're a shareholder or not, to access the Annual Report online. They're not just being targeted to investors now." In addition, an online report can be accessed by the entire globe, translated into other languages and "read" to the blind or vision-impaired with screen-reading software.

This global availability can even contribute to better design. If the whole world is looking at your company's Annual Report, you know you've got to make it appeal to potential investors, possible clients and, in this era of increased scrutiny of corporate malfeasance, even the media and general public. The options for achieving this goal really open up when publishing in the context of the internet. "SEC rules state that an online piece must include every single item that the printed piece has," explains Doug Hebert, Principal & Design Director at Savage Brands, "but the wonderful thing is you can add to an online piece…It allows the opportunity to support a lot of the information we have in the printed piece through other means, whether it be infographics or video."

Video, animation and other interactive features lend an Annual Report a personal touch, too. As an investor, imagine having the chairperson of a company speak directly to you (through a computer screen, of course) about his impression of the previous year, rather than reading a letter. A written letter simply doesn't achieve the same personalized effect as seeing a person's facial expressions and hearing her voice inflection or laughter. With all these benefits for the audience, let's also not forget about the substantial benefits online Reports present to the company itself. Production time and cost for online is significantly lower than for print. For International Security Exchange's (ISE) 2008 Annual Report, INC Design created an animation and video-heavy online Report with no print component. INC's Bill Ferguson and Art Director Alex Medina say the project took exactly 57 days from beginning to end, a time savings of 50% over the previous year's printed report. Ferguson says a typical project takes three and a half to four months. "That surprised even us," he explains, "because there were a lot of components that had to go into this." With no printed component, that also means there were no printing, no paper and no mailing costs. Ferguson states that the 2008 ISE Report had a cost savings of over 80% from the previous year's printed Annual Report.

Even companies that go for both a print and an online version still stand to save a substantial amount of money because they can print many fewer paper copies, especially if it's distributed on a print-on-demand basis. Additionally, by cutting back on printing costs, more money can be spent on the budget for the online portion while still keeping the total budget well under its original print-only price tag. Explains Tooms, "In a way, the total budget is reduced, but now within that budget, they get both a print and an online."

Beyond the cost-savings of going digital, there's also significant environmental impact. Paper production pollutes the air, water and land, and requires substantial amounts of energy and resources. Even recycled paper has its drawbacks, as the de-inking process creates a sludge by-product. Further environmental problems include the use of traditional petroleum-based ink, as well as the energy required to create and distribute the Report, and the likelihood that many a Report will end up in landfills instead of being recycled once its recipient no longer needs it. There are options to lessen the impact, such as using post-consumer or FSC (Forest Stewardship Council) certified paper and soy-based inks, but those options often cost more than their less environmentally responsible counterparts, and publishing a paper document still requires substantially more energy than publishing online.

There's a certain permanence when something's in print that just makes the experience a little bit more enjoyable.

Bill Ferguson

It's so much easier for anyone, whether you're a shareholder or not, to access the Annual Report online. They're not just being targeted to investors now.

Robin Tooms

Sysco Corporation 2008 Annual Report designed by Savage, Inc. | www.sysco.com/investor/OnlineAnnualReport/

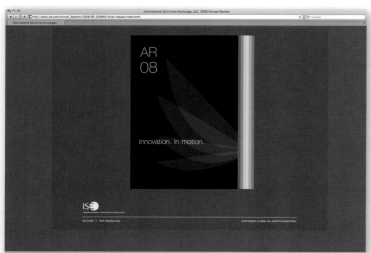

ISE Interactive Annual Review by INC Design | www.incdesign.com/portfolio/7

"We think it's important that companies are taking an environmental initiative and considering interactive experiences versus traditional print in terms of saving paper and energy," says Medina. By publishing online, or online in conjunction with distributing fewer printed Reports, a company is demonstrating its commitment to the environment as well as demonstrating that it is on the cutting edge of new, innovative technologies. A further advantage that online Reports present is that a document's popularity can be accurately tracked on the internet. The number of website visitors, where those visitors originate geographically, and which pages within the site get the most views, for example, can all be easily calculated. When a printed Report gets mailed out, there is no way to track who opened it and who threw it right into the trash, much less who read which parts of it. The internet also provides the opportunity to receive feedback. Visitors can submit comments in an online forum or through e-mail. The internet allows for instant communication with shareholders and other interested parties.

So where are Annual Reports going from here? Certainly, print will never fall entirely out of favor. It does have some major benefits, its impact on the environment is rapidly becoming less harmful and, of course, there will always be enthusiasts who simply prefer paper. But print and online don't have to be exclusive. Often, the print and online versions of a Report are most effective when they work together. An online Report married to a print-on-demand option makes a hard copy of the Report a mere click or phone call away. Or shareholders can be offered the choice to receive an online Report long before the printed copy is delivered. Next year, Graphis will also be ready to accept online submissions to its Annual Reports Annual as well as the traditional printed Report.

Online capabilities are also still developing. With e-books, cell phone applications and social networking tools becoming ever more ubiquitous, there's no telling what the next frontier will be. "It can be whatever you imagine," says Medina. "Obviously, you have to start with considering what the client needs and what's right for them. But other than that, you can take it anywhere you can think of." Perhaps in a few years, a printed brochure will be mailed to shareholders (or downloaded to their e-books), which will then lead them to additional online content: the shareholder can watch a company video, join the company's social network or sign up for instant text message updates. Now that's brand loyalty.

It's important that companies are taking an environmental initiative and considering interactive experiences versus traditional print in terms of saving paper and energy.

Alex Medina

Doug Hebert

Robin Tooms

Alex Medina

Bill Ferguson

Doug Hebert, Principal, Design Director, Savage Inc: *The tagline of the 1979 theatrical release, Alien, was "In Space, No One Can Hear You Scream." What most moviegoers didn't catch was that the second part of that tagline was "...but you can still hear Doug Hebert's laugh." His boisterous laugh and mere presence transcends space and time. He can be about as subtle as an air horn during a church service. With an intensity and passion for design turned up to 11, this constantly inspired, heavy metal loving, dessert affi cianado has applied his talents to the creation of multifaceted branding, marketing and communications programs for clients such as Baylor College of Medicine, Delta Airlines, Sysco, Lyondell Chemical Company and Anadarko Petroleum. Doug has extensive experience extending brands across a variety of different media – print and online. His work has been featured in, or recognized by,* HOW Magazine, Graphis, AIGA 365, Communication Arts, STEP Inside Design Magazine, Print, *the Type Director's Club, and he has lectured at design conferences across the country about designing for non-profits. Doug won a grant from Sappi Paper to create the highly publicized High Risk Handbook for the University of Texas Health Science Center at Houston. He won a second grant from Sappi Paper in 2006 to fi nance a project for DePelchin Children's Center.*

Robin Tooms, Principal, Managing Director, Brand/Web Strategist, Savage Inc: *Robin Tooms was born with a genetic gift that gave her eight hands and arms that she currently conceals beneath brightly colored, coordinated sweater sets. On any given day you can find her utilizing those extra appendages to her advantage by simultaneously holding conference calls with clients, mining business, serving as President of AIGA Houston, writing monthly articles for* STEP Magazine, *working with management to set the direction of the company, updating the company blog and emailing numerous contacts. This refined multitasker works closely with clients to develop brand positioning, core messaging, marketing strategies and brand identities. She is dedicated to staying on the forefront of innovative technologies that enhance communication and business. In her role as Managing Director, Robin is responsible for keeping internal operations running smoothly, especially in areas regarding human resources: managing, recruiting, training, mentoring and professional development for our talented employees. Robin has been with Savage for over a decade working with clients like Baker Hughes, Devon Energy, General Motors, Imperial Sugar, Tenaris and Weingarten Realty. Robin is an alumna of University of Houston and holds an MBA from the Rice University Jones Graduate School.*

Alex Medina, Art Director, INC Design: *Alejandro ("Alex") Medina was born in 1977 in Elizabeth, NJ. He received his BFA, graduating with honors, from Kean University. Early career engagements included internships in the creative service departments for MTV Networks and DMA Design Studio. In 2004, following four years as a designer working in Simon & Schuster's children's publishing division, Mr. Medina joined INC Design. He has since earned three promotions and today with the title of Senior Art Director, he manages a design team of five. Most recent projects have included annual reports, CSR's, corporate websites and branding identity programming for a diverse range of clients, including Hess Corporation, International Securities Exchange and Nova Chemicals. Mr. Medina has been an adjunct professor at Kean University since 2000. He holds memberships at AIGA and Art Directors Club of New Jersey, the latter where he was a former chapter vice president. His design achievements and awards have included recognition from Graphic Design USA, Art Directors Club of New York, Art Directors Club of New Jersey, and the NJ Advertising Club and New York Book Show.*

Bill Ferguson, Managing Partner, INC Design: *Bill Ferguson is one of the original founding partners of INC Design. He has worked with long-term client companies such as Merck, ARAMARK and International Securities Exchange. Prior to forming INC Design in 1988, Bill was Senior Vice President, Director of Marketing Services for Corporate Graphics International, having opened the company's first satellite office in Los Angeles, CA. He began his marketing communications career in 1984 as a project manager for CGI. As a member of IABC, American Institute for Graphic Arts (AIGA) and National Investor Relations Institute (NIRI), he has appeared at various graphic design industry forums and communications/investor relations conferences, including NIRI/New York and Sid Cato's Annual Report Conference, addressing such topics as "Integrating the Annual Report With the Corporate Identity System," "Technology and the Annual Report" and "Cost-Saving Tips for the Corporate Communicator." He is featured in the book, Creative Marketing: Finding and Keeping Your Best Clients, published by John Wiley & Sons, INC. (1999). He holds BA from Susquehanna University.*

Michael Weymouth

Dana Arnett

Jill Howry

Deanna Kulhmann-Leavitt

Tom Laidlaw

Douglas Oliver

Greg Samata

Graphis Annual Report Advisory Board

The role of the Graphis Annual Report Annual Advisory Board is to oversee the judging process for the competition and to work with the financial underwriters of the event, without whose generosity the judging process would not be possible. The Board is comprised of leading Annual Report designers whose body of work over the years has set the bar for creative excellence. As the world of information decimation continues to change and evolve, the Annual Report to shareholders remains a fixed point in an otherwise rapidly moving stream of information, and the skill with which that message is crafted is reflected in the many Annual Reports that appear in this year's Graphis Annual.

Michael Weymouth, *Weymouth Design, Advisory Board Founder*
Michael Weymouth is the founder of Weymouth Design in Boston, a 35-year old firm specializing in Annual Report design. Michael started as a graphic designer but quickly realized the important role photography plays in corporate communications and started shooting his own photography. It has been the mainstay of Weymouth-produced Annual Reports ever since. The firm has won numerous local, national and international awards for its work. Of late, the firm has expanded its business to include the full range of corporate communications needs, including branding projects, web development and video, and has recently opened an office in San Francisco.

Dana Arnett, *VSA Partners*
Dana Arnett is a founding Principal of the internationally recognized firm of VSA Partners, Inc., headquartered in Chicago. Arnett, along with his four partners, leads a group of 100 associates in the creation of design programs, film projects, interactive initiatives and brand marketing solutions for a diverse roster of clients, including: Harley-Davidson, IBM, General Electric, Coca-Cola, and Nike. Over the course of his 22 years in the field, Dana and the firm have been globally recognized by over 60 competitions and designations including: *Communication Arts*, AIGA, *Graphis*, The Type Directors Club, the American and British Art Directors Clubs, *ID*, The LA Film Festival, the AR100 and the American Marketing Association. Arnett was a 1999 inductee into the Alliance Graphic International, and holds the honor of being named to the ID40 – which has cited him as one of the 40 most important people shaping design internationally. Arnett is a former member of the AIGA National Board of Directors, where he was involved in leadership and policy making that shapes the design industry. A frequent lecturer and visiting professor, Arnett is also active in furthering the role of design in society through contributing publishing endeavors, conference chairmanships, and foundation activities.

Jill Howry, *Howry Design Associates*
Jill founded Howry Design Associates in 1988 to provide message-driven design communications to companies that range in size from start-ups to Fortune 100 corporations. With more than 20 years experience in visual design, Jill's career spans many communication art forms including brand identity, Annual Reports, integrated marketing programs, environmental graphics and packaging. Her design work in the area of corporate communications is recognized on a national scale. Her work has been widely published and she has received awards from the American Institute of Graphic Arts, American Corporate Identity, Black Book's AR 100, Print, *Communication Arts* Magazine, *Creativity* and *Graphis*. Jill has served as a judge for various national and international design competitions including Communications Arts, the American Institute of Graphic Arts and Graphis. She has held lectures at several universities and national AIGA events.

Deanna Kuhlmann-Leavitt, *Kuhlmann-Leavitt, Inc.*
Deanna Kuhlmann-Leavitt began her design career in Los Angeles eighteen years ago after completing a degree in Graphic Design at Art Center College of Design in Pasadena, California. In 2001, she established Kuhlmann-Leavitt, Inc., a St. Louis based, multi-faceted firm known for its work in print, new media and design for the built environment.
As principal of KLI, Deanna has been recognized by the American Institute of Graphic Design (AIGA), American Institute of Architects (AIA), New York Type Directors Club, Art Directors Clubs from New York to Los Angeles and AR100, including a Best of Show Award and the Mead Annual Report Show. Her studio's work has been featured in Communication Arts, Monsa books, International Trade Fair Design by Avedition and many other leading design publications. Design organizations across the U.S. and Canada have invited Deanna to address their membership and to jury numerous regional and national competitions.

Tom Laidlaw, *Laidlaw Group*
Tom Laidlaw has devoted his career to creating corporate Annual Reports that are engaging, thoughtful, intelligent, informative, honest, direct and personal. In return, this endeavor has provided him with a life experience profoundly enriched by the people he has met, the places he's visited and the institutions he's had the privilege of working for.
Since 2004, Tom has been principal of Laidlaw Group Boston, a multi-disciplined design firm creating corporate communications including print, web, environmental and structural design for a diverse group of national and international clients including TerraMark, Tru Corporation, DeWolf and InterDigital Communications. He attended Ohio University and graduated from the Art Institute of Boston in 1979. Very soon after, he discovered his calling while freelancing at Weymouth Design, Inc. He accepted a design position and for the next 22 years—first as a designer and eventually as a partner of the firm—he created Annual Reports and other corporate communications programs. His long-term relationships with clients such as MeadWestvaco, Northrop Grumman, Corning and US Trust produced award winning work that has helped set industry standards. This work has received recognition from the AIGA, *Communication Arts*, *Graphis*, Graphis Annual Reports, The Mead Annual Report Show and The BlackBook AR100 and is included in the Cooper-Hewitt National Design Museum of the Smithsonian Institution and Museums fur Kunst und Gewerbe Hamburg.

Douglas Oliver, *Douglas Oliver Design Office*
Douglas J. Oliver is President and Chief Creative Officer of Douglas Oliver Design Office, located in Santa Monica, California. His work has been recognized by all of the major design institutions, garnering awards from *Communication Arts* Design Annual, Graphis Annual Reports, The AR 100, *Critique Magazine*'s "The Big Crit," American Institute of Graphic Arts, New York Art Director's Club, The Los Angeles Art Director's Club, and The Western Art Director's Club. His work is also part of the Permanent Design Collection of the Library of Congress. The consistent excellence of Doug's design of Annual Reports also made him a perennial favorite in the prestigious Mead Annual Report Show. His Annuals were chosen among the best for 15 consecutive years, until the Mead Show came to an end in 2001. He began his professional career in Los Angeles, working with the legendary James Cross and the late Robert Miles Runyan, who is often called the "father of the modern Annual Report." In 1983, Doug opened his own studio to design for Fortune 500 companies, major universities, institutions and foundations across the US, Europe and Japan. Over the years, Doug has remained active in the larger design community. In 1998, he served as Chair of The Annual Report Design Conference held at the World Trade Center in New York City. More recently, he returned to his alma mater, the University of Kansas, as a Hallmark Symposium speaker. He has also maintained close ties with Art Center, serving as an alumni board member, teacher, guest speaker and consultant. In 2004, Doug was one of a handful of graphic designers included in Art Center's "Design Impact," which detailed the contributions of Art Center alumni over the past 75 years.

Greg Samata, *SamataMason*
Greg Samata formed Samata Associates in 1975 and subsequently co-founded SamataMason Inc. with partners Pat Samata and Dave Mason in 1995. His work has spanned across three decades of all creative media and disciplines from print to film making. Greg has been published in every major design and industry publication and honored with hundreds of awards for his work in competitions worldwide. He has lectured throughout North America and internationally and has served as a juror for books and national competitions. Greg is an untiring advocate and participant for national design relevancy, both independently and while serving as a past national board member of the American Institute of Graphic Arts, and is a current board member of the Evan's Life Foundation, a non-profit organization that aids children at risk.
Greg has helped launch numerous business ventures, co-founded OpinionLab, Inc., the leader in automated user feedback systems for the web, and founded the film production company NoisemakerFilms where he creates, directs and produces documentaries and feature films. Greg lives in the Chicago area with his wife Pat, son Parker, twin daughters Lane and Tate and Frank and Stella, six-year-old sister black labs. Greg would say: "It's a life worth living."

PlatinumWinners

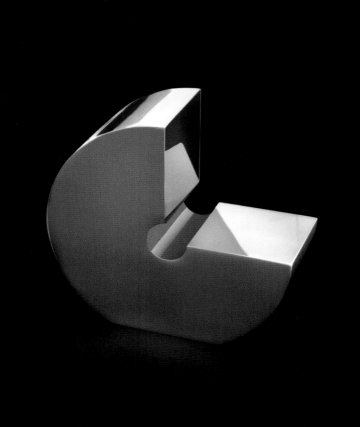

INFINITE POSSIBILITIES

UNIVERSITY OF VIRGINIA LIBRARY

2008 annual report

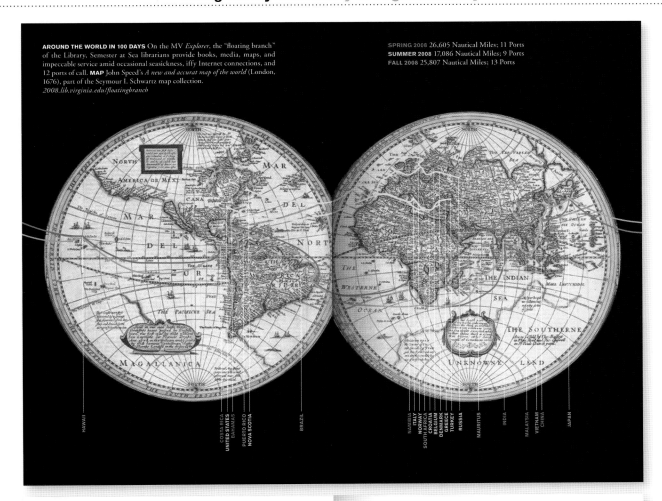

AROUND THE WORLD IN 100 DAYS On the MV *Explorer*, the "floating branch" of the Library, Semester at Sea librarians provide books, media, maps, and impeccable service amid occasional seasickness, iffy Internet connections, and 12 ports of call. **MAP** John Speed's *A new and accurat map of the world* (London, 1676), part of the Seymour I. Schwartz map collection. *2008.lib.virginia.edu/floatingbranch*

SPRING 2008 26,605 Nautical Miles; 11 Ports
SUMMER 2008 17,086 Nautical Miles; 9 Ports
FALL 2008 25,807 Nautical Miles; 13 Ports

FLOWERDEW HUNDRED COLLECTION Hundreds of years ago, an unsuspecting cat stepped on this clay roof tile. The tile is now one of more than 300,000 historical artifacts given to the Library by the Flowerdew Hundred Foundation, which was set up to administer research and access to this historic farm on the James River. The collection presents a one-of-a-kind archive of Virginia's history, from prehistoric times through the Civil War. The family of the late David and Mary Harrison chose the U.Va. Library to receive, catalog, and share this wide-ranging, unique resource. **OPPOSITE** From top, clockwise: a quartzite spearhead, A.D. 200–800; a tan Savannah River spearhead, 2500–300 B.C.; and various items from the 17th through 19th centuries—a candlewick trimmer; a wine bottle; a wine bottle seal; an iron key; the remains of a bottle; a pewter spoon; an iron ball padlock; and a gin case. *2008.lib.virginia.edu/flowerdew*

P. 20

Category: Education | **Location:** Washington, DC, United States | **Creative Director:** Jake Lefebure, Pum Lefebure | **Designer:** Scott Vadas | **Paper Type:** Cover Stock is Neenah Eames Canvas; Text Stock is Accent Opaque | **Print Run:** 12,500 | **Printer:** Worth Higgins Associates | **Project Manager:** Jake Lefebure

What was the client's directive?
We have been doing this report for 4 years now, and they want something different every year, yet familiar—that is our directive. They want every page to be fresh, a surprise, and informative. They want the audience to read it from cover to cover, and many do.

How did you define the problem?
This is one project we don't ever have many problems, other than it has to be a small format so it is easy for them to carry to events and meetings.

What was the approach?
Make the report distinct, engage the readers, and visually tell the story of the UVA Library; and since we get to work with fantastic images and artwork, it's like a dream project.

What disciplines or people helped you with the project?
Our clients are librarians—the most organized people in the world. They help us so much just by really caring about the work/product so much, it makes our lives super happy.

How involved was the CEO in your meetings, presentations, etc.?
They are very involved and hands on, each map, painting, or object is special to them. It is what they do, so they make sure we do it well!

What are clients looking for when it comes to designing an Annual Report?
We have yet to find any two clients that want the same thing, but I am pretty sure that they all want to have an amazing document that not only serves the basics of reporting their data/mission—but also serves as a marketing tool and collateral that can really stand out amongst their competitors.

Do you and the client both view the Annual Report as part of the company's communications strategy? And how important is it within the overall strategy?
There are two goals for this annual; one is to connect to the audience with meaningful verbal and visual messaging. The other is to get alumni, supporters and organizations to donate to the library so that they can continue to carry out their mission.

How do you define success in Annual Report design?
Annuals are about numbers for most, but a successful Annual is all about showing/telling what the organization is doing (or want to be doing) in a way that makes a strong connection to their audience. If the annual is designed in such a way, it will be successful.

In which direction do you see Annual Reports moving?
Unfortunately, paperless.

How large a role does environmental policy play in the design and production of your Annual Reports?
Some clients have to be green and others want to be green – thankfully the cost of 100PC sheets has become more affordable; and waterless soy-based inks are still around. Some clients have to have FSC while others do not care. It's quite a mix at our studio, but we do try to be as green as budgets allow on every project.

Annual Reports are about numbers but a successful one is about showing what the organization is doing so the audience can connect.

MEDUSA **ABOVE** That's the name of a "sonic spatial" instrument created by faculty and students in a "Robotic Ecologies" class. The creators presented the instrument at the New Horizons conference, a collaboration between the Library and the University's Information Technology group that brought the U.Va. community together to explore technology in teaching and research. A touch to the *Medusa's* tentacles begins a cascade of drum-like sounds corresponding with flashes of light—kinetic, computer-created music. **OPPOSITE** The *Panta Rhei*, another Robotic Ecologies project, uses a light system to translate human interaction into music and robotic choreography.

P. 23

"PEOPLE ARE CAPABLE OF INFINITE CHANGE."

William Faulkner as quoted in the Charlottesville *Daily Progress*, May 8, 1957. From *Conversations with William Faulkner*, edited by M. Thomas Inge.

SO MUCH TO READ, SO LITTLE TIME Alderman Library's Periodicals Room, offering almost 3,000 journals and 50 newspapers, was renovated to make researching, browsing, reading (and even napping in the comfortable chairs) a more enjoyable experience.

QUOTH THE RAVEN

NEVER MORE

EDGAR ALLAN POE Before he was the father of the detective novel, the 19th-century author Edgar Allan Poe attended U.Va. for a year. He lived in one of the Lawn's Range rooms, went to classes, checked out books, and even got an overdue notice from the Library. In celebration of his 200th birthday, the Mary and David Harrison Institute for American History, Literature, and Culture began working with the University of Texas to produce a major exhibition in 2009, "From Out that Shadow: The Life of Edgar Allan Poe." **ABOVE** The namesake of Edgar Allan Poe's poem "The Raven," as illustrated by Edouard Manet in the French translation, "Le Corbeau" (Paris, 1875).
2008.lib.virginia.edu/nevermore

P. 36

"TADPOLES IN THE STREETS" This year Library staff gave talks on particularly interesting items in the collection, including the papers of author John Dos Passos. This letter includes the writer's own illustrations as well as the observation, "if it keeps up [raining] there will be tadpoles in the streets." **ABOVE** An eager dog from another Dos Passos letter.

P. 55

VF's business model combines the **strength** to overcome current challenges, the **vision** to capture future opportunities and the **diversity** of businesses and brands to excel in all markets. Our **team** continues to deliver on the promise, producing uncompromising results in unprecedented times.

Strength

Size and strength were once synonymous. But as recent events have taught us, that's no longer true. So while we're proud that so many people know us as the "world's largest apparel company," there's really so much more that makes VF strong. Like our ability to connect globally with consumers. Our adaptability to fast-changing markets and opportunities. And our discipline for balancing risk and reward. During 2008, we combined these qualities to deliver excellent results in the face of extraordinary challenges—and that's the best definition of strength that we know.

(opposite)
Bob Shearer
Senior Vice President & Chief Financial Officer

"At VF, we take nothing for granted. We keep our costs and inventories low, plan conservatively and keep our balance sheet strong. It's a discipline that's embedded in our culture—and that's giving us a competitive advantage in these very difficult times."

Karl Heinz Salzburger
President—VF International

"We have some of the best-known brands in the world. But we still have great potential for international growth. We're leveraging our global infrastructure to continue to extend our reach across Europe, while investing heavily to capitalize on opportunities in large and growing markets like China."

Nautica

Eastpak®

Category: Fashion | **Location:** New York, United States | **Art Director:** Nicholas Davidson (print) Brian Crooks (interactive) | **Creative Director:** David Schimmel | **Designer:** Nicholas Davidson, Brian Crooks | **Paper Type:** Neenah Classic Crest | **Photographer:** Julian Dufort | **Print Run:** 25,000 | **Printer:** Lithographix | **Project Manager:** Lauren Gabbe | **Writer:** Frank Oswald

Since 2005, our jeanswear business has reduced the amount of water used in the wet processing of its products by 35%.

Throughout our company, VF people are applying their ingenuity to reduce waste, conserve water and resources, and promote a more eco-conscious way of living and working:

—Through its "water miser" program, our jeanswear business has reduced the amount of water used in wet processing garments by 35% since 2005. The business recycles 40% of the water used at its Torreón, Mexico manufacturing division. In addition, this division sells denim scrap from its three facilities, thereby keeping it out of local landfills.

—Our *Reef®* brand's unique *Reef Redemption®* initiative offers consumers products made with organic and sustainable materials, pledging 1% of the proceeds to support global conservation and humanitarian efforts.

—Our *Nautica®* brand is a passionate supporter of marine conservation and a corporate sponsor of Oceana— an organization dedicated to reducing pollution and preventing the collapse of fish populations and other sea life.

Additionally, the VF Foundation provides financial support for charitable organizations in many of our local communities. We also encourage and celebrate volunteerism through the VF 100 program, which annually recognizes the 100 VF associates who have contributed the most community service hours. The VF Foundation donates $1,000 on behalf of each VF 100 winner to their charity of choice.

(top)
Reef Redemption® products incorporate sustainable materials such as recycled car tires, post-consumer plastics and water-based cements.

Nautica's marine conservation efforts have included cleanup of a section of the Hudson River in New York City on World Ocean Day.

16

In the past, print has driven the online AR—we see that reversing in the future.

Q&A with And Partners NY

What was the client's directive?
To present VF's business model in a compelling manner that illustrates why they are strong in challenging times. Traditionally, the annual report showcases their brands, but this year the focus is on the company's strengths, vision, diversity and team.

How did you define the problem?
VF's solid foundation is built on key principles and qualities that enable them to stay competitive through good times and bad.

What was the approach?
Straightforward copy combined with quotes and black and white portraits of senior management complemented by beautiful color photos of product.

What disciplines or people helped you with the project?
In addition to our creative team, we worked with an independent writer and photographer.

What are clients looking for when it comes to designing an Annual Report?
They are looking for an accurate depiction of the year's events with some style added.

Do you and the client both view the Annual Report as part of the company's communications strategy? And how important is it within the overall strategy?
The annual report is a very important part of the overall communications strategy, especially because the AR and the website are the only corporate communications. All other communications are brand-based.

How do you define success in Annual Report design?
Mainly, when the client hires us for the next one.

In which direction do you see Annual Reports moving?
n the past, the print has driven the online AR—we see that reversing in the future.

Vans manufactured the first skate shoe in 1966 and has been an off-the-wall original ever since.

Vans

Leveraging its authentic Southern California heritage, our *Vans®* brand has successfully expanded into apparel and accessories, which now represent more than 20% of its sales. As it does with footwear, the *Vans®* brand has collaborated with marquis skateboarders and surfers to create a meaningful assortment of T-shirts, denim, fleece, wovens and accessories. World-renowned skaters such as Anthony Van Engelen and Johnny Layton and surfers such as Joel Tudor and Karina Petroni work with *Vans®* designers to create signature collections inspired by their performance, style and deep ties to their cultures.

Bulwark

Millions of people go to work every day in our Imagewear coalition's workwear products.

Customization and speed to market are hallmarks of our Imagewear businesses. Positioned for global expansion, our *Bulwark®* brand demonstrated its service capabilities in 2008 by rapidly fulfilling an urgent order for 10,000 customized flame-resistant coveralls, bibs and jackets for a mining company. Using its innovative Imagine It™ customization technology, our *Bulwark®* business was able to make an initial delivery to the customer in mere days, completing the entire order within eight weeks.

Bulwark FR

Reef   41   *lucy®*

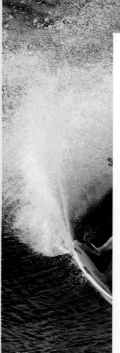

Our *7 For All Mankind®* brand continues to grow and evolve as a true denim lifestyle brand.

Seven For All Mankind

Acquired in 2007, our *7 For All Mankind®* brand opened 13 showcase retail stores in 2008, located in the best luxury shopping streets, malls and resort locations worldwide. The brand plans to open up to 15 additional stores in 2009. Successful product extensions into sportswear and handbags are expanding the "luxury denim-lifestyle" appeal of the brand. In eight short years, Seven For All Mankind, LLC has built a substantial global business, with one-third of its revenues coming from international markets.

for all mankind

Lee

Founded in 1899, our *Lee®* brand is one of the most popular work and casual brands on the planet.

Our *Lee®* brand's Fitinnovations™ design approach is winning over enthusiastic female customers with contemporary styled jeans for every body shape. Since its launch in 2006, Fitinnovations™ has helped the *Lee®* brand increase its market share in mid-tier department stores by more than 35%, making it one of the best performing denim brands in that channel. This approach is driving exciting new product developments across the brand—including *Lee® Slender Secret™*, a close-fitting jean offered in an ultra-stretch fabric that maintains its shape and fit. Fitinnovations™ is also helping the brand add new customers, including department stores, with the introduction of *Lee®* Platinum Label products.

Lee

Reef   42   *lucy®*

Wrangler Riggs Wear™   Vans®

Operating Committee

Eric Wiseman
Chairman, President
& Chief Executive
Officer

Robert Shearer
Senior Vice
President &
Chief Financial
Officer

Bradley Batten
Vice President
Controller &
Chief Accounting
Officer

Candace Cummings
Vice President
Administration,
General Counsel
& Secretary

Stephen Dull
Vice President
Strategy

Michael Gannaway
Vice President
VF Direct
Customer Team

Frank Pickard III
Vice President
Treasurer

Boyd Rogers
Vice President &
President
Supply Chain

Karl Heinz Salzburger
Vice President &
President
VF International

Martin Schneider
Vice President &
Chief Information
Officer

Franklin Terkelsen
Vice President
Mergers &
Acquisitions

Susan Larson Williams
Vice President
Human Resources

HOLD FAST

HARBOR POINT LIMITED

ANNUAL REPORT 2008

< 6 >

HOLD FAST

HARBOR POINT ON
Staying the Course

< 7 >

HARBOR POINT ON
STAYING THE COURSE

A
SEASONED
CREW

Our knowledgeable and experienced staff has
worked together for years and is highly regarded
by their industry peers. We work as a team with
a clear commitment to our principles.

< 8 >

< 9 >

Category: Financial Services | **Location:** Pennsylvania, United States | **Account Director:** Patti Monaco | **Art Director:** Justin Moll | **Associate Creative Director:** Justin Moll, Charles Smolover |
Chief Creative Officer: Bradley Gast | **Creative Director:** Joanne de Menna | **Paper Type:** Via Felt Cover, Cougar Natural Text | **Print Producer:** Susan Trickel | **Print Run:** 2000 |
Printer: Brilliant Graphics | **Writer:** Charles Smolover

MAINTAIN A SHARP LOOKOUT

The unexpected is to be expected. We anticipate this with our proprietary modeling and meticulous approach to risk management. This enables us to withstand inevitable surprises.

< 16 >

< 17 >

< 14 >

KEEP an EVEN KEEL

Over-exposure to any particular business segment is a risk we avoid. By continuing to focus on product, geographic and line diversity we maintain our balance and position ourselves for growth.

< 15 >

What was the client's directive?
Our client's directive was to communicate that their core rules for conducting business continue to serve them well, even during the most economically challenging year in decades. Their desire was to inspire confidence in their constituent audiences.

How did you define the problem?
The challenge was one of balance. The tone of the 2008 annual had to walk a very fine line between communicating confidence in the future, without appearing to be insensitive to the realities of the current economic environment. It needed to acknowledge the world as it is, without dwelling on it.

What was the approach?
Our approach used the metaphor of a ship's journal to underscore that, even in the worst of conditions, the right principles will serve a vessel well. In this case, Harbor Point's commitment to their underwriting precepts and their ability to navigate any environment led to a stable fiscal year for them and their clients.

What disciplines or people helped you with the project?
We partnered with a printer who specializes in both commercially printed materials and limited edition prints for fine artists. With his artistic eye, our printer was able to help us achieve the look we were trying to create with "Hold Fast." In addition, our bindery partner made a significant contribution to the final annual report with their skilled craftsmanship and attention to detail.

Our goal was to produce an Annual Report that had the appearance of belonging to a ship's crew over 200 years ago. The production process involved press testing to create just the right color and texture for the pages, along with the creation of a sculpted die to bring depth and dimension to the felt-textured cover. To further substantiate the weathered feel, a fabric strip was added to the spine area.

Were you happy with the result? What could have been better?
We are extremely pleased with the result. The simplicity of the communication and layout really keeps the focus on the content, which is where it belongs. Also, the modest approach to production values gives the piece an understated, bare-bones impact that is especially appropriate in this economy. There is nothing that we would change in this annual report.

What was the client's response?
As President & CFO Andrew Cook said, "Once again, great job, Mangos. They look even better in final form than all the proofs would have suggested. I really like them. I am sure we will get a lot of great comments again this year from our readers."

It met all of their criteria, including capturing their story and vision; reflecting their success modestly in an uncertain time; adhering to a smaller budget; minimal copy to read; and smallness of size.

What are clients looking for when it comes to designing an Annual Report?
We believe that clients want a report that presents their company in a way that is genuine, human and relevant, as well as helps to distinguish them from their competition. And also inspires confidence in their vision for the future.

Do you and the client both view the Annual Report as part of the company's communications strategy? And how important is it within the overall strategy?
Our client views their annual report as the cornerstone of their communications outreach. It serves as their primary marketing tool.

How do you define success in Annual Report design?
When the client receives glowing response from their constituent groups. And when we feel that we've done our best work.

In which direction do you see Annual Reports moving?
We think the trend toward less exotic annual reports with a brief editorial overview and a 10k wrap is going to continue. The online world will also continue to play a more and more significant role. However, we don't feel that the opportunity to create fresh, exciting annual reports will ever diminish.

How large a role does environmental policy play in the design and production of your Annual Reports?
Care for the environment is considered in the production of all of our printed materials. Our printing partner for "Hold Fast" is an FSC-certified printer. In addition, all of their inks are soybean-based and recycling plays a major role in their operations. Paper, board, waste inks, solvents and aluminum plates are all recycled.

Environmental concerns are also addressed when selecting papers. Our text paper for "Hold Fast" contained 10% recycled content and was manufactured by a paper company who is part of the Sustainable Forestry Initiative. The cover stock for "Hold Fast" featured 30% post-consumer waste and was manufactured using electricity offset with certified wind power certificates.

We believe that clients want a report that presents their company in a way that is genuine, human and relevant, as well as helps to distinguish them from their competition.

< 20 >

SHIP'S LOG

HARBOR POINT 2008

< 21 >

On June 14, 2006, the Company acquired 62,500, or 13.8%, of the common shares and 2,750, or 9.2%, of the preferred shares of Bay Point for a total purchase price of $9.0 million. The Company has accounted for these investments at fair value, since the investments do not have a readily determinable market value and the Company does not exercise significant influence over the activities of Bay Point. For the year ended December 31, 2008, the Company accrued $0.3 million (year ended December 31, 2007: $0.4 million) of dividends on the preferred shares and has recorded a $4.2 million (for the year ended December 31, 2007: $nil) increase in the fair value of its investment in the common shares of Bay Point. During 2008, Bay Point returned common and preferred capital to its investors. The Company has received $8.6 million related to its common and preferred investments in Bay Point.

In conjunction with the Company's investments in Bay Point, the Company entered into a quota share reinsurance agreement to cede 30% of its property-related lines of business to Bay Point Re Limited, a wholly-owned subsidiary of Bay Point ("Bay Point Re"). This quota share reinsurance agreement expired on December 31, 2007.

The following is a summary of the amounts recognized in the accompanying financial statements for the years ended December 31, 2008 and 2007 related to this agreement:

	2008	2007
Premiums ceded	$ (1,471)	$99,495
Ceded commissions	11,607	29,527
Ceded losses	4,006	26,361

In December 2008, Harbor Point acquired all of the common shares of New Point III Limited ("New Point III") for $35.0 million. The results

As of December 31, 2008, $0.2 million was included in reinsurance balances receivable (December 31, 2007: $33.1 million included in reinsurance balances payable) and $25.4 million (December 31, 2007: $29.2 million) in reinsurance losses recoverable under this agreement.

On December 17, 2007, the Company acquired 125,000 of common shares of New Point Limited ("New Point") for $12.5 million. On June 30, 2008, the Company acquired an additional 75,000 of common shares of New Point for $7.5 million. These investments relate to the Company's investment in the 2008 underwriting year of New Point. On December 31, 2007, New Point agreed to repurchase all of the Company's shares associated with its investment in the 2007 underwriting year of New Point. During 2008, the Company received $48.2 million related to the repurchased shares. For the year ended December 31, 2008, the Company recorded $2.5 million (for the year ended December 31, 2007: $9.1 million) to reflect the equity earnings on these investments.

In conjunction with the Company's investments in New Point, the Company entered into an underwriting services agreement to provide certain underwriting, actuarial and other administrative services to New Point Re, a wholly-owned subsidiary of New Point. Under the underwriting services agreement, New Point Re has agreed to pay the Company an underwriting fee based on gross written premium, a performance fee based on adjusted net income (as defined) and a fixed management fee. For the year ended December 31, 2008, the Company recorded $2.5 million (for the year ended December 31, 2007: $7.8 million) related to these agreements. These amounts are included in other income in the Consolidated Statements of Operations.

< 42 >

---

of New Point III are included in the consolidated results of the Company. This investment relates to the Company's investment in the 2009 underwriting year of New Point Re III Limited, a wholly owned subsidiary of New Point III.

In May 2008, the Company purchased a catastrophe bond for $25.0 million. The bond has a face value of $25.0 million and has a scheduled redemption date of May 24, 2011. The Company receives quarterly interest payments of U.S. Libor (3 months) plus 4.4% (6.6% as of December 31, 2008) on the bond. For the year ended December 31, 2008, the Company recorded $0.9 million of net investment income and a $1.4 million decrease in the estimated fair value of the catastrophe bond. The redemption value of the bond will adjust based on the occurrence of a covered event. A covered event would be an earthquake occurring in Japan.

The Company uses interest rate swaps and futures to adjust the curve and/or duration positioning of the investment portfolio, to obtain risk neutral substitutes for physical securities and to manage the overall risk exposure of the investment portfolio. The interest rate swap contracts have a cost basis of $1.2 million, a notional value of $189.8 million and expire between 2 and 30 years (December 31, 2007: $4.8 million cost, $658.0 million notional, expire between 1 and 11 years). The fair value of these interest rate swaps is based on the present value of the net cashflows of underlying interest payments. The interest rate futures have no cost basis and changes in the market value settle daily through a cash margin account. As of December 31, 2008, the Company held 1,731 interest rate futures contracts each with an equivalent of $1 million exposure to changes in the underlying interest rates.

6. LOSSES AND LOSS EXPENSES

The reserve for losses and loss expenses as of December 31, 2008 and 2007:

	2008	2007
Reported but unpaid losses and loss expenses	$ 141,090	$ 58,361
Losses incurred but not reported	465,141	303,285
	$ 606,231	$ 361,646

Net loss and loss expenses for the years ended December 31, 2008 and 2007:

	2008	2007
Loss and loss expenses paid	$ 125,239	$ 40,482
Loss and loss expenses recovered	(8,590)	(3,773)
Change in unpaid loss and loss expenses	245,972	239,573
Change in reinsurance losses recoverable	544	(24,448)
	$ 363,165	$ 251,834

< 43 >

HARBOR POINT LIMITED

CONSOLIDATED STATEMENTS OF CHANGES IN SHAREHOLDERS' EQUITY

For the years ended December 31, 2008 and 2007   *(Expressed in thousands of U.S. dollars)*

	2008	2007
COMMON SHARES		
Balance at beginning of period	$ 13,652	$ 13,565
Conversion of convertible note	2,000	–
Issued during the period	317	87
Balance at end of period	15,969	13,652
ADDITIONAL PAID-IN CAPITAL		
Balance at beginning of period	1,410,753	1,393,581
Conversion of convertible note	198,000	–
Repayment of employee loans to purchase shares	260	313
Issued during the period	22,551	(87)
Stock compensation expense, net of tax	11,385	16,946
Balance at end of period	1,642,949	1,410,753
ACCUMULATED OTHER COMPREHENSIVE INCOME (LOSS)		
Balance at beginning of period	10,318	(1,328)
Net unrealized investment gain	–	11,646
Cumulative effect of adoption of fair value option	(10,318)	–
Balance at end of period	–	10,318
RETAINED EARNINGS		
Balance at beginning of period	144,269	56,114
Common share dividends	(109,058)	(72,999)
Cumulative effect of adoption of fair value option	10,318	–
Net (loss) income	(12,975)	161,154
Balance at end of period	32,554	144,269
Total shareholders' equity	$1,691,472	$1,578,992

See accompanying notes to consolidated financial statements.

< 26 >

HARBOR POINT LIMITED

CONSOLIDATED STATEMENTS OF CASH FLOWS

For the years ended December 31, 2008 and 2007   *(Expressed in thousands of U.S. dollars)*

	2008	2007
CASH FLOWS PROVIDED BY (USED IN) OPERATING ACTIVITIES:		
Net (loss) income	$ (12,975)	$ 161,154
ADJUSTMENTS TO RECONCILE NET (LOSS) INCOME TO NET CASH PROVIDED BY OPERATING ACTIVITIES:		
Stock compensation expense	11,607	19,026
Deferred tax benefit associated with stock compensation expense	(222)	(2,080)
Net realized investment gains	(9,424)	(525)
Net unrealized investment losses	80,987	–
Net accretion on investments	(2,965)	(2,019)
Equity earnings and change in fair value of other investments	(6,706)	(9,220)
Net foreign exchange losses (gains) on cash and cash equivalents	5,789	(916)
Amortization of intangible assets	8,975	8,975
Amortization of runoff obligation	(2,411)	(3,270)
Change in:		
Accrued interest receivable	2,124	(3,287)
Reinsurance balances receivable	28,517	(18,691)
Deferred acquisition costs	6,128	(23,676)
Prepaid reinsurance premiums	26,842	(15,066)
Reinsurance balances recoverable	544	(21,448)
Other assets	1,169	(2,882)
Reserve for losses and loss expenses	244,585	237,371
Unearned premiums	(39,263)	50,843
Accounts payable and accrued expenses	(7,402)	6,421
Reinsurance balances payable	(33,063)	14,819
Cash provided by operating activities	302,836	395,529
CASH FLOWS PROVIDED BY (USED IN) INVESTING ACTIVITIES:		
Purchase of Harbor Point Reinsurance U.S., Inc.	–	(27,541)
Purchases of fixed maturity investments	(787,060)	(1,565,157)
Sales and maturities of fixed maturity investments	655,813	1,441,360
Purchase of short-term investments, net	(140,874)	(45,538)
Purchases of other investments	(95,396)	(16,574)
Proceeds from sales of other investments	83,749	543
Cash used in investing activities	(283,768)	(212,907)
CASH FLOWS PROVIDED BY (USED IN) FINANCING ACTIVITIES:		
Proceeds from sale of shares	24,143	–
Repurchase of shares to satisfy minimum tax withholding obligation	(1,275)	–
Proceeds from short-term debt	–	200,000
Dividends paid	(109,058)	(72,999)
Repayment of employee loans to purchase common shares	260	313
Cash (used in) provided by financing activities	(85,930)	127,314
Effect of exchange rate changes on foreign currency cash	(5,789)	916
Net (decrease) increase in cash and cash equivalents	(72,651)	310,852
Cash and cash equivalents at beginning of the period	577,768	266,916
Cash and cash equivalents at end of the period	$ 505,117	$ 577,768
SUPPLEMENTAL DISCLOSURE OF CASH FLOW INFORMATION:		
Interest paid	$ 15,348	$ 14,751
Income taxes paid	$ 1	$ 3,769

See accompanying notes to consolidated financial statements.

< 27 >

HARBOR POINT LIMITED

FINANCIAL HIGHLIGHTS

GROSS WRITTEN PREMIUMS

2008	$511,714
2007	$672,476
2006	$642,610

SHAREHOLDERS' EQUITY

2008	$1,691,472
2007	$1,578,992
2006	$1,461,932

OPERATING INCOME

2008	$64,053
2007	$170,106
2006	$84,585

COMBINED RATIO

2008	103.2%
2007	86.0%
2006	92.8%

< 22 >

HARBOR POINT LIMITED

FINANCIAL HIGHLIGHTS

For the years ended and as of December 31, 2008, 2007 and 2006   *(Expressed in thousands of U.S. dollars)*

	2008	2007	2006
INCOME STATEMENT HIGHLIGHTS			
Gross premiums written	$ 511,714	$ 672,476	$ 642,610
Net premiums earned	519,210	532,156	299,188
Net investment income	95,311	98,310	68,666
Operating income	64,053	170,106	84,585
Operating return on equity	4.3%	10.8%	6.0%
UNDERWRITING RATIOS			
Loss ratio	69.9%	47.3%	43.7%
Expense ratio	33.3%	38.7%	49.1%
Combined ratio	103.2%	86.0%	92.8%
BALANCE SHEET HIGHLIGHTS			
Invested assets	$2,232,068	$2,036,692	$1,537,932
Shareholders' equity	1,691,472	1,578,992	1,461,932
FINANCIAL STRENGTH RATINGS			
A.M. Best	A (Excellent)		
Standard & Poor's	A- (Strong)		

< 23 >

Times ARE Tough. Prices ARE RISing. Values ARE Falling.

The MORTGAGE and Energy CRISES ARE DRIVING THE ECONOMY into THE Ground.

TOO MANY PEOPIE ARE LOSING THEIR Jobs and THEIR HOMES. THE FUTURE LOOKS BIEAK. PEOPIE NEED HEIP.

Category: Non-Profit | **Location:** Illinois, United States | **Design Director:** Tim Bruce | **Designer:** Tim Bruce, Emilia Klimiuk | **Paper Type:** Mohawk Superfine | **Photographer:** Lisa Miller - Tony Armour Photography | **Print Run:** 7500 | **Printer:** Blanchette Press | **Writer:** Margaret Benson

What was the client's directive?

CVLS accepts no direct government funding; their work is made possible through grants and the generous support of law firms, corporations and individual donors. CVLS's annual report plays a critical role in communicating the quality, depth and breadth of CVLS's pro bono representation of individual clients from the ranks of Chicago area's poor and working poor. CVLS's directive is to make a good case for their work.

How did you define the problem?

How can we make a good case for their work?

What was the approach?

We listen, we talk and we identify possible themes but we don't generate ideas or commit to a direction. Instead, we meet and photograph the clients and lawyers and other constituents, dig into their stories, ideas and perceptions. The design direction flows from what we've gathered.

How involved was the CEO in your meetings, presentations, etc.?

The Executive Director (CEO) is the lead on the client side.

Were you happy with the result? What could have been better?

Certainly elements could be better. Our aim isn't better, however, it's a thoughtful, functional book that captures the energy and direction of CVLS at the time. A snap shot in time in an ever-changing environment for the practice of law and the complexities of the clients they serve.

What was the client's response?

CVLS is happy with the book, but more importantly, CVLS sees results. Consider a note from a donor they passed on: "We've just sent off a modest donation to CVLS. We'd like to thank you for thinking of us, but, more importantly, thank you for participating in what looks to be an amazing program. By the way, we've received many of these appeals over the years and the CVLS booklet is the most impressive we've ever seen."

What are clients looking for when it comes to designing an Annual Report?

Completely depends on the people, the business and the industry. The best relationships come from clients who are the most personally vested in the goals of the organization. Those clients look for an annual that reflects their story uniquely and passionately.

Do you and the client both view the Annual Report as part of the company's communications strategy? And how important is it within the overall strategy?

Yes, certainly. It's an important part. Years ago, we noticed a client's sales force using the annual report instead of the sales collateral that the company produced when pitching large contract work. We asked why. They told us that their prospects believed the annual report but not the collateral. They reasoned that if the annual report content was driven by the executive branch, reviewed by accounting and law, and followed the standards set aside for public reporting, then the annual represented the most accurate and truthful view of the company.

How do you define success in Annual Report design?

If we can produce an annual report that is an accurate and compelling portrait of an organization, that makes a good case, and still has a little of that undefinable, but perceptible energy and freshness, we think we've done well.

In which direction do you see Annual Reports moving?

As the low tide of the economy draws further out to sea, the beach is littered with unsightly surprises. Public companies have a lot to answer for. They need to build trust in a climate disinclined to trust them and they have to compete in for resources and talent in markets that shift rapidly. Annual reports, like the companies they portray, need to be integrated, intelligent, honest and adaptive. Annual reports' role as voice for the organization—one held to higher reporting standards than other communications—will continue to be relevant. Relevant and important even as the channels and the form change to the times.

Annual reports, like the companies they portray, need to be integrated, intelligent, honest and adaptive.

GREEDY RELATIVES, IN FINANCIAL TROUBLE, CONNED 93-YEAR Old ARMETTA INTO TAKING OUT A MORTGAGE FOR THEM ON THE HOME SHE OWNED FREE AND CLEAR.

Armetta

When They Stiffed her on The payments the HOUSE fell into Foreclosure.

Armetta's grandDaughter Melissa moved from Georgia to help, and went to COURT TO TRY to Stop The Foreclosure. When Judge Carolynn Quinn appointed CVLS to Represent the elderly homeOWNER, volunteer Albert Matthews, WORKing closely with CVLS ATTORNEY PATTY NELSON, found The ANSWER. They helped ARMETTA GET A REVERSE MORtgage which allowed her to USE The equity in her home TO PAY The mortgage with a little bit left over FOR FUN. ARMETTA is happy in her home and MELISSA feels good Knowing That her grandmother's FiNAL YEARS ARE SECURE.

IT WAS TIME FOR SHIRLEY TO MAKE A PERMANENT FAMILY WITH THE GRANDSON SHE'D RAISED AND LOVED HIS ENTIRE LIFE.

VOLUNTEER JONNA McGINLEY AND SUMMER ASSOCIATE ERICA RICHMAN GOT THE PLUM ADOPTION ASSIGNMENT THANKS TO THE CVLS/NEAL GERBER SUMMER ASSOCIATE PROJECT.

JACOBY WAS THRILLED, AND RESPECTFUL DURING HIS COURT APPEARANCE, TALKING WITH THE JUDGE ABOUT SCHOOL AND HIS FUTURE. SHIRLEY WAS CLEARLY PROUD OF HER SON, INFORMING THE JUDGE AND HER ATTORNEYS ABOUT HIS INTEREST IN HIS EDUCATION, EXCELLENT GRADES AND FUTURE PLANS. AND JONNA AND ERICA DISCOVERED THAT PRO BONO WORK CAN BE FUN AND FEEL GOOD—FOR LAWYERS AND FOR CLIENTS.

Erica Richman, Summer Associate
Jonna McGinley, Attorney

Shirley

Jacoby

DONORS

Maria M. Troxclair
J.H. Twinam & Associates
John & Virginia Ulaszek
Darlene A. Vorachek
  & Clifford J. Shapiro
Deborah S. Wahl
David A. Weininger
Robert B. Wilcox Living Trust
Daniel A. & Terri B. Zazove

Under $100
Reva B. Auerbach
In Honor of Alfred Baker
Scott P. Benson
Susan L. Boyd
Keith C. & Denise M. Brennan
Janice A. Childs
Jean G. Cleveland
Paul J. & Catherine
  R. Compernolle
Paul M. & Joanne A. Coogan
Daniel J. & Margaret
  Sulita Creed
Hon. Richard D. & Janet S. Cudahy
Margaret E. Currin
CustomInk.com
Eric S. Donahue
Mark B. and Eve C. Epstein
Fred I. & Judy C. Feinstein
Elizabeth A. Ferrari
Barbara J. Finder
Susan J. Friedman & Marc
  A. Primack
Cheryl Garrett
Victor M. Gryniewicz
James T. & Carol A. Haddon
Susan I. Hammerman
Stephen Harrington
Robert J. & Wendy N. Kopka
Keri S. Kotsonis
Patricia A. & Ivan M. Kralik
Robert J. Krull
Ann Bashook & Marvin D. Leiner
Anne C. Keays & Michael E.
  Leonard
Eileen M. Letts
Samuel H. Levine & Amy A. Levy
Barbara Levine
Melvoin Foundation
Patricia L. McCarthy
John P. McGovern
M. McGuinness
Julie-April Montgomery

John H. & Barbara B. Morrison
Christopher J. Moss
Dr. & Mrs. Willaim Nelson
Robin J. Omahana
Gwendolyn B. Palermini
Charles W. & Diane W. Perkins
Rachel D. & Jonathan M. Powell
Hon. Lee Preston
Imad I. Qasim
Steven M. & Mary R. Ravid
Lindsay P. Reichmann & Linda
  M. Rio
Village of Riverside
Pierre & Margaret Roche
Courtney C. Shea
Ann Marie Slater
John F. & Julie Dressel Stahl
Stephanie L. Uhlarik
George Vernon & Nancy Baker
Fay L. Walker
Ethan York

In Kind
Tony Armour Photography
Tim Bruce
Burrito Beach
Chicago Spine and Joint Care
Crowe Chizek
Deloitte
Fullline Printing
David Goldhaber
Al Goldman
Gravitas Marketing
IKON
Illinois Sports Facilities Authority
Law Bulletin Publishing Company
LOWERCASE, Inc.
Mayer Brown
My Bad Blues Band
owater
Schiff Hardin
Shefsky & Froelich
Swanson Martin & Bell
Universal Sole
Veritext Deposition and Litigation
  Services
White Deer Run
George Yedinak

44

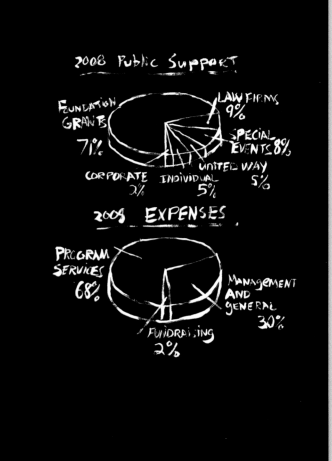

2008 Public Support

Foundation Grants 71%

Law Firms 9%

Special Events 8%

United Way 5%

Corporate 2%

Individual 5%

2008 Expenses

Program Services 68%

Management and General 30%

Fundraising 2%

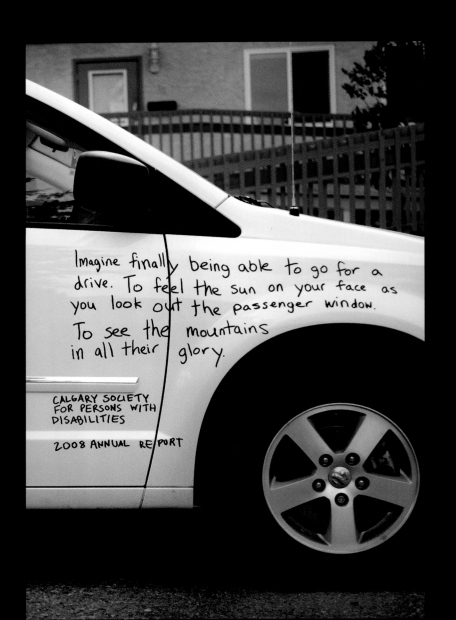

Imagine coming home to where everything feels right. Where the dishwasher washes the dishes and the bed is made with clean, crisp linens.

Imagine having the ability to complete daily activities without feeling uncomfortable and with a sense of dignity. Activities like eating and bathing, things that most of us take for granted.

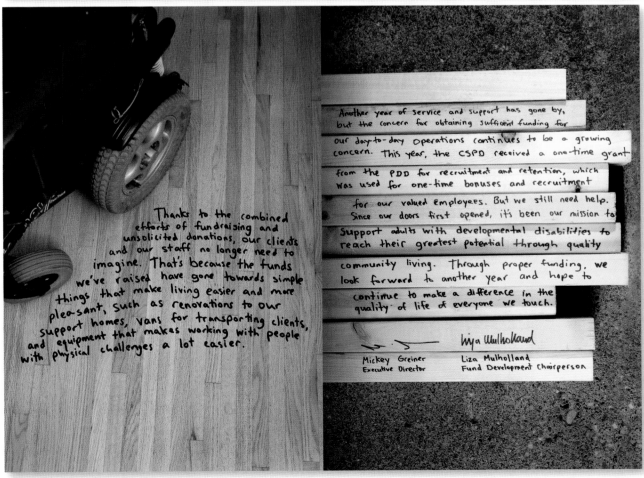

Thanks to the combined efforts of fundraising and unsolicited donations, our clients and our staff no longer need to imagine. That's because the funds we've raised have gone towards simple things that make living easier and more pleasant, such as renovations to our support homes, vans for transporting clients, and equipment that makes working with people with physical challenges a lot easier.

Another year of service and support has gone by, but the concern for obtaining sufficient funding for our day-to-day operations continues to be a growing concern. This year, the CSPD received a one-time grant from the PDD for recruitment and retention, which was used for one-time bonuses and recruitment for our valued employees. But we still need help. Since our doors first opened, it's been our mission to support adults with developmental disabilities to reach their greatest potential through quality community living. Through proper funding, we look forward to another year and hope to continue to make a difference in the quality of life of everyone we touch.

Mickey Greiner
Executive Director

Liza Mulholland
Fund Development Chairperson

Category: Non-Profit | **Location:** Alberta, Canada | **Art Director:** Jonathan Herman | **Creative Director:** Monique Gamache, Joe Hospodarec | **Paper Type:** Mohawk Options 80 lb Text |
Photographer: Justen Lacoursiere | **Print Run:** 500 | **Printer:** Blanchette Press | **Writer:** Saro Ghazarian

RESIDENTIAL SUPPORT

We provide three types of residential supports: Community Homes, Independent Living, and Community Support. Since our first home opened over 30 years ago, we've placed great importance on the compatability between roommates, support workers, and service providers. Because of our dedicated staff, our 45 clients have been able to reach personal bests that have gone beyond expectations.

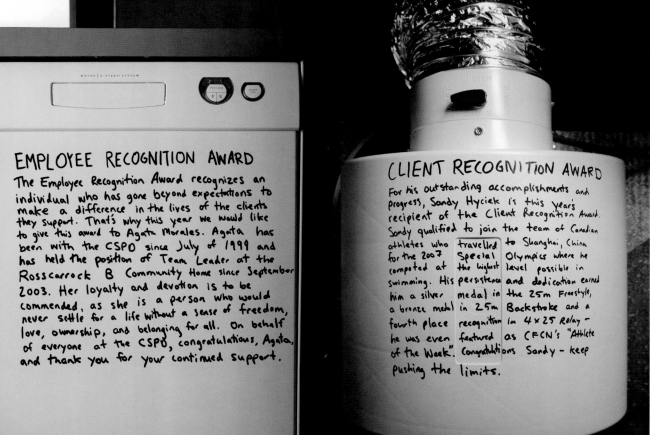

EMPLOYEE RECOGNITION AWARD

The Employee Recognition Award recognizes an individual who has gone beyond expectations to make a difference in the lives of the clients they support. That's why this year we would like to give this award to Agata Morales. Agata has been with the CSPO since July of 1999 and has held the position of Team Leader at the Rosscarrock B Community Home since September 2003. Her loyalty and devotion is to be commended, as she is a person who would never settle for a life without a sense of freedom, love, ownership, and belonging for all. On behalf of everyone at the CSPO, congratulations, Agata, and thank you for your continued support.

CLIENT RECOGNITION AWARD

For his outstanding accomplishments and progress, Sandy Hyciek is this year's recipient of the Client Recognition Award. Sandy qualified to join the team of Canadian athletes who travelled to Shanghai, China for the 2007 Special Olympics where he competed at the highest level possible in swimming. His persistence and dedication earned him a silver medal in the 25m Freestyle, a bronze medal in 25m Backstroke and a fourth place recognition in 4×25 Relay – he was even featured as CFCN's "Athlete of the Week". Congratulations Sandy – keep pushing the limits.

What was the client's directive?
The Calgary Society for Persons with Disabilities (CSPD) wanted people to know how their donations made an impact on the lives of their clients.

How did you define the problem?
Communicate how donations make an impact in the lives of CSPD residents and caregivers.

What was the approach?
We wrote the entire annual report using dry erase markers on objects that were purchased through donations that year.

What disciplines or people helped you with the project?
This was team effort—from brainstorming the idea to the execution. In fact, the writer was enlisted to help remove his writing from the objects after each shot. It helped keep things brief and on message—because the more he wrote, the more he had to wipe off afterward.

How involved was the CEO in your meetings, presentations, etc.?
This was the fourth annual report we've created for the CSPD, and over the years we've earned a lot of their trust. Mickey Greiner, the Executive Director of the CSPD, was involved in the process and never stood in the way of our unconventional concept.

Were you happy with the result? What could have been better?
We were very happy with the result. The only time we couldn't handwrite on objects was when it came to financials—they have to be printed. We handled that by putting them in a typewriter and on a computer screen so the auditors would sign off on them. It made the report better in hindsight.

What was the client's response?
They were thrilled. We attended their annual general meeting and received a standing ovation from the Board and the staff. It was very humbling and gratifying.

What are clients looking for when it comes to designing an Annual Report?
Whether it's in the numbers or in telling the details of their operations they're always looking to us to tell their story in a memorable way.

Do you and the client both view the Annual Report as part of the company's communications strategy? And how important is it within the overall strategy?
Annual reports are a huge part of the overall communications strategy. This annual was used as a fund-raising tool for the upcoming year. One employee of the CSPD talked about how she used this annual to help explain to their family what she does every day at work.

How do you define success in Annual Report design?
While this annual won a large handful of awards, what truly made this annual a success was the reception it was given at their annual general meeting.

In which direction do you see Annual Reports moving?
Annual reports exist to tell the financials—which we respect and embrace—but they also need to tell a larger story. Something that gets people to understand your business goals and objectives.

We attended [the client's] annual general meeting and received a standing ovation from the Board and the staff. It was very humbling and gratifying.

TEAM RECOGNITION AWARD

This year, we would like to express our appreciation to the efforts of a group of employees through a special Team Award. The team recognized with this award has consistently demonstrated how to be creative, caring, respectful, and flexible to clients and their families at all times. It is with great pleasure to honour the members of the 38th Street home - Tammy Budlong-Rietveld, Patrick Franke, Chloe McBean, Rachel Seever, Karen Bignell, Hannah Durodola and Emmanuel Ojewole - for all their hard work with this special award. Congratulations team.

SERVICE PROVIDERS AWARD

It is with great pleasure to present this year's Service Provider Recognition Award to Crystal Sabados. Crystal started her career with the CSPD over 25 years ago and has been a supportive roommate to John and Lynn for the last 13 years. Thanks to her help, patience, understanding, and sense of humour, both John and Lynn have been able to achieve their goals and pursue their dreams. On behalf of John, Lynn, and their parents and guardians, we would like to thank you, Crystal, for your ongoing dedication to the CSPD and our clients.

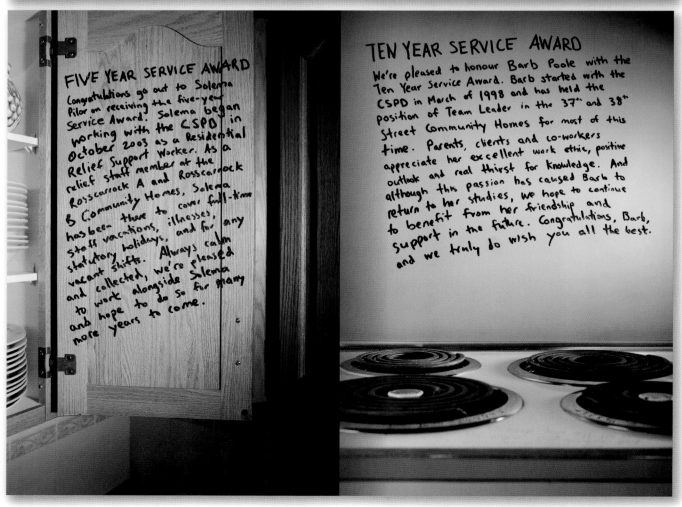

FIVE YEAR SERVICE AWARD

Congratulations go out to Solema Pilor on receiving the five-year Service Award. Solema began working with the CSPD in October 2003 as a Residential Relief Support Worker. As a relief staff member at the Rosscarrock A and Rosscarrock B Community Homes, Solema has been there to cover full-time staff vacations, illnesses, statutory holidays, and for any vacant shifts. Always calm and collected, we're pleased to work alongside Solema and hope to do so for many more years to come.

TEN YEAR SERVICE AWARD

We're pleased to honour Barb Poole with the Ten Year Service Award. Barb started with the CSPD in March of 1998 and has held the position of Team Leader in the 37th and 38th Street Community Homes for most of this time. Parents, clients and co-workers appreciate her excellent work ethic, positive outlook and real thirst for knowledge. And although this passion has caused Barb to return to her studies, we hope to continue to benefit from her friendship and support in the future. Congratulations, Barb, and we truly do wish you all the best.

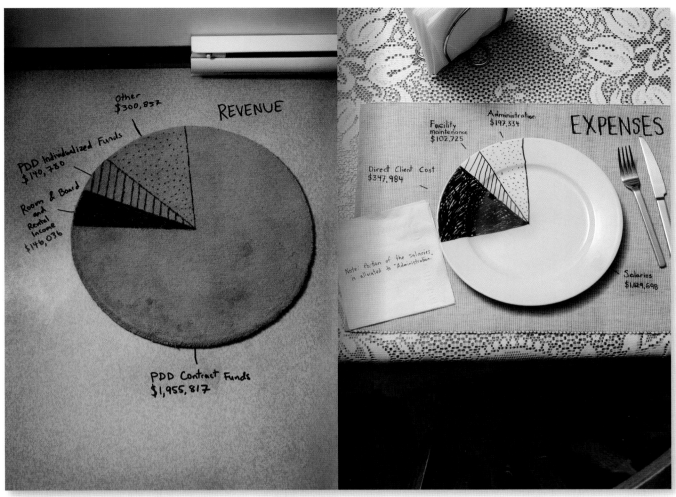

NEENAH PAPER, INC.
2008 ANNUAL REPORT

Category: Paper Companies | **Location:** New York, United States | **Creative Director:** Richard Colbourne | **Design Director:** Jason Miller | **Designer:** Jason Miller | **Illustrator:** Ilovedust, Raymond Biesinger, Mario Hugo, Faiyaz Jafri | **Paper Type:** Various Neenah stocks | **Photographer:** Dean Kaufman, Aakash Nihalani, Horacio Salinas, Corriette Schoenaerts | **Print Producer:** Nicole Anello, Georgiann Baran | **Print Run:** 19,000 copies | **Printer:** Lake County Press | **Project Manager:** Michelle Steg Faranda | **Set Designer & Props:** Sarah Illenberger | **Writer:** Edward Nebb

[The report] is very straightforward in message, yet at the same time highly expressive from a visual standpoint.

Q&A with Addison

What was the client's directive?
To communicate all the ways in which Neenah Paper had executed its strategic plan in becoming a more focused and agile fine paper company.

How did you define the problem?
To express bot the specialized niche focu of Neenah's products and culture as well as the straightforward accountability of their strategic planning and execution.

What was the approach?
We found that in many ways, the qualities that made Neenah a more interesting and competitive company also positioned them strongly to weather the economic downturn.

We developed a typographic solution based on a series of terms that communicate these differentiators—which are simple and direct—and then executed the typography in unique and surprising ways, relevant to each topic. It is very straightforward in message, yet at the same time highly expressive from a visual standpoint.

What disciplines or people helped you with the project?
We collaborated with a different artist, illustrator, or photographer on each spread. Their specific disciplines ranged from a high-end architectural photographer to a site-specific street artist.

How involved was the CEO in your meetings, presentations, etc.?
Very involved for a CEO, particularly in the formative stages.

How important is the Annual Report within the company's overall communications strategy?
The annual report is very important, particularly for this client, as they make premium uncoated paper, used in many annual reports.

Net Sales by Segment
dollars in millions, from left
Technical Products: $397
Fine Paper: $336

Technical Products Sales by SBU
dollars in millions, from left
Wall Covering: $44
Graphics & Identification: $51
Component Materials: $78
Tape: $90
Filtration: $133

26

Neenah Paper At A Glance

At Neenah Paper, our mission is to be the first choice for premium branded and customized paper products.

Our goal is to create value for our customers and stockholders through innovation, service and excellence in execution; and it is our employees who drive this value.

27

TECHNICAL PRODUCTS –
GLOBAL BUSINESS UNITS

Filtration
Transportation
Other (Home, Industrial)

Component Materials
Medical Packaging
Abrasives
Release Base
Application Masking
Veneer Backings

Tape
Crepe Base
Specialty Flatbacks

Graphics & Identification
Label & Tag
Image Transfer
Decorative Components
Clean Room
Durable Printing

Wall Covering
Nonwoven
Saturated Wetlaids

Neenah Technical Products

Neenah's Technical Products business is a leading producer of specialty papers and substrates for complex commercial applications that require saturating, coating and other engineered solutions. The segment consists of five global business units: Filtration, Specialty Tape, Component Materials, Graphics & Identification and Wall Covering. Our products might be found in the car you drive, the wall covering in your office, the personalized t-shirt you wear, or the tapes you use in a painting project. Specific uses include automotive, household and industrial filters, masking and industrial tapes, coated abrasives, medical packaging, heat transfer and book covers. Other graphics applications include specialty papers and labels that provide printability, durability and security. The technical products group serves customers in more than 35 countries through manufacturing facilities in the U.S. and Germany, supported by R&D efforts focused on developing the new processes and products that will meet customers' needs and drive our growth.

31

Neenah Fine Paper

Neenah's fine paper business is the undisputed leader in the premium fine paper market. We are recognized as a world-class manufacturer of premium writing, text and cover materials, cotton fiber papers and specialty items. Our well-known brands, such as CLASSIC®, NEENAH®, STARWHITE® and ESSE® Papers, set the gold standard for quality and consistently rank as number one and two in sales in their categories. A pioneer in eco-friendly paper products, our ENVIRONMENT® Paper is the premier offering of recycled content papers in the market. Neenah's leadership role in fine paper is supported by our broad range of colors, textures and other product features, as well as our reputation for attentive customer service. Our products are in demand wherever image counts: for letterhead, business cards, private watermark stationery, annual reports, brochures and such specialized uses as upscale retail packaging and wine labels – even the Presidential Inaugural Invitation.

29

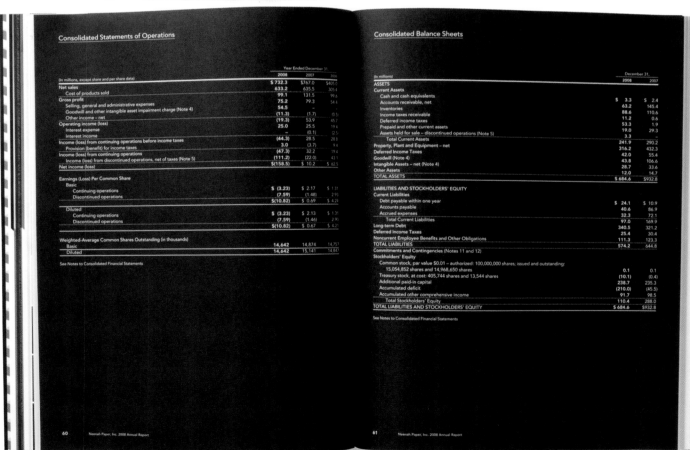

Consolidated Statements of Operations

	Year Ended December 31		
(In millions, except share and per share data)	2008	2007	2006
Net sales	$ 732.3	$767.0	$405.0
Cost of products sold	633.2	635.5	305.4
Gross profit	99.1	131.5	99.6
Selling, general and administrative expenses	75.2	79.3	54.4
Goodwill and other intangible asset impairment charge (Note 4)	54.5	–	–
Other income – net	(11.3)	(1.7)	(0.5)
Operating income (loss)	(19.3)	53.9	45.7
Interest expense	25.0	25.5	19.4
Interest income	–	(0.1)	(2.5)
Income (loss) from continuing operations before income taxes	(44.3)	28.5	28.8
Provision (benefit) for income taxes	3.0	(3.7)	9.4
Income (loss) from continuing operations	(47.3)	32.2	19.4
Income (loss) from discontinued operations, net of taxes (Note 5)	(111.2)	(22.0)	43.1
Net income (loss)	$(158.5)	$ 10.2	$ 62.5
Earnings (Loss) Per Common Share			
Basic			
Continuing operations	$ (3.23)	$ 2.17	$ 1.31
Discontinued operations	(7.59)	(1.48)	2.93
	$(10.82)	$ 0.69	$ 4.24
Diluted			
Continuing operations	$ (3.23)	$ 2.13	$ 1.31
Discontinued operations	(7.59)	(1.46)	2.90
	$(10.82)	$ 0.67	$ 4.21
Weighted-Average Common Shares Outstanding (in thousands)			
Basic	14,642	14,874	14,757
Diluted	14,642	15,141	14,847

See Notes to Consolidated Financial Statements

Consolidated Balance Sheets

	December 31,	
(In millions)	2008	2007
ASSETS		
Current Assets		
Cash and cash equivalents	$ 3.3	$ 2.4
Accounts receivable, net	63.2	145.4
Inventories	88.6	110.6
Income taxes receivable	11.2	0.6
Deferred income taxes	53.3	1.9
Prepaid and other current assets	19.0	29.3
Assets held for sale – discontinued operations (Note 5)	3.3	
Total Current Assets	241.9	290.2
Property, Plant and Equipment – net	316.2	432.3
Deferred Income Taxes	42.0	55.4
Goodwill (Note 4)	43.8	106.6
Intangible Assets – net (Note 4)	28.7	33.6
Other Assets	12.0	14.7
TOTAL ASSETS	$ 684.6	$932.8
LIABILITIES AND STOCKHOLDERS' EQUITY		
Current Liabilities		
Debt payable within one year	$ 24.1	$ 10.9
Accounts payable	40.6	86.9
Accrued expenses	32.3	72.1
Total Current Liabilities	97.0	169.9
Long-term Debt	340.5	321.2
Deferred Income Taxes	25.4	30.4
Noncurrent Employee Benefits and Other Obligations	111.3	123.3
TOTAL LIABILITIES	574.2	644.8
Commitments and Contingencies (Notes 11 and 12)		
Stockholders' Equity		
Common stock, par value $0.01 – authorized: 100,000,000 shares; issued and outstanding:		
15,054,852 shares and 14,968,650 shares	0.1	0.1
Treasury stock, at cost: 405,744 shares and 13,544 shares	(10.1)	(0.4)
Additional paid-in capital	238.7	235.3
Accumulated deficit	(210.0)	(45.5)
Accumulated other comprehensive income	91.7	98.5
Total Stockholders' Equity	110.4	288.0
TOTAL LIABILITIES AND STOCKHOLDERS' EQUITY	$ 684.6	$932.8

See Notes to Consolidated Financial Statements

We're here

COURIER 2008 ANNUAL REPORT

Category: Publishing | **Location:** Massachusetts, United States | **Creative Director:** Robert Krivicich | **Model:** Azatuhi Ayrikyan, Jose Lizardo | **Paper Type:** Monadnock Astrolite PC 100 80C/80T Finch Casablanca 60T | **Photographer:** Tim Llewellyn, William Geddes, Gary Pikovsky | **Print Producer:** Dynagraf | **Print Run:** 5,500 | **Printer:** Kirkwood Printing | **Senior Designer:** Gary Pikovsky | **Writer:** John Temple

What was the client's directive?
Amidst a turbulent year, Courier, a local book publisher and manufacturer, relied on its 184 years of experience and business community presence to come through strong during the global economic recession. This experience is what Courier wanted to highlight in the 2008 annual report.

How did you define the problem?
Our thought was to focus the book on the very things that created Courier's reputation over the years—consistent and stable publishing presence in the home remodeling, religion and education sectors.

What was the approach?
The cover phrase, "We're here." set the tone for the book. The phrase re-appears within a photo runway that summarizes Courier's audiences. Suggesting stability, these two words helped unite the visuals across a variety of pages.

What disciplines or people helped you with the project?
Photographers, writers, printers and friends (as models). John Temple was the writer for the project, with Tim Llewellyn as the main photographer and Kirkwood Printing as the printer.

How involved was the CEO in your meetings, presentations, etc.?
Jim Conway, Courier's CEO, is involved by shaping the overall messaging and the tone of the book. He is present at all the design presentations and is open to the creativity of the book, but knew this year the annual should be simple and direct.

Were you happy with the result? What could have been better?
The original idea we developed remained intact throughout the whole process. As designers, we always see ways of adding to the books we design, no matter what the final outcome is. In this particular case, it would have been great to add a few more tactile references to the classic printed books—mix of papers, finishes, hard cover, etc. In this economy, however, we thought the design was strong and efficient.

What was the client's response?
"I think it's a perfect fit for us this year!"

What are clients looking for when it comes to designing an Annual Report?
Four things: design, guidance, service and value.

Do you and the client both view the Annual Report as part of the company's communications strategy? And how important is it within the overall strategy?
We tend to feel that annual reports can play a number of roles for a company. Outside of providing investor information, the annual report can easily double as a company brochure, serve as a connection into the company's website and present some great illustration, photography and typography along with the above.

How do you define success in Annual Report design?
Happy clients and happy designers. Has to work both ways.

In which direction do you see Annual Reports moving?
The annual report, in its original nature, is a static entity. The information presented within the book is usually outdated the moment the annual reaches the shareholder. We think annuals are going to become more dynamic, with complementary websites providing updatable viewpoints from the CEO, along with rich multimedia experiences that one will want to visit more than once. The printed book, however, will always serve as a physical validation of the company's direction, while pointing you toward the website.

How large a role does environmental policy play in the design and production of your Annual Reports?
As the green movement permeates all aspects of our lives, the annual reports tend to shrink and begin to rely on FSC and recycled stocks for paper. Our goal is to educate clients about newly available options, as well to migrate sections of annuals onto the web in the form of video and easily updatable content.

We think annuals are going to become more dynamic, with complementary websites providing updatable viewpoints from the CEO, along with rich multimedia experiences that one will want to visit more than once.

and here.

AND WE'RE HERE TO STAY.

It was a turbulent year for our company, our industry and the national economy. Over 185 years, we've learned to work through turbulence, but it's never easy. Fortunately, we faced the task with a strong balance sheet, a disciplined organization, a state-of-the-art infrastructure and a golden reputation among our customers. We're confident that these assets will continue to serve us well when the economy turns and new opportunities arise.

FINANCIAL HIGHLIGHTS	2008	2007
Dollars in millions except net income (loss) per diluted share		
Sales	$ 280.4	$ 294.5
Net income (loss)	$ (0.4)*	$ 24.7
Net income (loss) per share	$ (0.40)*	$ 2.25

*Includes a non-cash, non-tax impairment charge of $12.1 million or $1.12 per share.

ADAPTING QUICKLY,

operating efficiently

AND ANTICIPATING

CUSTOMER NEEDS

HAVE SUSTAINED COURIER

THROUGH NEARLY

two centuries

OF ECONOMIC UPS

AND DOWNS.

Fiscal 2008 presented serious challenges, but we responded effectively, making necessary course corrections while maintaining our focus on excellent products, outstanding service and responsible management.

As a result, we were able to limit the damage while helping customers overcome adversities of their own. Along the way, we manufactured more than 175 million books, reached out to consumers at retailers nationwide, answered 32,000 direct queries from readers and established ourselves as a leader in implementing and promoting greener methods of book production. •

¶

MILLIONS OF SCRIPTURES, THOUSANDS OF
CLASSROOMS, HUNDREDS OF CUSTOMERS.

However you count, it was a busy year. In a down year for many businesses, we grew our share in two key manufacturing markets, helped bring scriptures to more than 100 countries, and attracted more than 40 new trade publishers into our customer ranks. Meanwhile, students and teachers at every level from elementary to graduate school made new discoveries every day with the help of millions of four-color textbooks made by Courier.

As the economy deteriorated, publishing sales were hit hard, with Creative Homeowner bearing the brunt of the housing collapse, but Dover Publications also down nearly 10 percent, and even Research & Education Association (REA) off slightly after three straight years of double-digit growth. Despite these headwinds, all **three brands** continued to reach out to readers with innovative titles and aggressive merchandising. REA helped more than half a million students prepare for SAT, AP and other high-stakes tests. Nearly a dozen Creative Homeowner titles held onto their positions as top sellers within their retail categories. And Dover released the first titles in its new **Calla Editions** line, combining environmental responsibility with stunningly beautiful four-color production. p

12

Calla Editions, *Stories from Hans Christian Anderson*, 2008

13

REMEMBERING
GEORGE NICHOLS
1929 – 2008

George Nichols' passing in the spring of 2008 deprived us of one of the most treasured members of the Courier family. As President of National Publishing Company for more than three decades, George created beautiful books and enduring relationships that strengthened our company, advanced our industry and made the world a better place. As colleague, mentor and friend, he was irreplaceable, but his inspiration lives on in the organization he built, the lives he touched—and the smile that continues to warm our days.

16

2008
FORM 10-K

ALREADY A LEADER IN FOUR-COLOR,
WE ADDED A FIFTH: GREEN.

Courier's superior technology and service are helping book publishers compete more effectively in challenging markets. Through years of working closely with customers, we've learned to anticipate trends and invest ahead of our peers. As a result, our plants in Indiana and Pennsylvania are widely recognized as the most efficient facilities in North America for the production of four-color books and religious scriptures. This year's improvements in **Kendallville** and **Philadelphia** closed out the largest program of capital investment in our history, leaving us well positioned for strong cash flow in an uncertain economy.

As our manufacturing footprint has grown, we've worked to make our carbon footprint smaller. Our all-digital workflow, high-yield presses and online proofing systems reduce paper demand, and we recycle 100 percent of paper waste as well as inks and solvents. We also promote environmental responsibility through our own books as well as those we manufacture for others. Creative Homeowner's *Green Up Your Cleanup* offers practical tips to reduce everyday use of harmful chemicals. And Courier's **Green Edition**™ seal adds marketing value for any publisher willing to comply with the environmental standards behind it. This Annual Report shows how colorful green can be. ▪

Creative Homeowner, *Green Up Your Cleanup*, 2008

14

15

REPORT OF INDEPENDENT REGISTERED PUBLIC ACCOUNTING FIRM

To the Board of Directors and Stockholders of Courier Corporation
North Chelmsford, Massachusetts

We have audited the accompanying consolidated balance sheets of Courier Corporation and subsidiaries (the "Company") as of September 27, 2008 and September 29, 2007, and the related consolidated statements of operations, changes in stockholders' equity, and cash flows for each of the three years in the period ended September 27, 2008. Our audits also included the financial statement schedule listed in the Index at Item 15(a)2. These financial statements and financial statement schedule are the responsibility of the Company's management. Our responsibility is to express an opinion on the financial statements and financial statement schedule based on our audits.

We conducted our audits in accordance with the standards of the Public Company Accounting Oversight Board (United States). Those standards require that we plan and perform the audit to obtain reasonable assurance about whether the financial statements are free of material misstatement. An audit includes examining, on a test basis, evidence supporting the amounts and disclosures in the financial statements. An audit also includes assessing the accounting principles used and significant estimates made by management, as well as evaluating the overall financial statement presentation. We believe that our audits provide a reasonable basis for our opinion.

In our opinion, such consolidated financial statements present fairly, in all material respects, the financial position of Courier Corporation and subsidiaries as of September 27, 2008 and September 29, 2007, and the results of their operations and their cash flows for each of the three years in the period ended September 27, 2008, in conformity with accounting principles generally accepted in the United States of America. Also, in our opinion, such financial statement schedule, when considered in relation to the basic consolidated financial statements taken as a whole, presents fairly, in all material respects, the information set forth therein.

We have also audited, in accordance with the standards of the Public Company Accounting Oversight Board (United States), the Company's internal control over financial reporting as of September 27, 2008, based on the criteria established in *Internal Control—Integrated Framework* issued by the Committee of Sponsoring Organizations of the Treadway Commission, and our report dated November 26, 2008 expressed an unqualified opinion on the Company's internal control over financial reporting.

As disclosed in Note G to the consolidated financial statements, the Company adopted on September 29, 2007 Statement of Financial Accounting Standards No. 158 "Employers' Accounting for Defined Benefit Pension and Other Postretirement Plans, an amendment of FASB Statements No. 87, 88, 106 and 132(R)."

/s/ Deloitte & Touche LLP

Boston, Massachusetts
November 26, 2008

F-1

COURIER CORPORATION

CONSOLIDATED STATEMENTS OF OPERATIONS

(Dollars in thousands except per share amounts)

	For the Years Ended		
	September 27, 2008	September 29, 2007	September 30, 2006
Net sales (Note A)	$ 280,324	$ 294,592	$ 269,051
Cost of sales	202,445	198,229	180,535
Gross profit	77,879	96,363	88,516
Selling and administrative expenses	53,034	53,926	50,144
Impairment charge (Note A)	23,643	-	-
Interest expense, net (Note A)	1,133	1,571	182
Pretax income	69	40,866	38,190
Provision for income taxes (Note C)	439	15,121	9,810
Net income (loss)	$ (370)	$ 25,745	$ 28,380
Net income (loss) per share (Notes A and J):			
Basic	$ (0.03)	$ 2.06	$ 2.30
Diluted	$ (0.03)	$ 2.03	$ 2.25
Cash dividends declared per share	$ 0.80	$ 0.72	$ 0.48

The accompanying notes are an integral part of the consolidated financial statements.

Fiscal year 2006 was a 53-week period.

F-2

Number ONE ——

Zukunft
Wachstum
Kunden
Profitabilität

———— Herausforderung Zukunft ————————

Category: Transportation | **Location:** Germany | **Art Director:** Stefan Kaderka | **Artist:** Günter Fidrich | **Creative Director:** Frank Wagner | **Designer:** Manuel Rigel | **Illustrator:** Adelgund Janik |
Print Producer: Melanie Sauer | **Printer:** Mediahaus Biering | **Project Manager:** Christian Finkenzeller, Frank Wagner

What was the client's directive?
The new strategic orientation of the BMW Group introduced last year should manifest itself as a meta theme of the annual report 2008.

How did you define the problem?
With the annual report 2008, a new trilogy was introduced, which newly defines the annual report of the BMW Group from scratch.

What was the approach?
The BMW group is reinventing itself. This is the principal statement of this annual report. To let the reader know this was the uppermost concern of the conceptual development.

The creative guide theme of "balance" re-interprets the strategic realignment of the group on almost every side of its 90-page image section in an innovative way. In this way, the report underlines the creative engineering spirit as well as the strategy of the company.

What disciplines or people helped you with the project?
Except for printing the report—controlled by our producer—everything was done within häfelinger + wagner design.

How involved was the CEO in your meetings, presentations, etc.?
The chairperson is the last authority to appraise the concept for the business report. There has been no direct contact between the agency and the CEO.

What are clients looking for when it comes to designing an Annual Report?
The company message must be implemented in a clearly established and visually harmonious way. It is necessary to stage the message in an emotionally appealing but at the same time serious way corresponding to the medium. It is very important that text body, graphics and tables are easy to read. Particular importance is also placed on a service-orientated organisation of complex and extensive content.

Do you and the client both view the Annual Report as part of the company's communications strategy? And how important is it within the overall strategy?
We view the annual report as a guide medium for all communication—its significance is correspondingly high.

How do you define success in Annual Report design?
The uppermost goal is to communicate the company message authentically and unmistakably. The appearance is harmonious from the title right up to the last detail, the optimum solution has been found for all formal and production technical aspects. As we supervise the report from conception, via the lithography, finished drawing right up to the final production, we have managed to produce a very harmonious, individual total picture. Generally, we are of the opinion that company communication must take place holistically and sustainably. We also use this standard when designing the annual reports.

How large a role does environmental policy play in the design and production of your Annual Reports?
Generally, we are very dependent on our customers in this regard. Many of them use FSC certified paper and we are very pleased that environmental awareness is growing in this area. At the same time, of course, there are forms of refinement such as varnish, which are less environmentally compatible, but achieve very beautiful optical and haptic effects.

The uppermost goal is to communicate the company message authentically and unmistakably.

So entstehen Fahrzeuge,
die Premium völlig neu
interpretieren.

Auf Basis technologischer
Innovationen. Und mit ei-
ner Effizienz, die mit Res-
sourcen und eingesetzten
Mitteln verantwortungsvoll
umgeht.

Zukunftsfähigkeit beweisen

Faszinierend bleiben

Profitabilität sichern

Weiter denken

Das Ziel: Wir wollen der
führende Anbieter von
Premium-Produkten
und Premium-Dienst-
leistungen für individuelle
Mobilität sein.

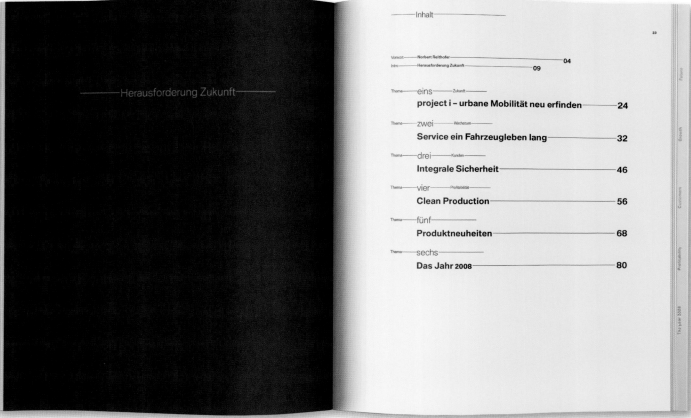

Herausforderung Zukunft

Inhalt

23

Rolls-Royce Phantom Coupé

Das Rolls-Royce Phantom Coupé ist das vierte und jüngste Modell in der Produktpalette von Rolls-Royce Motor Cars. Ein besonders leichtes und sehr festes Aluminiumchassis sorgt für optimale Sicherheit, der bewährte 6,75-Liter-V12-Motor für leistungsstarken Antrieb.

---

20 Geschäftsverlauf

Automobilabsatz erreicht das hohe Vorjahres-niveau nicht

Der Automobilabsatz der BMW Group war vor allem in der zweiten Jahreshälfte 2008 von der anhaltenden Finanz-krise und der damit einhergehenden Kaufzurückhaltung der Verbraucher beeinflusst. Insgesamt verkaufte die BMW Group im Berichtsjahr 1.435.876 Automobile der Marken BMW, MINI und Rolls-Royce, das sind 4,3% weniger als im Vorjahr.

Bei der Marke BMW beeinträchtigten zusätzlich modell-zyklusbedingte Effekte beim BMW 7er und Z4 den Absatz. Im Jahr 2008 lieferte das Unternehmen 1.202.239 Fahrzeuge der Marke BMW an Kunden aus, dies entspricht einem Rückgang von 5,8%. Mit 232.425 verkauften Automobilen der Marke MINI konnte der Vorjahreswert um 4,3% über-troffen werden, dazu trug auch der Erfolg des MINI Clubman bei. Von der Marke Rolls-Royce setzte die BMW Group 1.212 Fahrzeuge ab (+ 20,0%), dabei sorgte das seit Herbst 2008 für Kunden verfügbare Rolls-Royce Phantom Coupé für zusätzliche Impulse.

Viele Märkte mit sinkenden Absatzzahlen

Vor allem in der zweiten Jahreshälfte 2008 führte die Schwä-che der Weltwirtschaft in vielen Ländern zu erheblichen Einbußen beim Automobilabsatz. In Nordamerika verzeich-nete die BMW Group im Berichtszeitraum mit 331.796 an Kunden übergebenen Fahrzeugen ein Minus von 8,8% im Vergleich zum Vorjahr. Auch in den USA blieben die Ver-käufe im Jahr 2008 mit 303.639 Auslieferungen um 9,7% hin-ter dem Vorjahreswert zurück.

BMW Group – wichtigste Automobilmärkte 2008
in % vom Absatz

USA	27,1	China	5,3
Deutschland	19,0	Frankreich	4,9
Großbritannien	10,8	Spanien	4,2
Italien	6,3	Sonstige	28,0

In Europa waren die Auswirkungen der Finanzkrise vor allem ab der Jahresmitte deutlich spürbar. Negative Ten-denzen in Westeuropa konnten nicht vollständig durch die teilweise kräftigen Zuwachsraten in Osteuropa ausgegli-chen werden. Insgesamt lieferte die BMW Group in Europa im Berichtsjahr 954.583 Automobile der Marken BMW, MINI und Rolls-Royce aus, das entspricht einem Minus von 3,8%. In Deutschland konnte trotz des besonders schwie-rigen Umfelds mit 280.915 Verkäufen im Jahr 2008 das Vorjahresniveau erreicht werden (2007: 280.938). Dagegen

fiel der Absatzrückgang in Großbritannien mit 12,8% auf 151.527 Automobile deutlich aus. Auch in Italien und Spa-nien lagen die Verkäufe unter den Vorjahreswerten. Mit 90.470 Auslieferungen blieb der Absatz in Italien um 15,4% unter dem Vorjahres, in Spanien betrug der Rückgang 19,1% auf 59.658 Fahrzeuge. In Frankreich realisierte das Unternehmen im Jahr 2008 einen kräftigen Anstieg um 8,3% auf 70.516 Automobile. Dies ist auch das Ergebnis der dort bereits eingeführten emissionsbezogenen Fahr-zeugbesteuerung, von der die BMW Group durch das Innovationspaket Efficient Dynamics in besonderem Maße profitiert.

In Asien entwickelten sich die einzelnen Märkte überwie-gend positiv, insgesamt setzte die BMW Group in dieser Region im Berichtsjahr 165.745 Automobile ab und erzielte ein Plus von 3,9%. Auch wenn sich das Wachstum in der zweiten Jahreshälfte 2008 in den chinesischen Märkten (China, Hongkong, Taiwan) etwas abschwächte, stieg der Absatz in der Jahresbetrachtung um 23,3% auf 75.481 Fahr-zeuge. In Japan hingegen blieben die Auslieferungen mit 48.848 Automobilen der BMW Group deutlich unter dem Vorjahreswert (– 19,2%).

BMW Group Auslieferungen Automobile nach Regionen und Märkten
in Tsd.

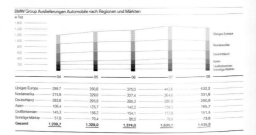

	04	05	06	07	08	
Übriges Europa	299,7	350,8	375,0	443,6	632,2	
Nordamerika	315,9	329,0	337,4	364,0	331,8	
Deutschland	283,6	295,9	295,3	280,9	280,9	
Asien	106,4	125,7	142,2	159,5	165,7	
Großbritannien	145,3	156,2	154,1	173,8	151,6	
Sonstige Märkte	57,9	70,4	80,0	78,9	73,8	
Gesamt	**1.208,7**	**1.328,0**	**1.374,0**	**1.500,7**	**1.435,9**	

Auslieferungen BMW Automobile nach Modellen
in Einheiten

	2008	2007	Veränderung in %	Anteil an BMW Auslieferungen 2008 in %
BMW 1er				
Dreitürer	49.559	30.984	60,0	
Fünftürer	122.666	133.525	– 8,1	
Coupé	26.304	1.287		
Cabrio	26.566	—		
	225.095	165.803	35,8	18,7
BMW 3er				
Limousine	246.231	310.278	– 20,6	
Touring	93.191	102.399	– 9,0	
Coupé	79.248	89.572	– 11,5	
Cabrio	55.538	52.970	4,8	
	474.208	555.219	– 14,6	39,5
BMW 5er				
Limousine	156.825	181.534	– 13,6	
Touring	45.462	49.311	– 7,8	
	202.287	230.845	– 12,4	16,8
BMW 6er				
Coupé	8.337	9.967	– 16,4	
Cabrio	7.962	9.659	– 17,6	
	16.299	19.626	– 17,0	1,4
BMW 7er				
	38.835	44.421	– 12,6	3,2
BMW X3				
	84.440	111.879	– 24,5	7,0
BMW X5				
	116.489	120.617	– 3,4	9,7
BMW X6				
	26.580	—		2,2
BMW Z4				
Coupé	4.035	8.361	– 51,7	
Roadster	13.971	20.022	– 30,2	
	18.006	28.383	– 36,6	1,5
BMW gesamt	1.202.239	1.276.793	– 5,8	100,0

GoldWinners

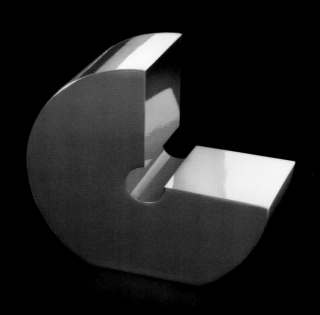

Take a Closer Look

Cover: Morphine Crystals. Morphine, named after Morpheus the god of dreams, relieves severe pain by blocking transmission of pain signals in the brain and spinal cord.

Contents

Review 2007–2008   1

Left: Pegylated interferon: a polymer linked to interferon (ribbons) by a bridge between two cysteine residues. Image by Dr Mire Zloh, Department of Pharmaceutical and Biological Chemistry.
Right: Bacteria in the gut digest the outer coating of a medicine, allowing the active ingredient to be released where it is needed, increasing efficacy and minimising side effects. Research by Matthew E A McGirr, Department of Pharmaceutics.

explores the basic concepts of miniaturisation. In the NanoMedicine modules, players are encouraged to build nanoscopic particles to treat human diseases. Professor Kostarelos and experts from other areas of nanoscience are steering the development of this creative initiative funded by the Wellcome Trust.

Making the cure for hepatitis C affordable
Approximately 180 million people worldwide have the life threatening liver infection, hepatitis C. But many can be cured with a combination of drugs including interferon alpha – a medicine based on a natural protein found in low levels in the blood.

To prolong the activity of interferon when it is used to treat hepatitis C, a chemical called polyethylene glycol (PEG) has been added, but the product is difficult to make and expensive to buy.

Dr Mire Zloh and Professor Steve Brocchini at the School, have discovered an innovative, more efficient way to produce PEG-interferon, which should make it more affordable to people with hepatitis C in developing countries.

They have designed a different type of chemical bridge between PEG and interferon alpha which makes the drug structure more stable so its biological activity is maintained. The process

also allows any interferon which is not used first time around to be recycled and used again.

"In making new medicines, we need to be innovative while ensuring that they can be affordable," says Professor Brocchini. "We hope that this new way of making PEG-interferon will ensure that even the poorest people can take advantage of a medicine which can help cure their hepatitis C and enable them to lead a normal life."

The technology for the new form of PEG-interferon has been licensed to the Indian company, Shantha Biotech, and it is being developed more broadly by PolyTherics, one of the School's spin out companies.

"The model for innovation and cost effectiveness goes a lot further than this one project or disease. It involves many people and organisations. In responding to the global challenges of disease and its effective treatment, we seek to innovate so that new treatments for disease can be developed," concludes Professor Brocchini.

Bacteria aid drug targeting in the gut
Using bacteria in the gut to digest the outer coating of a medicine for the common inflammatory bowel condition, ulcerative colitis, is proving an effective approach to drug targeting. Phase III clinical trials are underway

to test a novel formulation of the anti-inflammatory drug, prednisolone metasulphobenzoate, called COLAL-PRED™, which was developed by Dr Abdul Basit and his colleagues in the Department of Pharmaceutics.

The product uses the bacterial substrate, amylose, in the drug coating. When bacteria in the colon digest the amylose, holes form in the coating, allowing the active drug to be released from the formulation. As the bacteria are only found in the colon, the technology effectively targets the treatment to the part of the gut where it is most needed, thus improving its efficacy and reducing the risk of side effects.

"This technology is unique in the field of delivery of drugs to the gastro-intestinal tract, and we anticipate that it will provide a much more effective treatment for what is a painful and debilitating condition than those products currently available," says Dr Basit.

Rights to the core technology were assigned to Cambridge-based Alizyme Therapeutics Ltd in 2005 for £1.3m. The School of Pharmacy has been involved in the clinical development of the product in collaboration with Alizyme, from which it will receive royalty payments.

Category: Education | **Location:** United Kingdom | **Creative Director:** Neil Walker | **Designer:** Sam Stephens, Laura Taplin | **Printer:** Abba Litho | **Project Manager:** Candice Schneider

Expansion at the Square

The Square: now a multi-site operation
Over the past two years the School has invested in a significant increase in its space and, for the first time in its history, has become a multi-site operation.

We now lease two floors of BMA house in Tavistock Square to provide accommodation for the Department of Practice and Policy. Also, jointly with the School of Oriental and African Studies we have purchased the lease of a beautiful Georgian house in Russell Square. This now houses the work of the Joint Programmes Board and provides additional study space for MSc students.

The new accommodation in these two sites is well fitted and attractive – its users say that they enjoy it despite the occasional inconvenience of being a few minutes walk from the main building.

We also have the new molecular pharmacy extension in Brunswick Square.

All of this is good news. However, in the same period, staff and student numbers have grown and we are planning for continued growth, to be achieved primarily through research and taught masters provision. Thus, to both safeguard and develop the School we need to grow its income and its activities. This will require additional space and facilities. We also need to provide a professional and pleasant working environment for staff and for our students. Creating a safe, well-specified and professional environment is a priority in the next planning period. This will be helped by a recent grant of nearly £4m for research and teaching capital and infrastructure investment for the period 2008-2011.

Looking to the future
For the longer term, we have to recognise that the School has permanently outgrown its Brunswick Square building. The new space in BMA House and Russell Square provides immediate relief, but repeated addition of small satellite premises would be an expensive and unsatisfactory long-term solution. So we will need to consider whether there is unused capacity with the Brunswick Square building, what other options there might be, and how generally to ensure that the estate facilitates the long-term strategic growth of the School.

New molecular pharmacy wing – a centre for medicines research
The School's new molecular pharmacy wing was completed in the Spring of 2008. This is our first major building project since the Brunswick Square building was officially opened in 1960.

It will be a centre for collaborative research into the discovery, design and development of medicines.

The seven-storey 980m² wing has been built inside the School's footprint – a logistical nightmare for builders Kind & Co Ltd as all the internal debris had to be removed through a window-sized hole in the front wall of the School. New materials and equipment for building work entered through the same route.

Architects Day England Stevenson Marsh came up with an ingenious design that resembles connecting molecules. If you look up from the ground floor the metaphor is clear: coloured walkways criss-cross the connecting space joining the old building to the new. A glass roof allows light to flood down and at night spotlights are reflected by mirrored panels. Five floors of the new wing house research laboratories. There is also a teaching laboratory, a seminar room and space on the ground floor that will become a bright, modern venue for events. Each of the research floors is devoted to a particular discipline: Cancer pharmacology (led by Dr Andreas Schatzlein); microbiology and infectious diseases (Professor Peter Taylor); pharmaceutics and nanotechnology (Professor Ijeoma Uchegbu); pharmacognosy and phytotherapy (Dr Deniz Tasdemir); and molecular neuroscience and genetics (Professor Robert Harvey).

The building was funded by capital grants of £4.1m, with a further £1m donation from the Wolfson Foundation to enable the research laboratories to be equipped and furnished to the highest specifications.

Our Year

Income and expenditure account for the year ended 31 July 2007

Income	2007 £	2006 £
Funding Council Grants	7,907,175	7,284,386
Academic Fees and Support Grants	3,369,921	2,851,279
Research Grants and Contracts	5,270,411	5,771,785
Other Operating Income	591,397	521,825
Endowment and Investment Income	144,908	438,056
	17,283,812	16,867,931

Expenditure	2007 £	2006 £
Staff Costs	9,900,841	9,297,356
Depreciation	1,073,446	939,488
Other Operating Expenses	6,231,158	6,254,249
Interest Payable	12,825	-
	17,218,270	16,491,093

	2007	2006
Surplus on ordinary activities	65,542	376,838
Taxation	-	-
Surplus after tax	65,542	376,838

Extract from balance sheet as at 31 July 2007	2007 £	2006 £
Fixed Assets	9,717,538	7,819,474
Endowment Assets	560,268	546,521
Net current liabilities	(1,631,027)	(357,864)
Creditors falling due after more than a year	(489,185)	-
Total net assets	8,157,594	8,008,131

The full audited financial statements for 2006-2007 are available on request.

Average Staff Numbers (full time equivalents) by category: 2006–2007

Academic and research	117
Non-academic	95
	212

Student numbers 2006–2007

	Total	Home	EU	OS	Male	Female	Course
Undergraduate, full time	707	573	15	119	273	434	MPharm
Undergraduate, part time	17	17	0	0	0	17	Certificate in Medicines Management for Pharmacy Technicians
Postgraduate, taught full time	55	12	9	34	23	32	Clinical Pharmacy; Drug Delivery; Drug Discovery
Postgraduate, taught part time	312	312	0	0	64	248	Pharmacy Practice; General Pharmacy Practice
Postgraduate research full and part time	96	40	26	30	33	63	PhD
Visiting students	73	1	65	7	26	47	mainly incoming ERASMUS students
Total	1260	955	115	190	419	841	

Council 2006–2007

Chairman: Dr Philip J Brown

Vice-Chairman: Mr Nicholas Wood

Honorary Treasurer: Mr James Gemmell

Dean: Professor Anthony W Smith

Clerk to Council: Dr Julian C Axe

Members: Professor Nicholas D Barber, Ms Nafilia Daredia, Mrs Irene Dougherty, Professor Rod Flower, Professor Andreas Kortenkamp, Professor Quentin A McKellar, Miss Ann Lewis, OBE, Mr Julian Morris, Dr Brian Pearce, Mr Geoff Potter, Mr Alan Sanders, Mr Shahil Soni, Professor Kevin Taylor, Professor Alex Thomson, Professor David Thurston, Dr Lincoln Tsang

What was the client's directive?

As part of a new brand identity we have created for The School of Pharmacy, the annual report was seen as an integral part of communicating the School's vision and values to firmly place it at the heart of its communication strategy.

How did you define the problem?

The School of Pharmacy has a rich history of over 250 years; however, its image was seen as very dry and dated. The aim of the annual report was to reposition The School of Pharmacy and invite readers to take a closer look at the remarkable work the School is doing through its pioneering approach to education and research.

What disciplines or people helped you with the project?

We worked very closely with technical illustrators employed through The School of Pharmacy to bring a new dynamic to the way their illustrations were conceived and produced.

Were you happy with the result?

We were extremely happy with the result, especially as it sits at the heart of the new brand identity that we have created for The School of Pharmacy.

What was the client's response?

"We have found the design team at CDT truly inspirational in their approach and we are delighted with the work they have created for the School." From Professor Anthony Smith, Principal and Dean, The School of Pharmacy.

Do you and the client both view the Annual Report as part of the company's communications strategy? And how important is it within the overall strategy?

This is critical to both the business and brand strategies of any client and we are increasingly seeing annual reports playing a pivotal part in our clients' communications strategy. In some instances, the annual report is seen as the key driver of this strategy with many of our clients communicating where their businesses are now and where they are going to be in the future.

How do you define success in Annual Report design?

The success of any annual report is in the way that it communicates the key messages of the business, both strategic and financial to its target audiences. Transparency of disclosure and clarity of accounting policy are also key to its success.

CDT has won many awards both for design and production as well as accounting policy. We measure our success in annual reporting by the relationships we have built over the last 30 years with our clients, many of which return year in year out e.g. The British Land Company PLC, who we have worked with for the last 20 years on their annual reports.

In which direction do you see Annual Reports moving?

We are currently seeing significant change ns this market with the uptake of online reporting. However, both print and online are being used to support each other and aimed at different user groups. Printed reports are now an extension of the client's business and brand strategies, and are aimed at communicating the direction of the business as well as the hard financial facts. Our online reports are very much seen as tools of the trade aimed at analysts and investors.

How large a role does environmental policy play in the design and production of your Annual Reports?

This has been an integral part of our process for many years and it is now a pre-requisite for all annual reports designed and produced in the UK. All our reports have minimum use paper from sustainable sources and certified by the FCS and adhere to EMAS, ISO 14001 environmental and ISO 9001 quality standards. CDT also operates a studio-wide environmental policy and is also ISO 9001 accredited.

The success of any annual report is in the way that it communicates the key messages of the business, both strategic and financial to its target audiences.

HANNAH MORE SCHOOL
2007
ANNUAL REPORT
OUTSIDE THE BOX

IMPORTANT DOCUMENTS ENCLOSED

OUTSIDE THE BOX
Hannah More School 2007 Annual Report

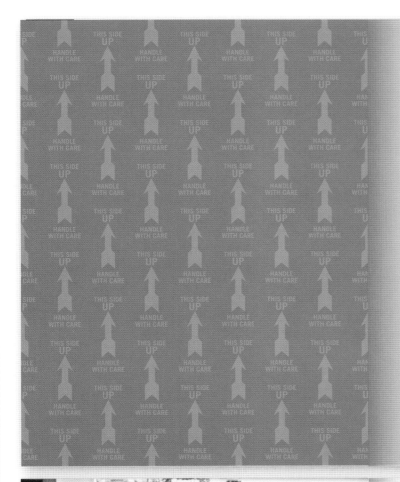

Hannah More School provides individualized academic, vocational, and therapeutic programs to elementary (grades 4 and 5), middle, and high school students who have been identified as emotionally disabled, autistic, learning disabled, or whose behaviors have interfered with their ability to be successful in public school.

The school is committed to providing such programs in a nurturing and educationally challenging environment so that students may develop the skills necessary to reach their greatest potential in an increasingly complex and culturally diverse society.

Dear Friends,

Each year we take a moment to remember the previous year, and reflect on student activities and successes.

In many ways, the 2006–2007 school year was similar to other years: students returned in late August, fresh with excitement from summer break and wondered, who are my teachers? Will I like them? How much homework will I have? The months unfolded, August to September, and beyond, with students gradually settling into a new routine.

While in some ways the school year was filled with predictability: bell schedules, lunch breaks, and gym class, other events happened as a result of some "outside the box" thinking on the part of school staff.

Shortly after school started, the first Pet Therapy Clinical Group was held. Every other Monday, a volunteer from Pets on Wheels arrived with an animal in tow, providing an opportunity for our students to meet and greet the four-legged guest. This new therapy proved extremely helpful for many of our students, especially

3

Category: Education | **Location:** Maryland, United States | **Art Director:** Kathryn Shagas | **Designer:** Priscilla Henderer | **Photographer:** Tracey Brown, André Chung, Joe Rubino | **Print Run:** 2500 | **Project Manager:** Kathryn Shagas | **Writer:** Joan Drebing

Four-Legged Friends

Hannah More School's Pet Therapy Group has had a very positive impact on our students and staff since it first began in the fall of 2006. School Social Workers Candice Thomas and Nicole Franklin co-lead the group, which meets each week and has a visit from an animal every other week. Many of the visits are scheduled through volunteers with the local Pets on Wheels chapter. All of the pets are certified after passing a temperament test, and are trained to participate in the pet therapy. Ms. Thomas came up with the idea of a Pet Therapy Group during conversations with students when she discovered a lot of them were animal lovers. "Research shows that patting and interacting with a pet can lower blood pressure and make people feel calm," says Ms. Thomas. "I thought that it would be a positive experience for our students to interact with animals and learn to de-stress and connect with something outside their own circle."

The group talks about the basics of caring for a pet, and the impact that pets have on the well-being of their

7

The Hannah More School Foundation 2006–2007

Revenue

Investments 30%
Contributions 70%

Expenses

Support 33%
Program 67%

24

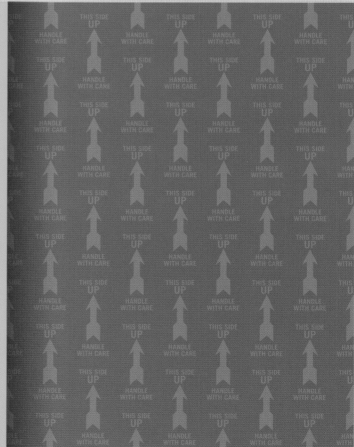

What was the client's directive?
The client wanted to tell the story of unusual programs, including drumming and pet therapy, that have produced positive results at a school for children with emotional and physical disabilities.

How did you define the problem?
Explain 3 different programs under the overall theme of "out of the box."

What was the approach?
First, we changed the concept to "outside the box," rather than "out of the box," which can mean ready-made (for example, a purchase from a store ready to use out of the box). Both are overused clichés (apparently, the term "outside the box" is used once every nine days in The New York Times).

To get a handle on what they were trying to communicate... 1) Not only is the report about the students with disabilities—unconventional, "outside the box" behavior. And they don't fit "inside the box" of a traditional classroom setting. 2) It's also about Hannah More's programs (drumming, pet therapy, etc.), which are outside the traditional classroom box. For example, an art exhibit held outside the building grounds. 3) But, most importantly (our focus), these programs are "outside the box" in terms of Hannah More's willingness to take new perspectives and openness to do things differently in teaching, in order to connect to students and teach them important life skills (sense of community, too) that they can apply to other situations and challenges.

After exploring several complicated and expensive solutions, we settled on a simple, cheaper, idea: a single sheet of corrugated cardboard with the clear envelope attached and the whole report as a small booklet inside the envelope. The contents of the clear envelope are literally "outside the box." Clear envelopes available for purchase with the copy: "important documents enclosed."

What disciplines or people helped you with the project?
Just research and the designer's brainpower.

Were you happy with the result? What could have been better?
We were pleased with the results. There was a time-consuming learning curve around manufacturing and printing the box material, and obtaining the correct color of pouches.

What was the client's response?
The response was very positive from the client and their donors.

What are clients looking for when it comes to designing an Annual Report?
Clients are looking to convey clear information, tell a good story and create an effective fund-raising tool.

Do you and the client both view the Annual Report as part of the company's communications strategy? And how important is it within the overall strategy?
Yes. This is a small school for middle and high school students with a primary disability of emotional disturbance, autism, specific learning disabilities, other health impairment, or multiple disabilities.
Budget considerations only allow an annual report to be produced every other year. The annual report becomes one of the school's primary marketing tools.

How do you define success in Annual Report design?
Readers develop or increase interest in a client and may choose to be involved in their success at some level.

In which direction do you see Annual Reports moving?
Fewer print copies, more web-based.

When it comes to designing an Annual Report, clients are looking to convey clear information, tell a good story and create an effective fund-raising tool.

IN MOTION

ANNUAL REPORT 2008

**Dallas Center
for the Performing Arts®**

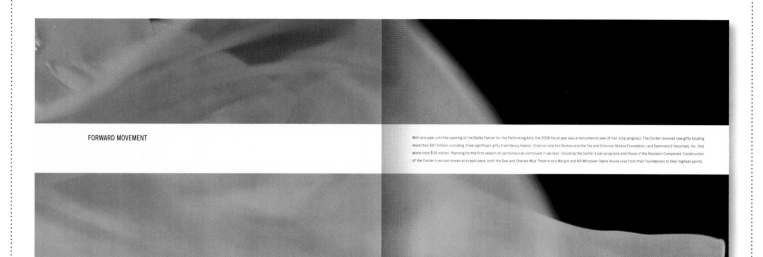

FORWARD MOVEMENT

With one year until the opening of the Dallas Center for the Performing Arts, the 2008 fiscal year was a monumental year of non-stop progress. The Center received new gifts totaling more than $67 million, including three significant gifts from Nancy Hamon, Shannon and Ted Skokos and the Ted and Shannon Skokos Foundation, and Sammons Enterprises, Inc. that alone total $35 million. Planning for the first season of performances continued in earnest, including the Center's own programs and those of the Resident Companies. Construction of the Center's venues moved at a rapid pace: both the Dee and Charles Wyly Theatre and Margot and Bill Winspear Opera House rose from their foundations to their highest points.

OUR PROGRESS

Dear Benefactors and Friends:

The Dallas Center for the Performing Arts' 2008 fiscal year, which concluded on July 31, 2008, was the second year in the campaign's three-year construction phase, the eighth year in the campaign's nine-year operation and the most successful and productive year since the campaign's inception in the fall of 2000.

Dallas families and organizations committed more than $67 million during the year in new gifts for construction, increasing total funding to $327 million, 96 percent of the campaign's publicly announced goal of $338 million. The number of gifts of $1 million and above increased during the year to 126, establishing the campaign as the most successful project of its kind in America's history.

Among the most remarkable new gifts committed during the 2008 fiscal year were a $10 million gift from Nancy Hamon to name the Nancy Hamon Education and Recital Hall in the Margot and Bill Winspear Opera House; a $10 million gift from Shannon and Ted Skokos and the Ted and Shannon Skokos Foundation to name the Shannon and Ted Skokos Pavilion in Annette Strauss Artist Square and the Shannon and Ted Skokos Stage in the Winspear Opera House; a new $6 million commitment for a total commitment of $8 million from Diane and Hal Brierley to name the Diane and Hal Brierley Esplanade at the entrance of the Wyly Theatre and the Brierley Encore Suite in the Winspear Opera House; and a remarkable $15 million gift from Sammons Enterprises to help construct the Center and name the Elaine D. and Charles A. Sammons Park.

During the year, design and construction continued on schedule and with cost containment unprecedented for a project of this scope, and both the Winspear Opera House and Wyly Theatre reached their highest levels of elevation and were topped out. By the year's end, more than 50 percent of the construction of the Winspear Opera House and 55 percent of the construction of the Wyly Theatre were completed, as were construction documents for the Elaine D. and Charles A. Sammons Park. Design development documents for the new Annette Strauss Artist Square were also completed. And, the Center purchased more than 96 percent of the materials required to construct the venues, reducing significantly the potential of cost-overruns through the remainder of the construction process.

From marketing and communications perspectives, the Center generated more than $4 million in media coverage during the 2008 fiscal year, including two front-page stories in The Dallas Morning News and numerous articles featured in local and national publications. The Center hosted a major media event in New York City featuring renowned architects Norman Foster, Rem Koolhaas, Joshua Prince-Ramus and Michel Desvigne that was attended by more than 30 representatives of the top national and international media based in New York.

The Center confirmed two of its important annual productions and title sponsors for both. Shorenstein Hays Nederlander was contracted to be the Center's Broadway consultant and Lexus was confirmed as the title sponsor of the new Lexus Broadway at the Center series.

Early in the fiscal year the Center hosted an announcement event in the Meyerson Symphony Center to announce Brinker International as the title sponsor of the Brinker International Forum and the Forum's unique partnership with National Geographic Live! During the year, the Forum's Board of Advisors was appointed and activated, and the Center sold season subscriptions amounting to more than 80 percent of the Meyerson's seating capacity, the venue of the inaugural 2008-2009 season.

From an operational perspective, the Center continued implementation of the Tessitura software system among all of the Resident Companies and other performing arts organizations, including the Dallas Children's Theater. The Center engaged in discussions with its Resident Companies on drafts of license agreements that will be executed prior to the Center's opening in the fall of 2009. The Center continued to work with its Resident Companies to identify core services that can be shared by the Center and the companies for cost-effectiveness and efficiency purposes. And the Center promoted Mike Riley to be Senior Vice President and Chief Operating Officer and authorized Mr. Riley to begin identifying and appointing operating personnel to be employed during the 2009 fiscal year in advance of the Center's Grand Opening.

The Center concluded the 2008 fiscal year with an eighth consecutive balanced budget and an audit with a clean opinion. During the year the Center revised its business model and long-term cash flow projections, and identified alternative refinancing options for its tax-exempt bonds to address the tough auction rate securities market resulting from the nation's sub-prime and real estate market crisis.

From the perspectives of fund-raising, design and construction, operations, communications and financial management, the Dallas Center for the Performing Arts' 2008 fiscal year was the most productive year since the campaign's beginning in the fall of 2000. More than 500 volunteers were directly involved throughout the year and thousands of other individuals in and beyond Dallas were aware of the campaign and its progress and forthcoming impact on Dallas and the region. With the understanding that more gifts were committed during the 2008 fiscal year than any year since the campaign's launch, design and construction remained on schedule and on budget, and campaign expenses were contained to less than four cents of each donor dollar, the state of the campaign is strong and the project is postured for continued progress.

Sincerely,

Howard Hallam
Chair, Board of Directors
Dallas Center for the Performing Arts

William H. Lively
President and CEO
Dallas Center for the Performing Arts

5 In March 2008, the Center held a briefing on the project for national and international media in New York City, focusing on the architecture and programming of the Center. Norman Foster, Rem Koolhaas, Joshua Prince-Ramus and Michel Desvigne presented their designs for the Center's venues. 6 Shannon and Ted Skokos and the Ted and Shannon Skokos Foundation contributed the second $10 million gift of fiscal year 2008. The Shannon and Ted Skokos Stage in the Winspear Opera House and the Shannon and Ted Skokos Pavilion at Annette Strauss Artist Square will be named in honor of their contributions. 7 In June 2008, Diane and Hal Brierley contributed a new $3.4 million gift, which pushed the campaign total past the $300 million mark. 8 TITAS, the Dallas-based presenter of the finest music and dance groups from around the world, announced plans to move its season to the Dallas Center for the Performing Arts, becoming the Center's Resident Fine Arts Presenter.

9 Fiscal year 2008 closed with the third-largest gift in the campaign: a $15 million gift from Sammons Enterprises, Inc. the largest ever made in the company's 70-year history. The Center's 10-acre park will be named the Elaine D. and Charles A. Sammons Park in honor of this gift. 10 The Capstone giving program, chaired by Sarah and Ross Perot, Jr. raised 22 new gifts of $1 million or more. By the end of fiscal year 2008, the Center had raised an unprecedented 126 gifts at this level, and a total of $327 million over all. 11 In its first year, the Center's Pillar program, designed for gifts from $25,000 to just under $1 million, raised more than $3 million. Board member Bess Enloe and her husband, Ted, chair the Pillar Action Team. 12 The Center launched its Step into the Spotlight campaign, to reach donors throughout the community. In the first year of the campaign, the Center raised nearly $1 million in gifts at all levels.

Category: Entertainment | **Location:** Texas, United States | **Chief Creative Officer:** Chris Rovillo | **Creative Director:** Samantha Reitmayer | **Designer:** Samantha Reitmayer | **Printer:** Williamson Printing

Gold83

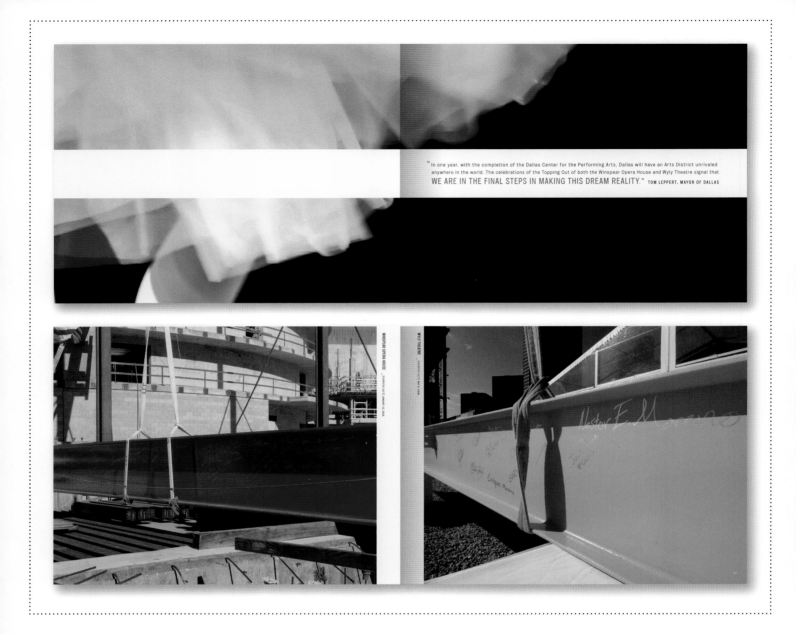

" In one year, with the completion of the Dallas Center for the Performing Arts, Dallas will have an Arts District unrivaled anywhere in the world. The celebrations of the Topping Out of both the Winspear Opera House and Wyly Theatre signal that **WE ARE IN THE FINAL STEPS IN MAKING THIS DREAM REALITY.**" TOM LEPPERT, MAYOR OF DALLAS

For us, success [in Annual Report design] is when the CEO is happy by way of the donors.

Q&A with Rovillo+Reitmayer

What was the client's directive?
Previous annual reports for the Dallas Center for the Performing Arts have focused on the donors, the fundraising efforts or the buildings. However, with the center nearing completion, this was the first year that began to focus on the performance aspect of the DCPA. The trick was alluding to the performing arts without focusing on one particular aspect since the DCPA will showcase ballet, dance, opera, theater, jazz and popular music.
The second mandatory was color. Most of their past annual reports had been fairly austere. They wanted this one to have more color and more excitement: Something that also alluded to the impending opening of the Dallas Center for the Performing Arts.

How did you define the problem?
We wanted to capture the arts without being specific. We settled on the idea of motion as a metaphor for performing arts.

What was the approach?
Photography was the best solution to show the idea of motion. The tight crops on the fabric allowed a great deal of abstraction as well as color.

What disciplines or people helped you with the project?
We're a small shop, so it was the six of us working to solve it. We also had to rely on stock photography since the actual performing art companies were not available to let us use their dancers, etc. As for production, we knew we wanted to bring in Williamson Printing. Their high impact printing techniques can achieve bright vivid color on an uncoated sheet. We liked the idea of vivid color pared with the tactile nature of uncoated paper.

What was the client's response?
Very positive. This was their first colorful annual report, and they were very pleased with the result.

What are clients looking for when it comes to designing an Annual Report?
With someone like the DCPA, it needs to look good but not be extravagant. They are a non-profit, so they want to put their best foot forward without looking like they're wasting their donor's money.

Do you and the client both view the Annual Report as part of the company's communications strategy? And how important is it within the overall strategy?
We do, and the CEO used it as a marketing piece. We were very aware that it would be placed in a folder with other materials. It was a good piece to use in conjunction with their other collateral or just as a stand-alone brochure.

How do you define success in Annual Report design?
For us, success was when the CEO was happy by way of the donors. When the donors would email the CEO that they liked the annual report, we knew we had succeeded.

In which direction do you see Annual Reports moving?
Like everything else, they're moving more and more online. That's not entirely a bad thing. It's just different. It doesn't mean that the design needs to be diluted, but the delivery needs to change. Plus, the economy is going to be a major factor hanging over annual reports for the next two to maybe three years. No company wants to look like they're spending too much money.

How large a role does environmental policy play in the design and production of your Annual Reports?
It's becoming more and more prevalent as consumers become more and more aware of the environment. It used to be enough to indicate that it was printed on 30% post-consumer stock, but now printed materials need to feature FSC certification and so forth.

GROUP

Our
game
plan

Geschäftsbericht 2008

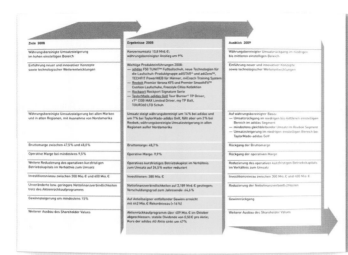

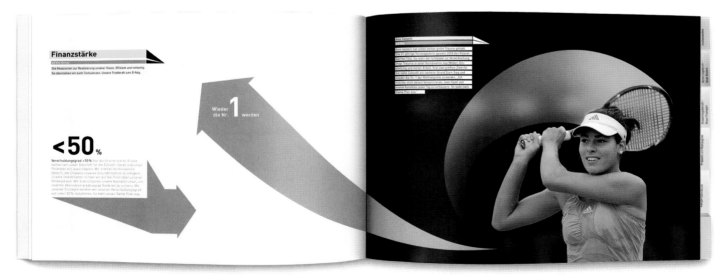

Category: Fashion | **Location:** Germany | **Art Director:** Christopher Biel | **Artist:** Andreas Rimmelspacher | **Creative Director:** Frank Wagner | **Illustrator:** Adelgund Janik | **Print Producer:** Melanie Sauer | **Project Manager:** Frederike Reinhold, Cornelia Metzger | **Printer:** Longo AG

What was the client's directive?

The conceptual job description was on the one hand to communicate the market position and the current success of the company. On the other hand, it was to manifest the achievement of future goals via the in-group market strategy.

How did you define the problem?

We defined the following key massage:

The adidas Group is a company that, unlike any other company, has turned the concept of performance in sports into the self-concept of its own corporate culture.

To set objectives as a company, to follow these objectives consistently, and to achieve the same is the decisive key message of the annual report.

What was the approach?

The adidas Group and its brands enjoy strong recognition power, bringing together athletes from around the world. The slogan "Our game plan" allows the company to identify with an athlete's goal: it develops a strategic game plan, enabling it to achieve the best possible performance.

What disciplines or people helped you with the project?

Except for printing the report—controlled by our producer—everything was done within häfelinger + wagner design. The scope of services in detail: Communication concept, Image texts, editorial of magazine/interviews, Design concept, Shootings, Realisation and Production.

Were you happy with the result? What could have been better?

Yes, we are happy. The budget that was available to us did not allow any particular refinement techniques. For example, for the presentation of the tartan track on the title page, we used comparatively low cost material (step protection varnish).

What was the client's response?

Enthusiastic.

In which direction do you see Annual Reports moving?

The annual report is lead publication of the year for many of our customers, with enormous appeal. In many cases, the report is replacing the image brochure which is compiled more and more rarely now.

The online medium is an equal alternative and addition to the print version. But one is not replacing the other. The online version enriches financial communication and translates the print version adequately for the internet, with added values that the internet offers, e.g. interactivity and functionality, service functions, downloads, links, multimedia features etc. Internal links between the online annual report and the group page additionally increase mutual attractiveness. Equally the demand from customers, primarily amongst DAX 30 representatives, for valuable company communication and its high quality implementation is higher than ever before. Here we can notice the trend "quality versus quantity."

To set objectives as a company, to follow these objectives consistently, and to achieve the same is the decisive key message of the annual report.

2005
2006
iStar Financial Annual Report > 2007
2008
2009

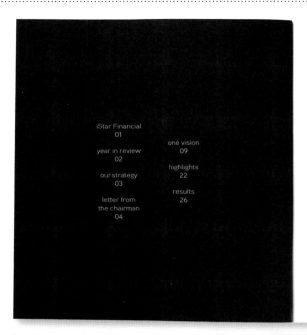

Having completed over $28 billion of commercial real estate investments over the past 15 years, iStar is now one of the most experienced companies in the U.S. commercial real estate finance markets. Our focus has always been long-term, building our business based on a forward-looking strategy that has made us a leader in the industry.

Today, iStar is a true "one-stop" private banker to high-end commercial real estate owners in the U.S. and internationally. We are primarily an on-balance-sheet lender with a full product range of capital solutions, from senior and mezzanine real estate debt to senior and mezzanine corporate capital, to corporate net lease financing and equity.

Our prudent approach to investing and operating our business has produced measurable results: a strong balance sheet; stable earnings and dividends; investment-grade ratings; a well-diversified portfolio; a low-leverage capital structure; deep in-house capabilities; a broad knowledge base; and a highly disciplined investment process.

iStar is also known for a strength that does not appear on the balance sheet: our continual drive at every level of the business to be a leader in our field and to build on our long-standing reputation for integrity, fairness and commitment to our customers and shareholders. These core strengths form our unique DNA, and serve as the foundation upon which we continue to build our business.

equity that supports our balance sheet and our investment grade ratings. It is now clear that these new, untested and dramatically higher leverage levels were also at play in many other parts of the capital markets, with the all too familiar outcome being a sharp and painful correction.

2008 will be full of challenges. We will continue to push hard to make sure iStar is one of the first and strongest companies to emerge from this period. There is no secret formula — we must work diligently, know our assets and borrowers inside out, be disciplined and thoughtful about how we access and invest capital, and find ways to deliver the solid returns our investors expect from us. We are a strong organization with a unique DNA. I certainly believe we are up to the challenge and I thank you for your continued support and commitment.

Jay Sugarman
Chairman and Chief Executive Officer

one vision

Deliver superior risk-adjusted returns

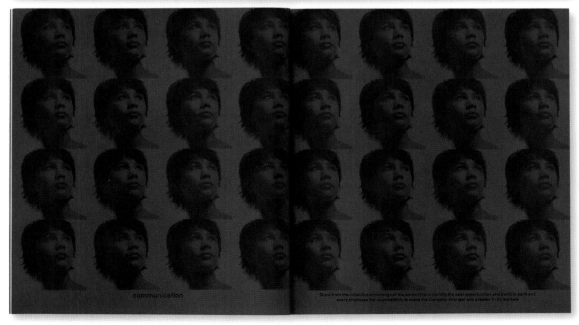

communication

Category: Financial Services | **Location:** New York, United States | **Account Director:** Renee Marmer | **Creative Director:** Christina Antonopoulos, Richard Colbourne | **Designer:** Christina Antonopoulos | **Photographer:** Chris Jones | **Print Producer:** Georgiann Baran, Joe Trupia | **Printer:** Innovation Printing

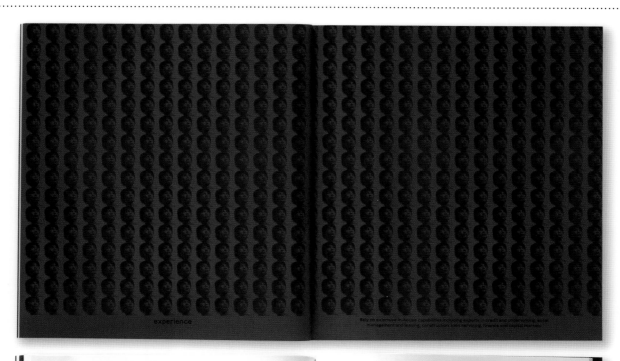

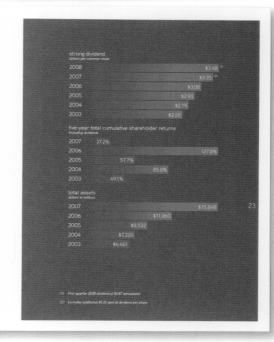

What was the client's directive?
iStar Financial is a finance company that is focused on the commercial real estate industry. They wanted to reassure their investors that the company is focusing on its core strengths.

How did you define the problem?
After creating the company's new tagline "Return on Ideas," our challenge was to create a concept for the annual report that would help establish the luxury brand, reflecting the new tagline and working across the entire company's guidelines. We defined iStar's core strengths as "iStar DNA."

What was the approach?
We created a visual metaphor for the exponential multiplication of "iStar DNA" across the company's business. A luxurious, innovative feel is established, which expresses the core attributes of creativity and intelligence that differentiates iStar from its competitors, and helps establish the company's unique position in the real estate investment marketplace.

How involved was the CEO in your meetings, presentations, etc.?
We benefited greatly by having access to and input from the CEO. He was involved in all critical presentations and decisions.

Were you happy with the result?
We were very happy with the result. It was strong, simple, and effective. The research we have conducted since clearly shows that our strategy is resonating with key audiences. All respondents rated iStar highest for sophistication, creativity, and intelligence in their sector.

How do you define success in Annual Report design?
If it communicates a big idea in an interesting (or even surprising) fashion, and if it's a book that someone would actually want to keep (or steal), then it's probably a success.

How large a role does environmental policy play in the design and production of your Annual Reports?
It varies depending on the client, but is something we increasingly plan for and encourage.

Our challenge was to create an annual report that would help establish the luxury brand. We benefited greatly by having access to and input from the CEO and the results were strong, simple, and effective.

AS THE LACK OF AFFORDABLE HOUSING
AFFECTS INCREASING NUMBERS OF INDIVIDUALS,
FAMILIES, AND COMMUNITIES, PROGRAMS THAT
EFFECTIVELY ADDRESS THE NEED ARE MORE
IMPORTANT THAN EVER.

FEDERAL HOME LOAN BANK OF SEATTLE
REPORT OF AFFORDABLE HOUSING AND COMMUNITY
INVESTMENT INITIATIVES
2008

HOUSING IS ONE OF OUR MOST BASIC HUMAN NEEDS.
SAFE, DECENT, AFFORDABLE HOUSING
AFFECTS THE VIABILITY AND WELL-BEING OF OUR FAMILIES,
OUR COMMUNITIES, AND OUR OVERALL ECONOMY. BUT ONE IN
SEVEN FAMILIES PAYS MORE THAN 50 PERCENT OF ITS INCOME
FOR HOUSING.

OUR PROGRAMS
TARGET THE NEEDS OF
INDIVIDUALS
AND FAMILIES WHO LIVE
IN URBAN AND RURAL
AREAS ACROSS THE REGION
WE SERVE:
FARMWORKERS,
TEACHERS,
AND CIVIL SERVANTS;
ALASKA NATIVES,
NATIVE AMERICANS, AND
NATIVE HAWAIIANS;
SENIORS, VETERANS,
HOMELESS INDIVIDUALS,
AND FAMILIES;
AND MANY MORE.

Category: Financial Services | **Location:** Washington, United States | **Creative Director:** Dale Hart | **Designer:** Minh Nguyen | **Editor:** Paula Thurman | **Photographer:** Bruce Gilden, Young Lee |
Print Producer: Derek Sullivan | **Project Manager:** Dacia Ray | **Strategy Director:** Janet DeDonato | **Writer:** Connie Waks

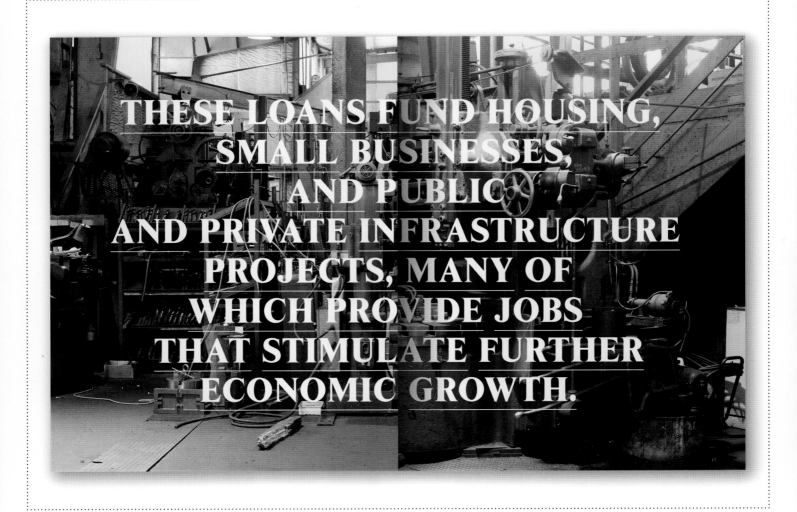

THESE LOANS FUND HOUSING, SMALL BUSINESSES, AND PUBLIC AND PRIVATE INFRASTRUCTURE PROJECTS, MANY OF WHICH PROVIDE JOBS THAT STIMULATE FURTHER ECONOMIC GROWTH.

This annual review is a critical part of their overall communications strategy. It's a multi-purpose piece that effectively tells their story in a very human way.

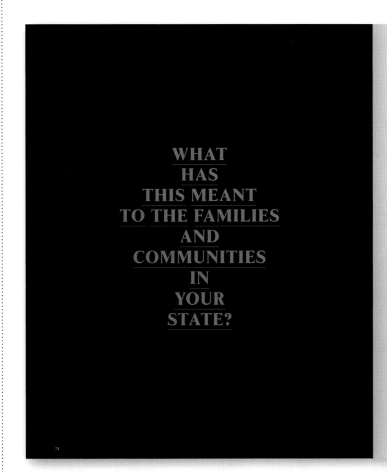

WHAT
HAS
THIS MEANT
TO THE FAMILIES
AND
COMMUNITIES
IN
YOUR
STATE?

WE PROVIDE AFFORDABLE HOUSING GRANTS
THROUGH OUR AFFORDABLE HOUSING PROGRAM (AHP)
AND OUR HOMESTART PROGRAMS.
DISCOUNTED LOANS FOR AFFORDABLE HOUSING
AND ECONOMIC DEVELOPMENT ARE OFFERED THROUGH OUR
COMMUNITY INVESTMENT PROGRAMS (CIP) AND OUR
ECONOMIC DEVELOPMENT FUND (EDF).

ALASKA

$8.95M / $.20M / 1,939
AHP / HOMESTART   CIP / EDF   HOUSEHOLDS
GRANTS   LOANS   SERVED

Q&A with Methodologie

What was the client's directive?
To create a communications piece that would hopefully motivate legislators/policy makers to continue to fund affordable housing programs.
How did you define the problem?
The problem was to make a compelling case for funding at a time when programs are being curtailed.
What was the approach?
Our approach was to frame the current crisis in affordable housing with relevant statistics and facts, for the front of the book. This brief intro presented the scope of the crisis. This intro was followed by information/statistics related to FHLB Seattle's funding initiatives, their impact and rate of success, and all the people and communities that benefit from their funding.
What disciplines or people helped you with the project?
In addition to the client, there were contacts within the field of affordable housing from academic institutions that helped with the statistics and data.

How involved was the CEO in your meetings, presentations, etc.?
The CEO was very involved during the initial design/concept meeting. After that, there were occasional check-ins with him.
What was the client's response?
They're very happy. It's a great outreach piece for them.
Do you and the client both view the Annual Report as part of the company's communications strategy? And how important is it within the overall strategy?
This annual review is a critical part of their overall communications strategy. It's a multi-purpose piece that effectively tells their story in a very human way.
How do you define success in Annual Report design?
A well-designed piece that motivates decision-making or action. And a happy client.
In which direction do you see Annual Reports moving?
Online. Clients are seeing the benefits of interactive reports.

FIRST REPUBLIC BANK
It's a privilege to serve you®

2008

NEW YORK, NEW YORK

"They take the time to understand my business. Having somebody who actually listens and understands is worth everything."

KENT SWIG
President
Swig Equities, LLC

Pictured at the Museum of American Finance, New York.

Kent Swig is a leader and innovator in the real estate industry. Through his various companies — including Swig Equities, Brown Harris Stevens and Halstead Property — he owns and operates more than $3 billion of commercial and residential properties in New York and California. Kent has made his mark by moving intelligently and quickly and he has chosen a bank that does the same. First Republic is proud of its long-term relationship with Swig Equities on both East and West coasts.

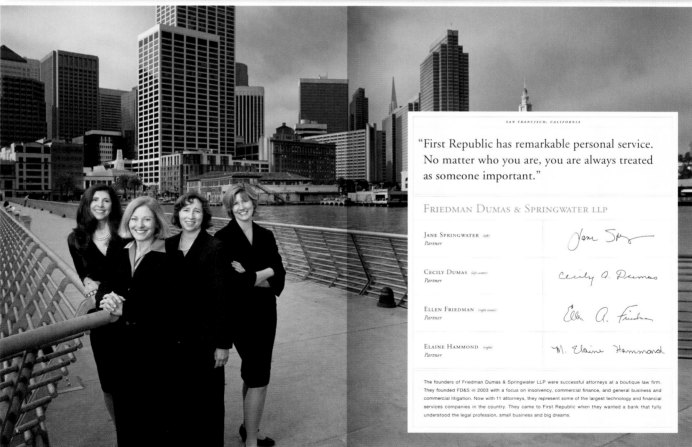

SAN FRANCISCO, CALIFORNIA

"First Republic has remarkable personal service. No matter who you are, you are always treated as someone important."

FRIEDMAN DUMAS & SPRINGWATER LLP

JANE SPRINGWATER *(left)*
Partner

CECILY DUMAS *(left center)*
Partner

ELLEN FRIEDMAN *(right center)*
Partner

ELAINE HAMMOND *(right)*
Partner

The founders of Friedman Dumas & Springwater LLP were successful attorneys at a boutique law firm. They founded FD&S in 2003 with a focus on insolvency, commercial finance, and general business and commercial litigation. Now with 11 attorneys, they represent some of the largest technology and financial services companies in the country. They came to First Republic when they wanted a bank that fully understood the legal profession, small business and big dreams.

Category: Financial Services | **Location:** California, United States | **Creative Director:** Jill Howry | **Designer:** Clay Williams | **Photographer:** Jamey Stillings | **Printer:** Cenveo | **Project Mgr.:** Paula Lucas

"Everything I do with First Republic is effortless. They are always there to support me and my business—just like family."

MYRTLE POTTER

CEO and President
Myrtle Potter and Company, LLC

Myrtle Potter was the first female African American president of a major pharmaceutical business and then COO at Genentech, Inc., the world's leading biotechnology company. She now advises through her own firm, Myrtle Potter and Company, which specializes in corporate strategy, personalized medicine and health care. In 2002 *Time* magazine named her as one of its 15 Young Global Business Influentials, in 2003 and 2004 she made *Fortune* magazine's list of the 50 Most Powerful Women In Business, and in 2008 *Directorship* magazine named her one of "50 Directors Under 50". Whatever she does, she moves quickly and she chose her bank for precisely these same reasons.

17.

FULL SERVICE PRIVATE BANKING AND WEALTH MANAGEMENT

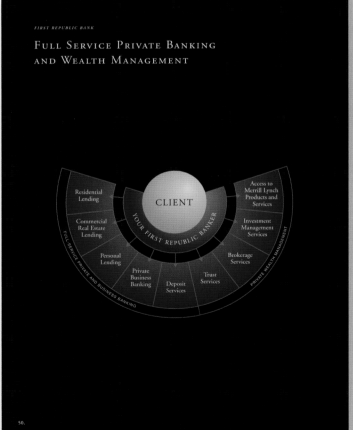

PRIVATE BANKING

A Relationship Manager works directly with each of our clients and directs a seamless flow of activities within First Republic. This Relationship Manager provides direct access to any bank function and coordinates communications and information. Relationship Managers at First Republic do just that: build long-term rewarding relationships with our clients.

A Distinctive Brand of Private Banking:

- Our approach to clients is based on advice and solutions—not products.
- We offer full-service banking on both coasts, including free Online Banking, free Bill Pay and free access to over 800,000 ATMs around the world. (We even rebate access fees charged by other banks whenever our clients use their ATMs.)
- We keep financial safety and privacy at the forefront.
- We believe in frequent, personal contact. Our bankers get to know our clients and are easy to reach.
- Our primary source of new clients is referrals from satisfied existing clients.

PRIVATE BUSINESS BANKING

We provide the same personalized, professional, and highly-responsive service to the business community as we do to personal banking clients. That's why we call it Private Business Banking.

Specialized Services offered for:

- Accounting Firms
- Architecture and Design
- Art and Antique Dealers
- Business Management Firms
- Business Partnerships
- Entertainment/Media
- Entrepreneurs

- Family Offices
- Financial Services
- Hedge Funds
- Independent Schools
- Investment Firms
- Law Firms
- Medical Firms

- Non-Profit Organizations
- Private Equity Funds/Firms
- Property Management Firms
- Real Estate Investors
- Venture Capital Funds/Firms
- Wineries

PRIVATE WEALTH MANAGEMENT*

Based on an Open Architecture model, First Republic Private Wealth Management enables a seamless interplay of internal and external investment options.

Wealth Management Services include:

- Asset Allocation
- Trust Administration, Custody, Asset Management
- Comprehensive Brokerage Services
- Fixed Income Management
- Financial and Estate Planning

- Access to Alternative Investments, including Private Equity, Hedge Funds, and Real Estate Funds**
- Socially Responsible Investing
- Hedging Strategies for Concentrated Stock Positions

- Multi-cap Equity Management
- Foreign Exchange
- Online Brokerage
- Access to Merrill Lynch Products and Services

* Investment Advisory services are provided by First Republic Investment Management, Inc. and First Republic Wealth Advisors, LLC. Trust services are provided by First Republic Trust Company. Brokerage services are offered through First Republic Securities Company, LLC, Member FINRA/SIPC.

** These products are offered on a private placement basis to clients who meet certain eligibility and suitability requirements.

What was the client's directive?

First Republic wants their annual report to help them attract new customers by conveying how their personal approach to banking provides stability and growth. Strategically, we needed to help the Bank define the characteristics that make them special. The report needed to reflect their motto, "It's a Privilege to Serve You," which is the basis of the Bank's dedication to a very personal form of customer service. The Bank displays these reports in their branches and sends them to customers. The Bank wanted a marketing piece was approachable, easy to read and visually compelling. While the Bank enjoys highlighting sample customers through photos, the hero of each client spread is the customer quote. These quotes tell the story of why First Republic Bank is unique.

How did you define the problem?

We have prepared this report for the Bank for 15 years. The challenge is to attract potential customers by highlighting the Bank's focus on personal service while also showing investors how this focus is a successful business model. This was particularly true for the 2008 report, which was produced in the midst of a severe banking crisis. The Bank does not want a radical departure in the design of the book from year to year since stability and consistency are important traits to communicate to customers and investors. But we also need to refresh the design each year so that the Bank is seen as continually moving forward in a positive direction.

What are clients looking for when it comes to designing an Annual Report?

It is easy to look at a finished annual report and think it's a straightforward document to produce. However, this underestimates what in reality is a very complex process, especially the role designers play in developing the theme of the report.

We lead off with a kick-off meeting with investor relations, marketing and/or finance. They may agree in general on what makes their company successful, but they often have very different ideas on what should receive the most emphasis or how the themes should be portrayed. We do extensive research in advance and come prepared with questions that help define their key communications needs. The client expects that we will take all of the input on themes and messaging from that download meeting and synthesize it into effective design directions. We then have a 45-minute meeting with management to present and explain the design solutions. New stakeholders, such as the CEO or CFO, often attend the design presentation and may raise new viewpoints. The design team needs to be fully prepared to strategically explain why our design solutions are appropriate. Getting agreement on how our visual design directions communicate the themes is more challenging than getting management to agree on the themes and messages. But getting consensus at this stage is critical—getting buy-off from the CEO but not from other departments often leads to problems down the road as the CEO bows out of the production process. How is this critical step accomplished? Research and preparation—fully understanding the company's strategy is necessary before we begin to design. We need to be aware of what the company's competitors are doing and current developments in the industry. New clients have remarked after our design presentation that we appear to understand the goals and strategies of the company as well as they do. Fortunately, we've always emerged from our design presentations to management with approval on a direction versus having to start over. Advance preparation is a key factor in this.

Agreeing on theme and messaging and getting sign-off on a design direction is just part of the battle—we must then manage the photography and printing and avoid the potential landmines that can arise in production. The above challenges are evident in every design project. However, 2008 brought a particular challenge. In the midst of the design process, the financial industry suffered a full-blown crisis—experts questioned whether many banks could even survive without a government bailout. This raised the stakes for our meetings with management.

To summarize, our clients expect that we will build consensus with respect to messages and themes among disparate stakeholders within a company, that our design solutions will effectively capture these themes while being visually attractive, and that we will seamlessly navigate the many potential production landmines and complete a report that the company can be proud to distribute to shareholders.

Do you and the client both view the Annual Report as part of the company's communications strategy? And how important is it within the overall strategy?

In many companies, the annual report serves both as a key marketing tool and employee morale builder. For First Republic Bank, the report is at the core of their communications strategy. The Bank selects many of the annual report testimonials for advertising within its branches, on its web site and in print ads. We also redesigned the Bank's marketing brochures and website, making the annual report client testimonials the central element of the home page. So the annual report is integral to the Bank's marketing and communication strategy.

How do you define success in Annual Report design?

There are a variety of ways that a report can be successful. For example, in recent years, First Republic Bank's annual report was recognized by an international annual report competition as the best annual report produced by a regional bank for three consecutive years. However, the only metric of success that matters in the end is that our client says that we effectively met (and hopefully exceeded) their expectations by successfully synthesizing the variety of themes presented at the kick-off meeting and navigating a smooth process to produce the report according to their expectations. For the Bank, the metrics of success also include getting positive feedback on the report from customers and having growth in new customers. For us, the best measure of success is that we have been partnering for the last 15 years to help First Republic build their image to where it is today. We have been able to extend the strong elements of the annual report's messaging and design into their entire corporate brand including advertising, marketing, branch communications and their website.

In which direction do you see Annual Reports moving?

The internet has played a significant role in the evolution of annual reports. Prior to the last decade, financial statements were an integral part of annual reports. However, now investors can access the financial statements from the electronic filings of companies well before they are produced in an annual report. Therefore, many companies have decided to no longer incur the expense of printing the financial statements when they can be accessed online. Some companies provide summary financial information but many others leave any mention of financial information to the letter to shareholders. We see this as a trend where annual reports are geared towards employees or customers as much as investors.

How large a role does environmental policy play in the design and production of your Annual Reports?

Printing annual reports involves paper, so it's important to be environmentally conscious. For First Republic's report, we use FSC (Forest Stewardship Council) certified paper—manufactured with renewable energy (wind, hydro or biogas) and includes post-consumer recovered fiber. Whenever possible, we work with environmentally sustainable printers. Such printers have "zero" landfill 100% recycling policy for waste byproducts. They generate their own electric/thermal power.

Another important element is that we produce web-enabled online versions of the annual report that users can access from the company's web site. This allows a company to minimize the number of annual reports that it has to print. For First Republic's online report (http://www.firstrepublic.com/aboutus/reports/2008/index.html), the benefits of using web features is apparent as the reader can use drop-down menus to immediately access information from the menu at the top of the screen. We also introduced a separate drop-down menu under the "Client Profiles" button, which allows users to sort the list of testimonial clients by profession, as well as by name. A real estate professional, for example, may just be interested in seeing what other real estate people are featured in the report without having to navigate through the entire client section. This trend towards printing fewer annual reports is helped by new SEC rules, which allows companies to poll their shareholders and send printed annual reports only to those shareholders that want it. Having an effective, web-enabled online annual report helps the client minimize their print quantity, which in turn reduces the cost of producing an annual report.

The only metric of success that matters in the end is that our client says that we effectively met (and hopefully exceeded) their expectations.

Nothing but Quality

A sound business strategy and strong customer relationships solidified SYSCO's position as the market leader in foodservice distribution with a record-setting year

The Quality of Our Food

With the largest Quality Assurance
team in the industry, SYSCO puts quality
on the menu

At SYSCO, the quality, safety and wholesomeness of the foods we distribute are our
paramount objectives. SYSCO's team of
highly qualified foodservice quality and food
safety experts work hand-in-hand with
growers, packers and processors who
supply fresh and processed foods to SYSCO
to ensure that every SYSCO Brand product
meets our quality standards. Products and
processes are constantly monitored to
ensure that our customers are receiving the
high quality and safe food products they
require to succeed in their business.

The quality and food safety of fresh produce
products start in the field. To maintain food
safety, we require suppliers of SYSCO Brand
products to undergo an annual third-party
Good Agricultural Process audit. In fiscal
2008, we extended this program to encom-
pass all growers of ready-to-eat produce
that SYSCO distributes under any brand.

*"We sum up our initiatives on quality, safety and wholesomeness
in just two words: good food."*

By taking this step, we are able to reassure
our customers that they are purchasing
products only from growers and suppliers
who have implemented stringent food
safety practices that are designed to
prevent food safety issues on the farm
before they develop.

More and more, our customers and the
clientele they serve are interested in not
only the taste of their food, but its impact
on the environment. SYSCO has been at
the forefront of the industry in this area.
As an active participant in the Sustainable
Food Laboratory, we are working toward
a sustainable food and agricultural system
that enhances soil fertility and water quality
and protects biodiversity while ensuring
that the food we eat is not only safe and
healthy, but affordable.

Part of this effort is our industry leading
Integrated Pest Management program.
Since 2002, this program has significantly
reduced the use of pesticides and fertilizer
on over 600,000 acres under cultivation
by SYSCO Brand growers and suppliers.
The result: quality products with lower
costs and reduced environmental impact.

We sum up our initiatives on quality, safety
and wholesomeness in just two words:
good food.

Under SYSCO's leadership,
suppliers such as Randall
Borgardt, Vice President
of Sales for Borzynski Farms
in Wisconsin, employed
sustainable agricultural
practices on thousands of
acres under cultivation in
the 2007 crop season.

SYSCO CORPORATION

2008 ANNUAL REPORT

Heavy Kitchen Equipment
From grills to stoves to condi-
ment stations, dependable
kitchen equipment is at
the heart of a hard-working
restaurant kitchen.

iCare Program
Employee benefits,
accounting software,
credit card services and
marketing advice are just
a few of the many services
provided through SYSCO's
iCare partners.

Chemicals and Kitchen Wear
SYSCO supplies many cleaning chemicals for the kitchen
and other areas. In addition,
there are many choices for
employee uniforms.

Dining Room Furnishings
SYSCO isn't just in the
kitchen. Trays, plates,
baskets and table center-
pieces add color and flair to
a table setting. Restaurant
owners can browse our catalog and find a wide selection
of serving ware that enables
each restaurant to show off
its own personality.

Technology
An electronic order track-
ing board is just one example
of the point of sale and marketing technology SYSCO
provides.

Disposables
Disposable dishes, cutlery
and paper products are
basics for many fast casual
restaurants. SYSCO is
helping these restaurants
become "greener" with
recycled and compostable
products, including corn-
resin-based cutlery as an
alternative to plastic.

Food and Beverages
From fresh meat and
produce to authentic ethnic
ingredients as well as any
coffee, soft drink, water,
and other non-alcoholic
beverages - quality SYSCO
products make every
restaurant's menu great.

Supplies and Equipment
Pots and pans, mixers and
bowls, stainless food prep
items ... where would a
restaurant be without these
essentials? SYSCO has
everything the most
discerning chef needs.

The Quality of Our Offering
The Whole Enchilada

Walk into a SYSCO customer's kitchen
and you will see our quality in more than
just the food. From eco-friendly paper and
packaging products to kitchen equipment,
we provide a wide array of restaurant
essentials. We also provide our customers
with access to third-party services that
they otherwise may not have been able to
access with the same advantages - liability
and health insurance, printing services,
even advertising air time.

For an independent restaurant like the
Flying Star Cafe in Albuquerque, SYSCO in
the kitchen means never having to fly solo.

SYSCO CORPORATION

2008 ANNUAL REPORT

Category: Food & Beverage | **Location:** Texas, United States | **Account Director:** Doug Hebert | **Art Director:** Doug Hebert | **Creative Director:** Dahlia Salazar | **Design Director:** Doug Hebert |
Designer: Ashley Ross | **Photographer:** Drew Donovan, Chris Shinn | **Print Producer:** Page International | **Printer:** Page International | **Programmer:** Jon Thompson | **Project Manager:**
Jackie Wilkerson | **Writer:** Alice Brink

What was the client's directive?

Savage was selected to design and produce print and online versions of the 2008 annual report and sustainability report for Sysco Corporation. The fully interactive online versions of both reports would be firsts for Sysco. As online communications begin to play a larger role in Sysco's communications efforts, the decision to introduce a corresponding online format was a natural one. This year, to ease the transition from print to online, the client wanted to create both versions. The online report was also viewed as an opportunity to provide a multitude of valuable information in a more accessible and timely manner.

How did you define the problem?

We decided to produce a traditional annual report, with a slightly shorter (16-page) narrative section and a bound 10K. For the sustainability report, we produced an 8-page summary, and used it as an introduction to Sysco's online sustainability report, where much more content was offered. In lieu of producing a PDF version of the reports on the website, we designed fully interactive online versions of both reports in Flash, complete with dynamic transitions and infographics, offering a more engaging user experience.

What was the approach?

The most used word in the annual report-focused interviews was Quality. Sysco states that the goal of every employee is to help the customer succeed by providing consistent quality services and products. They believe that the level of quality it provides its customers translates to a quality performance for shareholders.

Research for Sysco's sustainability efforts concluded with an overwhelming sense of Commitment to responsible business practices that meet the needs of the present without compromising the future. Overall, Sysco is committed to doing the right thing—for customers, employees, suppliers and society as a whole, and believes that this commitment to sustainability creates shareholder value. Commitment to doing the right thing and providing the best quality and nutrition, while being environmentally responsible and promoting economic fairness, was a message that Sysco was eager to communicate.

The creative objective for this project was to design and create a cohesive campaign that would tie together the message of Quality Sysco wished to communicate to their audiences in their annual report, and the theme of Commitment communicated in their sustainability report. The report concepts were created in tandem to seamlessly transition from one to the other. They are intended to be extensions of the other's message. The design concept, layout and photography style of both reports and their respective online components mirror each other in an aesthetically pleasing and visually dynamic way.

The strategy behind the design coordination of the reports was devised to help Sysco leverage its high standards of social responsibility in an effort and reinforce this brand message with the investment community and other key audiences. The narrative and photography woven throughout both reports reinforce and validate Sysco's corporate mission and values in terms of their products, employees, suppliers and service to consumers. In both reports, photography was styled and shot candidly to capture Sysco employees and vendors working, moving and living. Clean and simple graphs were used to illustrate the environmental strides Sysco is taking to ensure an environmentally responsible product and service. A bright and clean color palette was selected to evoke a cheerful, fresh, healthy living feeling.

What disciplines or people helped you with the project?

Internally at Savage, the Design Director designed the piece, and a print producer, programmer and copywriter were a part of the team. Two different photographers were also hired for imagery. On the client side, the Vice President of Investor Relations and Manager of Investor Relations were our main contacts, and an integral part of the team as well.

How involved was the CEO in your meetings, presentations, etc.?

The CEO was involved in the interview process at the beginning of the report, and after designs were submitted they were shown to him for his blessing. The COO and CFO were also involved in the interview process.

Were you happy with the result? What could have been better?

We were very happy with the resulting pieces. This is a company that is the global leader in what they do, but the quality of the customer experience is everything to them. They take a very personal, consultative approach with their customers and we felt that the pieces accurately captured that spirit.

What was the client's response?

The CEO's wife said it was the best report Sysco has ever produced, and we think that says a lot. The client was very happy with the pieces as they served as a nice visual transition to Sysco's new brand update introduced shortly thereafter, "Good Things Come From Sysco." Specifically, the sustainability report also demonstrated Sysco's commitment to the environment, not as a follower or because it's en vogue to say you are committed, but as a leader in its industry. This position has been supported for years from the CEO on down throughout the Sysco organization and its suppliers. Both reports were very well received and led to additional work including the refresh of Sysco's corporate website.

As online communications begin to play a larger role in Sysco's communications efforts, the decision to introduce a corresponding online format was a natural one.

The Quality of Our Relationships

By listening and offering strategic solutions, we build lasting connections with our customers

If there is one SYSCO advantage that our competitors find the most difficult to duplicate, it is the quality of the relationships with our customers. At SYSCO, we have invested in building strong customer relationships, and we see the return in a high level of customer loyalty and market share that continues to grow.

At the heart of our customer relationships is our ability to listen to our customers' needs and respond with tools that help them succeed.

We sit down one-on-one with customers every day in our local operating company offices to go through a structured Business Review. The key to the success of this program is listening to the customer. We identify a customer's points of pain and together we find solutions. For an independent restaurateur who may have to be the human resources department one minute and the chef and host the next, SYSCO is a trusted advisor that can review the situation and offer knowledge and expertise.

Some recommendations involve SYSCO products and services; others consist of professional advice from someone who has qualified experience in the food business. Menu planning is an area that customers have found extremely valuable, especially in this period of rising food costs. We may recommend a different cut of meat with less waste, or a way to rebalance a plate that offers better nutrition and lower food costs, or a way to take advantage of seasonal or less familiar fruits and vegetables. With our advice, a restaurant owner can maintain quality and improve profitability.

Business Reviews are an investment we make in many of our best and most promising customers – and the return is – as these customers succeed, we succeed with them.

Sharon Culligan
Marketing Associate

Adam Siegel
Executive Chef
Bartolotta Restaurant Group
Milwaukee

The recipient of the 2008 James Beard Award as Best Chef in the Midwest, Adam Siegel is at the top of the Milwaukee restaurant scene and one reason the city's tastes are becoming more upscale. Having worked in the kitchen since he was 14, Siegel just recently became more involved in the business end of restaurant management. SYSCO's Business Reviews are a valuable tool for independent restaurateurs like Siegel and Paul Bartolotta, the restaurants' owner.

Vanessa Pena
Assistant Manager
Flying Star Cafe
Albuquerque

The Flying Star Cafe has had multiple Business Reviews and several mini product shows with SYSCO Foodservices of Albuquerque. With the help of the culinary consultants at SYSCO, the Flying Star Cafe recently identified two particular products that have had a great impact on their menu offering: cage-free, drug-free eggs and wild haddock. Both items have become very popular on the restaurant's menu, primarily due to their high quality and uniqueness. This is just one of many examples where Business Reviews and mini product shows have produced good results for both SYSCO and our customers.

"That's terrific. Thank you for your help."

SYSCO
CONSOLIDATED RESULTS OF OPERATIONS

	Year Ended		
	June 28, 2008	June 30, 2007	July 1, 2006
	(In thousands except for share data)		
Sales	$ 37,522,111	$ 35,042,075	$ 32,628,438
Cost of sales	30,327,254	28,284,603	26,337,107
Gross margin	7,194,857	6,757,472	6,291,331
Operating expenses	5,314,908	5,048,990	4,796,301
Operating income	1,879,949	1,708,482	1,495,030
Interest expense	111,541	105,002	109,100
Other income, net	(22,930)	(17,735)	(9,016)
Earnings before income taxes and cumulative effect of accounting change	1,791,338	1,621,215	1,394,946
Income taxes	685,187	620,139	548,906
Earnings before cumulative effect of accounting change	1,106,151	1,001,076	846,040
Cumulative effect of accounting change	—	—	9,285
Net earnings	$ 1,106,151	$ 1,001,076	$ 855,325
Earnings before cumulative effect of accounting change:			
Basic earnings per share	$ 1.83	$ 1.62	$ 1.36
Diluted earnings per share	1.81	1.60	1.35
Net earnings:			
Basic earnings per share	$ 1.83	$ 1.62	$ 1.38
Diluted earnings per share	1.81	1.60	1.36

See Notes to Consolidated Financial Statements

SYSCO
CONSOLIDATED SHAREHOLDERS' EQUITY

	Common Stock		Paid-in Capital	Retained Earnings	Accumulated Other Comprehensive Income (Loss)	Treasury Stock		Total
	Shares	Amount				Shares	Amount	
	(In thousands except for share data)							
Balance as of July 2, 2005	765,174,900	$765,175	$389,053	$4,552,379	$ (13,677)	136,607,370	$2,934,091	$2,758,839
Net earnings				855,325				855,325
Minimum pension liability adjustment					43,180			43,180
Foreign currency translation adjustment					47,718			47,718
Change in fair value of interest rate swap					7,064			7,064
Amortization of cash flow hedge					333			333
Comprehensive income								953,620
Dividends declared				(408,264)				(408,264)
Treasury stock purchases						16,104,600	530,563	(530,563)
Treasury stock issued for acquisitions						(126,027)	(1,305)	3,055
Share-based compensation awards			134,881			(6,306,823)	(140,716)	275,597
Balance as of July 1, 2006	765,174,900	$765,175	$525,684	$4,999,440	$ 84,618	146,279,320	$3,322,633	$3,052,294
Net earnings				1,001,076				1,001,076
Minimum pension liability adjustment					3,469			3,469
Foreign currency translation adjustment					25,052			25,052
Amortization of cash flow hedge					428			428
Comprehensive income								1,030,025
Dividends declared				(456,438)				(456,438)
Treasury stock purchases						16,501,200	559,788	(559,788)
Share-based compensation awards			111,470			(9,445,997)	(218,475)	329,945
Adoption of SFAS 158 recognition provision					(117,628)			(117,628)
Balance as of June 30, 2007	765,174,900	$765,175	$637,154	$5,544,078	$ (4,061)	153,334,523	$3,663,946	$3,278,400
Net earnings				1,106,151				1,106,151
Foreign currency translation adjustment					30,514			30,514
Amortization of cash flow hedge					427			427
Amortization of prior service cost					3,777			3,777
Amortization of net actuarial losses					2,003			2,003
Amortization of transition obligation					93			93
Pension funded status adjustment					(124,301)			(124,301)
Comprehensive income								1,018,664
Dividends declared				(513,593)				(513,593)
Treasury stock purchases						16,499,900	520,255	(520,255)
Share-based compensation awards			75,054			(5,892,065)	(143,143)	218,197
Adoption of FIN 48				(91,635)				(91,635)
Adoption of SFAS 158 measurement date provision				(3,572)	22,780			19,208
Balance as of June 28, 2008	765,174,900	$765,175	$712,208	$6,041,429	$ (68,768)	163,942,358	$4,041,058	$3,408,986

See Notes to Consolidated Financial Statements

Parkland's
story is
one that
affects the
entire
community

17

at Parkland

Parkland has the only psychiatric ER in the region for those who need critical and timely intervention.

18

Parkland provides numerous programs essential to Dallas and influential nationally, including disaster preparedness. Highly trained teams stand ready to respond to a crisis, including a chemical or biological incident.

Category: Healthcare | **Location:** Texas, United States | **Art Director:** Kevin Bailey | **Creative Director:** Brian Boyd | **Designer:** Kevin Bailey | **Illustrator:** Kevin Bailey | **Paper Type:** Utopia
Photographer: Skeeter Hagler | **Print Run:** 5,000 | **Printer:** Allcraft Printing, Inc. | **Typographer:** Kevin Bailey

What was the client's directive?

The directive was to demonstrate how Parkland affects the community and the region; and by doing so, to build the case for building a new public hospital that is desperately needed.

How did you define the problem?

To identify the areas where Parkland is unique, that are demonstrable to its profound outreach to all areas of the community and even in some cases to the country. To further identify the deficiencies in space and modern technologies the current hospital has and how these deficiencies hurt the future needs of the community. By highlighting why the hospital is important and by demonstrating its physical deficiencies, we would be able to make the case for the new hospital.

What was the approach?

To subdivide the annual's theme to the key areas of Parkland's excellence; "training," "prevention" and "top-ranked programs," and lead into the last section category of "challenges." Using the classic metaphor of the ripple effect superimposed and juxtaposed to specific programs where the hospital excels, many unique to Parkland, to demonstrate its outreach. We used strong and direct sound bites to clearly delineate the subdivision of segments.

What disciplines or people helped you with the project?

Strong writing and photography coupled with the hospital's smart, motivated marketing director and staff. The hospital team had a clear vision of what the annual needed to be to succeed and were extremely helpful and opened minded with the creative.

What was the client's response?

The client was thrilled with the final result; it hit the mark.

What are clients looking for when it comes to designing an Annual Report?

The reasons are varied depending on the client. Obviously, clients want creativity, and, like all good Annual Report design, it needs to communicate the CEO's vision for the direction of the company. They want effective communication.

Do you and the client both view the Annual Report as part of the company's communications strategy? And how important is it within the overall strategy?

The Annual Report is always a part of a company's communication strategy, usually on a number of levels. An annual is unique to a company's brand in the sense that it blends the CEO's personal brand with that of the company; this is a rather ethereal quality an annual possesses. It's the designers charge to effectively wield the two, to communicate the CEO's vision and flair, and be true to the corporate brand in its expression and communication. It's a very important tool to literally gauge "who you're dealing with."

In which direction do you see Annual Reports moving?

Sadly, I believe the printed Annual Report is going to continue to sdiminish as a communications tool beyond the strict reporting of numbers. It will certainly continue on in the digital realm. Print is a medium that possesses unique advantages, however, so I hope there will always be a need for it.

It's the designer's charge to effectively communicate the CEO's vision and flair and at the same time, be true to the corporate brand.

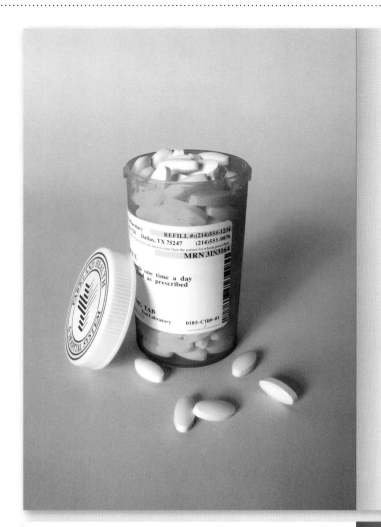

CHALLENGES

at Parkland

A pharmacy designed decades ago must struggle to keep up with today's patient volumes and needs.

32

2007 Financial and Statistical Summary (refer to website for complete financials)

Parkland applies its limited resources to meet the most acute needs in the most effective and responsible way possible. We are proud to report that Parkland is one of the most financially stable public hospitals in the country, operating in the black and debt-free. Parkland's tax rate has not increased in the last seven years.

Volume Statistics

Adult inpatient discharges	41,645
Neonatal inpatient discharges	1,143
Total outpatient visits	914,042
ER visits	142,723
Pathology procedures	7,403,810
Prescriptions filled	5,467,178
Radiology examinations	356,405
Surgeries	
Main operating room	13,524
Simmons Ambulatory Surgery Center	1,520
Total	15,044

Ad Valorem Taxes (thousands)

Fiscal Year	Tax Base	Tax (per $100 valuation)	Net Tax Revenue	Cost of Uncompensated Care	Cost of Uncompensated Care Over Tax Revenue
2007	$149,914,000	0.254	$373,624	$511,984	$138,360

Net tax revenue includes adjustments for actual collection performance.

For complete audited financial statements, please visit parklandhospital.com.

Payor Mix

32% Charity**
10% Commercial insurance
11% Self-pay*
32% Medicaid
15% Medicare

*Self-pay patients have no identified third-party payor source and do not qualify for the Parkland Healthplus program.
**Charity patients are Dallas County residents who qualify for Parkland Healthplus program or other charitable payor source.

Sources of Revenue (millions)

$344 Patient revenue
$312 Premium revenue
$137 Government
$60 Other
$29 Interest
$374 Property taxes

Uses of Revenue (millions)

$494 Salaries & benefits
$332 Supplies, purchased services & other
$268 Claims expense
$61 Pharmaceuticals
$35 Depreciation & amortization

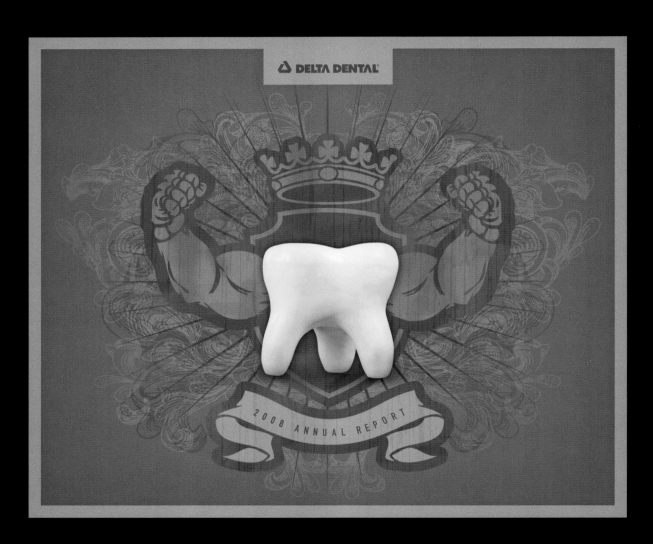

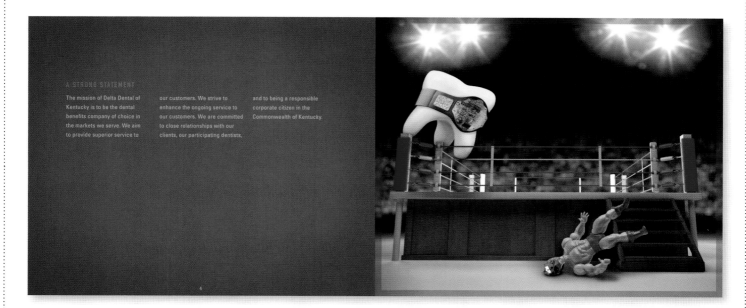

A STRONG STATEMENT

The mission of Delta Dental of Kentucky is to be the dental benefits company of choice in the markets we serve. We aim to provide superior service to our customers. We strive to enhance the ongoing service to our customers. We are committed to close relationships with our clients, our participating dentists, and to being a responsible corporate citizen in the Commonwealth of Kentucky.

SERVICE IS OUR STRENGTH

We are dedicated to providing our employer clients, members and dentists the best service possible. Our statistics tell a story of success. During 2008, our customer service representatives answered calls within 19 seconds on average, with an abandonment rate of only 2.6%. During the same period, 99.6% of our claims were processed within 15 days, with a 99.9% financial accuracy rate. A 2007 survey of over 300 benefit managers found that 98% were satisfied or very satisfied.

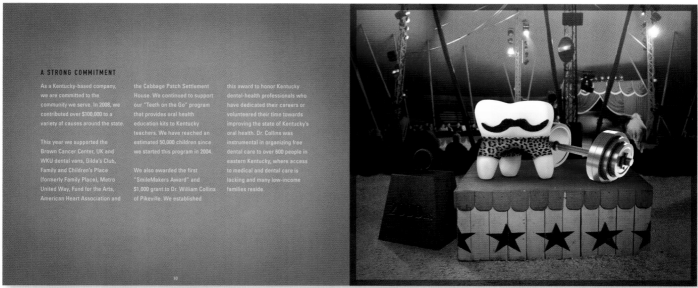

A STRONG COMMITMENT

As a Kentucky-based company, we are committed to the community we serve. In 2008, we contributed over $100,000 to a variety of causes around the state.

This year we supported the Brown Cancer Center, UK and WKU dental vans, Gilda's Club, Family and Children's Place (formerly Family Place), Metro United Way, Fund for the Arts, American Heart Association and the Cabbage Patch Settlement House. We continued to support our "Teeth on the Go" program that provides oral health education kits to Kentucky teachers. We have reached an estimated 50,000 children since we started this program in 2004.

We also awarded the first "SmileMakers Award" and $1,000 grant to Dr. William Collins of Pikeville. We established this award to honor Kentucky dental-health professionals who have dedicated their careers or volunteered their time towards improving the state of Kentucky's oral health. Dr. Collins was instrumental in organizing free dental care to over 600 people in eastern Kentucky, where access to medical and dental care is lacking and many low-income families reside.

Category: Insurance | **Location:** Kentucky, United States | **Art Director:** Brian Garr | **Author:** Ted Eckel | **Creative Director:** Gary Sloboda | **Photographer:** Brian Garr | **Printer:** Vivid Impact

Gold**111**

What was the client's directive?

As in any annual report, Delta Dental of Kentucky (DDKY) needed to supply updates of relevant events of the previous year, as well as the year's financials. But the client wanted to convey their commitment to dental research and preventative care that benefits both DDKY and their clients. They also wanted have an annual report that conveyed a friendly personality; since the recipients of the report also include client prospects, DDKY wanted them to know that not only were they proficient but a pleasure to work with.

How did you define the problem?

That DDKY is committed to helping their clients create and maintain good dental healthcare.

What was the approach?

The agency decided to represent DDKY's commitment to their clients' oral health through humorous vignettes of "strong teeth." A miniature setting of a "strong tooth" would be displayed on the right side of a spread while report information could be read on the left. Allowing for an efficient read for any audience; business on the left, fun on the right, letting the reader decide how involved they wanted to be.

What disciplines or people helped you with the project?

The imagery is a blend of built and photographed miniature sets and composite photography. Most everything was handled in-house. Miniature sets were built and photographed by the art director as well as any image compositing. Stock photography was also coupled with items shot in-house for final images. Collaboration between the agency creative team and the printer led to the selection of paper stock and the use of a clear foil stamp to accent the tooth in each image.

How involved was the CEO in your meetings, presentations, etc.?

DDKY's CEO, Clifford Maesaka, has always taken an active role in the annual report. He looks to make sure that the agency continues to communicate DDKY's personality in a creative, friendly and appropriate manner.

Were you happy with the result? What could have been better?

We were very pleased. We had tossed around the idea of creating a microsite web version of the report to supplement the printed piece to help viewing reach beyond the print run.

What was the client's response?

They were very pleased and proud to use the piece.

What are clients looking for when it comes to designing an Annual Report?

Clients want a piece that easily communicates their dealings for the year in a way that represents their corporate culture. I think some clients are more brave in letting their culture/personality show through than others, but underneath it all that's their goal.

Do you and the client both view the Annual Report as part of the company's communications strategy? And how important is it within the overall strategy?

For DDKY, the annual report is a large part of their communications strategy. They have a limited marketing budget and use the annual report as a platform to separate themselves from all of the healthcare providers vying for the attention of CEO's and Human Resource Managers. DDKY's annual report works as a mnemonic for their sales staff to build and maintain relationships with prospects. The report's tradition of being humorous and personable also serves as a good tool in maintaining relationships with current clients.

How do you define success in Annual Report design?

A successful annual report should come across as more than a stodgy collection of numbers and facts. My hope would be that a reader wouldn't just take a quick glance to make sure the financials look solid and that the 5 to 10 year revenues are headed in the right direction, but that they got a feeling and a personality from the piece as well. Whatever feeling and personality is appropriate for that brand.

In which direction do you see Annual Reports moving?

I think the internet will be a new arena for annual reports, and not just a downloadable PDF version of a printed piece.

How large a role does environmental policy play in the design and production of your Annual Reports?

It is a role that is increasing—from electronic-only Annual Reports to the use of recycled paper.

A successful annual report should come across as more than a stodgy collection of numbers and facts.

BEEFY PLANS, PUMPED UP NETWORK

A comprehensive network of dentists. A variety of network options. Cost-efficient plans tailored to each client's individual needs. These are the reasons Delta Dental of Kentucky continues to be the preferred carrier in Kentucky, covering more families in the Bluegrass State than any other carrier.

DELTA DENTAL PREMIER *(Fee for Service)* – Provides the maximum flexibility of coverage for those who prefer the freedom to go anywhere they choose. Receive services from any dentist, though this program has the largest network of dentists in the nation – approximately 194,900 dentist locations (some dentists have more than one office). Dentists

under this plan agree not to balance bill our members and will file all claim forms.

DELTA DENTAL PPO – The ultimate balance of cost and flexibility. Perfect for those who are comfortable with the many skilled providers who comprise the biggest dental PPO network in Kentucky and across the nation. Members in this popular plan enjoy up to 25% savings with approximately 116,500 dentist locations nation wide.

DELTA DENTAL PPO PLUS PREMIER – We are the only carrier in the nation that can offer two extensive provider networks simultaneously: the Premier and PPO networks.

We have combined these two networks into a plan we call Delta Dental PPO Plus Premier. For large employers, we can design programs with a choice of benefit levels and network fee schedules, both in and out of network, to meet specific cost and provider network needs.

DELTACARE (DHMO) – When affordability and quality of care are the primary factors, DeltaCare may be the right choice. The network size is reduced, along with the cost of benefits. Limited choice is offset with a credentialed network and the increased predictability of a fixed co-pay. Nationally, the DeltaCare USA network has nearly 22,000 dentist locations.

12

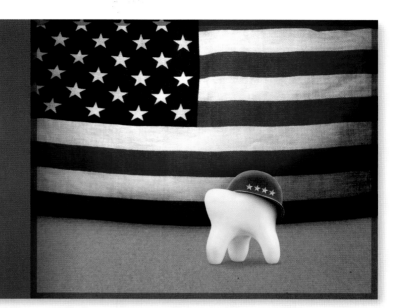

2008 FINANCIALS

Delta Dental of Kentucky, Inc. and Subsidiaries
Consolidated Balance Sheets (Unaudited)

	December 31 2008	2007
	(In Thousands)	
Assets		
Investments and cash	$ 35,206	$ 35,876
Subscriber dues receivable	5,915	6,172
Property and equipment	10,650	10,998
Other assets	435	770
Total assets	**$ 52,206**	**$ 53,816**
Liabilities and amount retained for protection of subscribers		
Estimated claims liability	$ 5,422	$ 4,795
Claim checks outstanding	3,951	5,924
Other liabilities	4,627	4,726
Total liabilities	**14,000**	**15,445**
Amount retained for protection of subscribers	38,206	38,371
Total liabilities and amount retained for protection of subscribers	**$ 52,206**	**$ 53,816**

5-Year Revenue Comparison
(In Thousands)

2004	2005	2006	2007	2008
$91,430	$94,629	$105,308	$115,888	$124,050

16

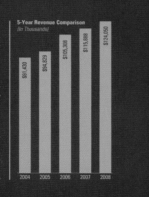

2008 BOARD OF DIRECTORS AND OFFICERS

BOARD OFFICERS

Carrie Bell Brown, DMD
Chairman of the Board

John Norton Williams, Jr., DMD
Vice Chairman

BOARD OF DIRECTORS

Carrie Bell Brown, DMD
Lexington, Kentucky

Michael Childers, DMD
Louisville, Kentucky

Mary Michael Corbett
Vice President Health Policy & Government Relations
Norton Healthcare
Louisville, Kentucky

Richard L. Feltner, PhD
New Ross, Indiana

Franklin Pierce Justice, Jr.
Pawleys Island
South Carolina

Olivia Faulkner Kirtley
Business Consultant
Louisville, Kentucky

Clifford T. Maesaka, Jr., DDS
President & Chief Executive Officer
Delta Dental of Kentucky
Louisville, Kentucky

Michael Bartlett Mountjoy
Managing Partner
Mountjoy & Bressler LLP
Louisville, Kentucky

John Lindsay Gordon Richards
Louisville, Kentucky

Jeffrey Charles Smith, DMD
Florence, Kentucky

John Norton Williams, Jr., DMD
Dean
University of NC School of Dentistry
Chapel Hill, North Carolina

CORPORATE OFFICERS

Stephen Charles Day
Vice President & Chief Marketing Officer

Curtis Randal Ladig
Vice President, Chief Operating & Financial Officer & Treasurer

Clifford T. Maesaka, Jr., DDS
President & Chief Executive Officer

Angela Jean Nenni
Vice President
Professional Services & Information Technology

Barbara Faust Stonebraker
Assistant Secretary

John Linton Weeks III
Vice President, General Counsel & Secretary

Gina Renee Whitlow
Assistant Secretary

18

HISCOX

2007
Hiscox Ltd
Report and
Accounts

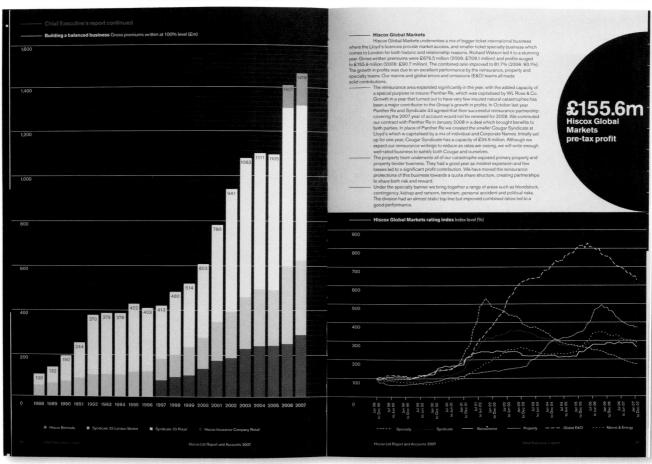

Category: Insurance | **Location:** United Kingdom | **Creative Director:** Jonathan Ellery | **Editor:** Kylie O'Connor | **Paper Type:** Challenger Offset FSC, Flamingo Pink Kaskad | **Photographer:** John Ross | **Print Producer:** Westerham Press | **Print Run:** 10,000 | **Project Manager:** Rebecca Rollin | **Senior Designer:** Claire Warner

Gold115

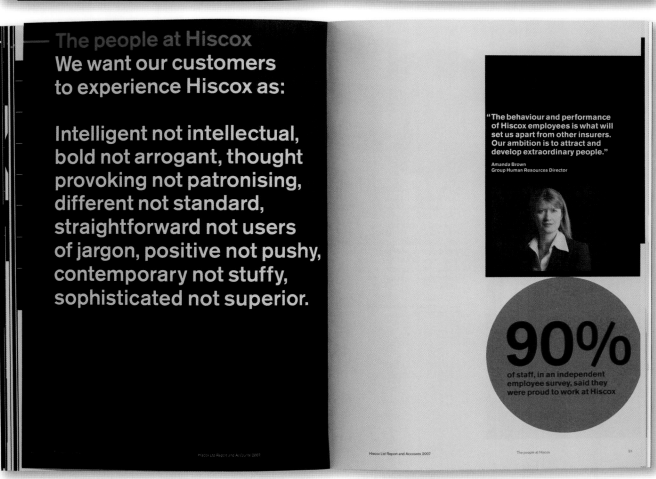

What was the client's directive?
To design and produce an annual report which developed the previous years' minimal and pared back aesthetic, therefore making a timely statement, both economically and environmentally.

What was the approach?
The approach was a document printed in 1-colour—from an aesthetic point of view, it was very much "less is more."
This met the client's objectives from an economic and environmental point of view, yet fulfilled our creative need to do something unconventional within annual reporting.

How involved was the CEO in your meetings, presentations, etc.?
The Chairman attended the first 2 creative presentations and stepped back in at the end to approve the final version. The CEO, however, took more of a backseat and fed back to us via our main client contact.

What was the client's response?
Very happy—they felt it had met their objectives.

What are clients looking for when it comes to designing an Annual Report?
An understanding of their business at that time, thorough knowledge of Best Practise for annual reporting, a smooth and fluid project management process, and ultimately a R&A which represents their business accurately.

Do you and the client both view the Annual Report as part of the company's communications strategy? And how important is it within the overall strategy?
Yes, it is a vital part of their overall communications strategy, as it is seen by key stakeholders and acts as a financial review of the past year.

How do you define success in Annual Report design?
A happy client, acknowledgement through awards (Investor Relations, etc.), and being asked to produce the report the following year.

In which direction do you see Annual Reports moving?
Online.

How large a role does environmental policy play in the design and production of your Annual Reports?
It is usually a given that the production of the R&A will have as minimal impact on the environment as possible. Clients need to be seen to be doing the right thing, so 100% recycled paper, an FSC logo or a Carbon Neutral printer's logo are all considerations.

This [Annual Report] met the client's objectives from an economic and environmental point of view, yet fulfilled our creative need to do something unconventional.

NATIONAL GALLERY OF ART 2008 ANNUAL REPORT

Category: Non-Profit | **Location:** New York, United States | **Art Director:** Michael Gericke | **Designer:** Michael Gericke, Seong Im Yang | **Printer:** Finlay Printing

Visitors view the Gallery's 2008
acquisition *Swamp Maple (4:30)*
by Alex Katz in the East Building
Concourse Galleries.

COLLECTING

THE GALLERY ACTIVELY SEEKS WORKS OF ART IN THE AREAS
IN WHICH IT COLLECTS, IN KEEPING WITH THE HIGH
STANDARDS ESTABLISHED BY ITS FOUNDING BENEFACTORS.
THROUGH THE GENEROSITY OF MANY INDIVIDUALS,
THE GALLERY BUILT ITS RENOWNED COLLECTION WITH
SOME SEVEN HUNDRED SIGNIFICANT ACQUISITIONS IN 2008.

☐ ALFRED THOMPSON
BRICHER
A Quiet Day near Manchester
Paul Mellon Fund, Avalon
Fund, and Gift of Jo Ann
and Julian Ganz, Jr.

PAINTINGS Three highly
important nineteenth-century
American paintings were acquired
in 2008: two by the celebrated
genre painter Eastman Johnson,
and a third by Alfred Thompson
Bricher, best known for his depictions of coastal New England.

Johnson's *Gathering Lilies*, 1865, and *On Their Way to Camp*,
1873, date from the post-Civil War period during which the
artist was at the height of his powers. During the early 1860s
Johnson undertook numerous trips to Maine to make studies of
maple sugar camps. His intention was to compose a large genre
painting that would rival history paintings in scale and ambition,
but he never succeeded in completing the work. He set that
project aside in 1865 and turned his attention to painting ideal-
ized views of women in various pursuits. The masterpiece of these
works, *Gathering Lilies* shows a solitary woman bending down to
pick the flower of a water lily from the surface of a tranquil
pond with her right hand while holding others in her left.
Johnson perfectly captured the graceful elegance of her motion

as she balances on the log and turns
to grasp the stem of the flower.

The subject of *On Their Way to
Camp* was derived from Johnson's
earlier study of maple sugar camps
in Maine. Although his interests
had previously centered on the busy activities of making sugar,
in this work he shows only three boys—two towing a sled with
a sap barrel through snowy woods while a third, younger boy
rides atop the barrel holding a wooden bucket. The trees
around the boys have been tapped to gather the maple sap, and
in the background a wooden lean-to and the red flames of a
fire are visible. *On Their Way to Camp*—signed and dated "E.
Johnson/1873"—is the only picture related to the sugar-making
theme that Johnson seems to have regarded as fully finished
and complete.

Alfred Thompson Bricher began his career as a painter of
autumnal landscapes, but by the late 1860s, he had become a
specialist in seascapes. His favorite subjects were the beaches
and headlands of the New England coast, and he excelled at

depicting such scenes in calm weather and lit by
serene, luminous skies. At his best, as in the radi-
antly beautiful *A Quiet Day near Manchester*, 1873,
which depicts a scene on the Massachusetts coast
north of Boston, he was capable of equaling the
finest work of his fellow marine painters, John
Frederick Kensett, Sanford Robinson Gifford,
and Martin Johnson Heade. Although Bricher
painted many pictures over the course of his long
career, he created nothing that surpasses the
superb quality of *A Quiet Day near Manchester*.

These three important paintings join the
American collection through the Paul Mellon Fund,
Avalon Fund, and the generous gift of Jo Ann and
Julian Ganz, Jr.

Two striking European paintings were added to
the collection this year. Abraham de Verwer's
atmospheric *View of Hoorn*, c. 1645, depicts Hoorn
from the south, the view that greeted ships as they
sailed the Zuiderzee towards this important Dutch
port, a major center for trade to the Baltic, the
West Indies, and the East Indies. A bank of clouds
stretches across the late-afternoon sky, with only the

water's ripples, some fluttering flags, and a gliding
sailboat to suggest the gentle breezes passing over
the broad roadstead. De Verwer suggested the
water's expanse by modulating the way light
reflects against its surface, moving from a darker
foreground to lighter tonalities near the horizon.
From de Verwer's low and distant vantage point,
Hoorn's distinctive city profile is barely distin-
guishable. Visible above the buildings lining the
harbour are masts of ships, silhouetted in muted
browns against the grey sky. The only activity of
note in this serene image occurs on the deck of
the large sailing ship at the left, where sailors grasp
lines from a block and tackle attached to the square
rigging to load cargo into the ship's hold. No
commission for *View of Hoorn* is known, so the
circumstances under which de Verwer executed
this remarkable work remain a mystery. This
painting was acquired through the generosity of
the Derald H. Ruttenberg Memorial Fund.

The third work by an artist of the Danish Golden
Age to enter the Gallery's collection, *View of
Bregentved Forest, Sjaelland*, mid 1830s, is a characteristic work by the Danish landscape painter
Frederik Sødring. In contrast to the majority of
artists associated with the period, Sødring devoted
himself almost exclusively to landscape painting.
This painting, which is believed to depict the lush
forested region around Bregentved Manor in central
Sjaelland, the largest island of Denmark, displays
the keen observation, rigorous attention to detail,
and sensitivity to light and atmosphere that were
the hallmark of the Golden Age. Although meticulously composed, the scene has a charming air of
spontaneity due to Sødring's handling of paint. This
painting is a gift of Jean-François and Véronique
Heim in memory of Philip Conisbee.

☐ EASTMAN JOHNSON
Gathering Lilies
Paul Mellon Fund
and Gift of Jo Ann and
Julian Ganz, Jr.

☐ ABRAHAM DE VERWER
View of Hoorn
The Derald H. Ruttenberg
Memorial Fund

{12}

{13}

What was the client's directive?

The National Gallery of Art asked us to create a report that reflects its rich history and legacy as one of the country's most important and long-standing art institutions. The book presents the year's recent acquisitions, galleries, ever-changing exhibitions, donors, staff and detailed information about the management of the Gallery.

The audience for the book includes the President of the United States, Members of Congress, Trustees (including the Supreme Court Justices, the Secretary of State, etc.) and the public-at-large.

How did you define the problem?

We've designed the National Gallery of Art's Annual Reports for the past eight years. Each year, we meet with the Director and senior curators to review the past year's events, shows, acquisitions and upcoming plans.

What was the approach?

We've designed the books to be perceived as an ongoing and connected series of annual reviews. Linked by attitude, typography and approach—but uniquely designed to celebrate the events of each year.

Like the Gallery's architecture—a classic West Building opened by Andrew Mellon, and a modern East Building designed by I.M. Pei—the book design carefully balances its visual attitude for a broad audience.

How involved was the CEO in your meetings, presentations, etc.?

The Gallery Director, Earl A. Powell III, was very involved in the development of the book. He attended briefings, presentations and presented the book to the Board of Trustees.

Were you happy with the result? What could have been better?

This year's annual report was a success. The design is optimistic and uplifting. We overcame several challenges to produce this year's Annual Report. The overall production budget was reduced considerably. With careful planning and research, the paper specifications and printing processes were optimized to reduce costs—without a noticeable change in quality.

We could continue to push for better images of gallery installations that are photographed during the year (before we begin the book design).

What are clients looking for when it comes to designing an Annual Report?

The National Gallery of Art is looking for an Annual Report that evolves year to year, but also maintains a forward-looking view of the institution. Each report is part of a collection and fits into the series of past reports.

Do you and the client both view the Annual Report as part of the company's communications strategy? And how important is it within the overall strategy?

The National Gallery of Art's Annual Report is sent to thousands of donors and supporters of the institution. The report plays an integral role as part of the institution's communication strategy, serving as an educational piece and keepsake.

How do you define success in Annual Report design?

A successful annual report should be compelling, memorable, and capture the spirit of the institution, while communicating all pertinent information.

In which direction do you see Annual Reports moving?

Annual reports will move more and more towards solely online communication. There will continue to be a need (for some audiences, like the National Gallery's) to have a physical and lasting object to define and remember its history.

How large a role does environmental policy play in the design and production of your Annual Reports?

We work closely with an environmentally conscious offset printer and carefully determine the exact quantity required to reach the audience.

A successful annual report should be compelling, memorable, and capture the spirit of the institution, while communicating all pertinent information.

AFGHANISTAN: HIDDEN
TREASURES FROM THE
NATIONAL MUSEUM, KABUL

+ GEORGE DE FOREST
BRUSH: THE INDIAN
PAINTINGS

+ MARTIN PURYEAR

During the fiscal year, the Gallery lent 778 works of art to 226 sites. Among these significant works were portraits of the Prince and Princess of Saxony by Lucas Cranach the Elder lent to the Städelsches Kunstinstitut und Städtische Galerie, Frankfurt and the Royal Academy of Arts, London. The Gallery also sent three works by sixteenth-century Italian artist Sebastiano del Piombo to the Palazzo di Venezia in Rome and the Kulturforum in Berlin. Two important paintings by Albrecht Dürer, *Madonna and Child* and *Portrait of a Clergyman* were included in *Durero y Cranach: Arte y Humanismo en la Alemania del Renacimiento* at the Museo Thyssen-Bornemisza in Madrid. Jean Siméon Chardin's *The House of Cards* was featured as a focus installation, in the series *Masterpieces from the World's Museums at the Hermitage,* at the State Hermitage Museum in St. Petersburg. The Gallery lent eighteen works by Mark Rothko to an exhibition organized by the Tate Modern and twelve Rothko works to an exhibition that traveled to Rome, Munich, and Hamburg.

The Gallery also sent large groups of loans to domestic exhibitions. Sixty-eight prints were lent to *Colorful Impressions: The Printmaking Revolution in Eighteenth-Century France* at the Yale University Art Gallery. Another exceptionally large group of loans, 110 photographs, was included in *The Art of the American Snapshot, 1888–1978: From the Collection of Robert E. Jackson,* which traveled to the Amon Carter Museum in Fort Worth. Thirty-three collection pieces by Eugène Boudin were seen in *Eugène Boudin at the National Gallery of Art* at the Virginia Museum of Fine Arts, Richmond.

{28}

{29}

REPORT OF INDEPENDENT AUDITORS

TO THE BOARD OF TRUSTEES OF THE NATIONAL GALLERY OF ART

In our opinion, the accompanying statements of financial position and the related statements of activities and cash flows present fairly, in all material respects, the financial position of the National Gallery of Art (the Gallery) at September 30, 2008, and the changes in its net assets and its cash flows for the year then ended in conformity with accounting principles generally accepted in the United States of America. These financial statements are the responsibility of the Gallery's management; our responsibility is to express an opinion on these financial statements based on our audit. The prior year summarized comparative information has been derived from the Gallery's 2007 financial statements, and in our report dated November 9, 2007, we expressed an unqualified opinion on those financial statements. We conducted our audit of these statements in accordance with auditing standards generally accepted in the United States of America and Government Auditing Standards issued by the Comptroller General of the United States, which require that we plan and perform the audit to obtain reasonable assurance about whether the financial statements are free of material misstatement. An audit includes examining, on a test basis, evidence supporting the amounts and disclosures in the financial statements, assessing the accounting principles used and significant estimates made by management, and evaluating the overall financial statement presentation. We believe that our audit provides a reasonable basis for our opinion.

In accordance with Government Auditing Standards, we have also issued a report dated November 13, 2008, on our consideration of the Gallery's internal control structure and its compliance with laws and regulations.

PricewaterhouseCoopers LLP

Washington, D.C.
November 13, 2008

[44]

FINANCIAL STATEMENTS

STATEMENTS OF FINANCIAL POSITION
September 30, 2008 and 2007

ASSETS	2008	2007
Cash and cash equivalents	$ 38,537,082	$ 34,331,102
Accounts receivable, net	2,487,440	1,817,339
Pledges receivable, net	21,739,700	39,090,880
Investments	609,641,948	724,092,677
Trusts held by others	11,439,562	19,063,039
Publications inventory, net	1,671,784	1,612,308
Deferred charges	1,253,084	1,204,710
Fixed assets, net	191,790,381	183,234,343
Art collections	–	–
Total assets	**$ 878,560,981**	**$ 1,004,446,398**

LIABILITIES AND NET ASSETS	2008	2007
LIABILITIES		
Accounts payable and accrued expenses	$ 42,419,962	$ 39,736,611
Capital lease obligation	1,883,955	2,037,403
Contractual obligations	31,808,398	39,435,357
Asset retirement obligation	19,149,837	19,368,200
Total liabilities	95,262,152	100,577,571
NET ASSETS:		
Unrestricted		
Designated for collections and art purchases	15,054,671	21,869,501
Designated for special exhibitions	10,292,464	10,424,172
Designated for capital projects	–	25,926,161
Designated for education and public programs	5,346,311	24,239,280
Designated for other operating purposes	41,184,478	67,663,091
Designated for publications, including systematic catalogues	20,562,474	26,510,524
Designated for fixed assets	189,906,426	181,350,388
Total unrestricted	282,346,824	357,983,117
Temporarily restricted	128,223,946	177,040,132
Permanently restricted	372,728,059	368,845,578
Total net assets	783,298,829	903,868,827
Total liabilities and net assets	**$ 878,560,981**	**$ 1,004,446,398**

The accompanying notes are an integral part of these financial statements.

[45]

2008 REVIEW

Northwestern University
Feinberg School of Medicine
150 Years of Advancing Science, Improving Health

A SESQUICENTENNIAL TIMELINE

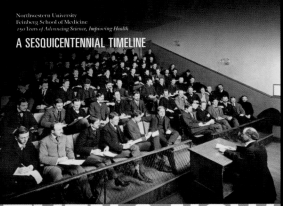

THEN & NOW

Northwestern University
Feinberg School of Medicine
150 Years of Advancing Science, Improving Health

ANNUAL REPORT 2007-08

THEN & NOW

150 YEARS
1859–2009
NORTHWESTERN
FEINBERG
SCHOOL *of*
MEDICINE

FROM THE DEAN

This year we celebrate our sesquicentennial—150 years of excellence.

We continue to build on this foundation as we move into the future of medicine as leaders and innovators. Our strategic vision can be summed up in three words: *Alignment, Innovation,* and *Impact.*

Alignment

Alignment involves the nurturing and expansion of pragmatic alliances with our clinical affiliates. This effort intensifies as Children's Memorial Medical Center prepares to move onto our campus in 2012 and as we strengthen our partnership with Northwestern Memorial Hospital. As many of you know, in June 2009, the Feinberg School and Evanston Northwestern Healthcare (ENH) will terminate their affiliation. We are moving forward with an amicable separation (details are provided in the Clinical Services section of this annual report) and are exploring exciting new affiliations.

Innovation

Our search for innovation has led us to initiate a process to redesign the curriculum (discussed in the Education section of this report). It also has led us to our vision of The Great Academic Medical Center, which grew out of a Joint Planning Committee of senior leaders from the medical school, Northwestern Memorial Hospital, and the Northwestern Medical Faculty Foundation. It had become evident to us all that more opportunities were available through better alignment and joint planning. After more than a year of work, we recently reported our findings to an external group of senior academic leaders from leading institutions and are awaiting their feedback.

Innovation is also the causative impulse behind "One Northwestern," a novel budgeting and planning process that reflects the increasingly interdisciplinary nature of biomedical education and research. The final report contains several transformational themes including a new process for joint faculty hiring across schools, the creation of new University-wide departments, the redefinition of the focus of existing basic science departments, and the integration of the graduate programs.

Impact

In all these endeavors, we will guide our activities by assessing impact, whether in clinical care, research, teaching, or community outreach. We want to measure what we have accomplished, not how much time or money we have spent.

It is my very great pleasure to announce the following key leadership appointments that were made during the year.

Nathaniel J. Soper, MD, the immediate past-president of the International Society of Digestive Surgery, nationally known as an expert and innovator in minimally invasive and natural orifice surgery and as a surgical educator, was selected as Loyal and Edith Davis Professor and chair, Department of Surgery.

William A. Muller, MD, PhD, was recruited to the Feinberg School of Medicine (FSM) and was named the Magerstadt Professor and chair, Department of Pathology. Dr. Muller had been on the faculty of Weill Cornell Medical College, where he was professor of pathology and laboratory medicine and attending pathologist at New York Presbyterian Hospital. He is the editor of the *Journal of Experimental Medicine* and is distinguished for his research in leukocyte–endothelial cell interactions in inflammation.

John G. Csernansky, MD, was recruited from Washington University in St. Louis where he was Gregory B. Couch Professor of Psychiatry and professor of anatomy and neurobiology. He joined FSM as the Lizzie Gilman Professor and chair, Department of Psychiatry and Behavioral Sciences. He is a nationally respected physician-scientist whose research utilizes sophisticated neuroimaging techniques to study how abnormalities in brain structures relate to symptoms, cognitive defects, and responses to drug therapies in patients with schizophrenia and Alzheimer's disease and other dementias.

Douglas E. Vaughan, MD, was recruited to FSM from Vanderbilt University where he was the C. Sidney Burwell Professor of Medicine and chief of the Division of Cardiovascular Medicine. Dr. Vaughan came to Northwestern as professor and chair, Department of Medicine. He has been invested as the Irving S. Cutter Professor of Medicine. Dr. Vaughan currently is principal investigator on four major grants from the National Heart, Lung, and Blood Institute that address research questions ranging from the basic mechanisms to the potential innovative therapies of cardiovascular disease.

In closing, I would like to reassure you that the Feinberg School remains financially solid. Like all medical schools, we have been impacted by the recent economic downturn. However, the careful stewardship of our Board of Trustees and the generosity of our many donors enabled us to weather these difficulties. I sometimes think of the medical school as a high speed train. We have enormous momentum, all the signals are pointing in the same direction, we know where we want to go, and we are getting there fast. We have always been known for excellence and for leadership. There is no doubt in my mind that we will intensify that tradition during the next 150 years and beyond.

Regards,

J. Larry Jameson, MD, PhD
Vice President for Medical Affairs
and Lewis Landsberg Dean,
Feinberg School of Medicine
Northwestern University

FINANCIALS

Total 2008 Revenue (in millions) for the Period Ending August 31, 2008

$1,139.3

Revenue Comparison 2007–08 (in millions)	2007	2008	Change
Faculty Practice Plans, Clinical Income	$ 446.8	$ 469.5[1]	5.1%
Research Grants & Contracts	266.1	290.0[2]	9.0%
Support from Affiliated Hospitals	203.6	187.3[3]	-8.0%
Endowment Income	52.2	58.3	11.5%
All Other Sources	47.2	48.3	2.2%
Support for Graduate Medical Education	66.7	67.5	1.3%
Tuition & Fees	42.8	46.0	7.6%
Support from Northwestern Medical Faculty Foundation	37.2	34.8[4]	-6.6%
Expendable Gifts	19.3	25.5	31.9%
Less: Consolidating Entries	(91.0)	(87.9)[4]	
Total Revenue	**$ 1,091.0**	**$ 1,139.3**	**4.4%**

[1] Revenues reported by Northwestern Medical Faculty Foundation (NMFF) and Pediatric Faculty Foundation (PFF).

[2] Includes $85.0 million in extramural funding for research by FSM faculty members at affiliated hospitals.

[3] FY08 includes contributions of $140.0 million reported by hospitals not reflected on FSM books, offset by $6.4 million in VA support to Graduate Medical Education (GME), $3.7 million in FSM support to GME, $2.6 million in NMFF support to GME, and $0.4 million in other support to GME. These offsets are accounted for in the category "Support for Graduate Medical Education."

[4] Reflects only contributions actually processed through FSM books; excludes in-kind contributions to teaching and research.

[5] Includes $24.39 million in NMFF support to FSM and $53.1 million in additional NMFF support to NMFF. These amounts are eliminated since they are duplicated in various revenue categories listed above.

1859

c.1870 Located at Prairie and 26th Street and adjacent to Mercy Hospital, this newly completed teaching allowed for the continued growth of the Chicago Medical College that would later become today's Feinberg School of Medicine.

c.1870 Founder of the American Medical Association and founding editor of its prestigious journal, Dr. Nathan Smith Davis served as the medical school's first dean from 1870–98. Gifted deeply, renowned in their fields, wrote to follow in his footsteps.

1881 On the steps of the medical school, faculty members and students from the Class of 1881 pose for a photo—a tradition graduating classes have upheld throughout the years. Owning a top hat, Dr. Nathan Smith Davis stands at the top of the steps behind the railing.

1905 Go Medics! Members of one of the medical school's first football teams, these students managed to combine sports and medicine into their studies. Today Northwestern's competency-based education framework encourages students to balance all that goes into becoming competent physicians and leaders, including personal awareness and self-care.

1927 The publication *Alumni News* featured news and information about the University and helped update graduates on their alma mater much like today's alumni magazine *Ward Rounds.*

1925 Mrs. Montgomery Ward (right) and her daughter, Marjorie, participate in the ground breaking ceremony for the Montgomery Ward Memorial.

c.1927 An early view of the newly completed Montgomery Ward Memorial (right) and Wieboldt Hall serves as reminders that while much has physically changed at Northwestern, much of the medical school's rich tradition remains the same.

ALUMNI NEWS
September 1927

Category: Non-Profit | **Location:** Illinois, United States | **Associate Creative Director:** Liz Haldeman | **Creative Director:** Brock Haldeman | **Designer:** Don Emery | **Printer:** Lake County Press

Gold**125**

2008 New technology demands multitasking — a skill that today's medical students have wholeheartedly embraced. Studying placenta previa, this student combines her "old-fashioned" textbook with his high-tech PC tablet and iPod tunes.

2008 One of only three such facilities in the United States, Northwestern's new Nikon Imaging Center is equipped with the latest technology in the light microscopy imaging systems that are instrumental in ongoing biomedical research.

2008 Dr. Lewis Landsberg served as dean from 1990–2007. Irving S. Cutter Professor Emeritus of Medicine, he is the founder and director of the new Northwestern University Comprehensive Center on Obesity. Completed in 2008, this oil painting honors his service to the institution.

2008 Using the center's Nikon C1si confocal microscopes, researchers can obtain high resolution micrographs such as these images showing the three major cytoskeletal networks within the endothelial cell: actin (red), intermediate filament (blue), and microtubule (green).

2008 Dr. Sandro Mussa-Ivaldi (foreground), professor of physiology and of physical medicine and rehabilitation, is advancing human-machine convergence by leveraging robotics to decipher the human motor control system. His work blurs the lines between biology and technology —critical to advancing 21st century medicine.

2008 Interested in cell adhesion and the role it plays in cell behavior and tissue morphogenesis, Dr. Kathleen Green, Joseph L. Mayberry, Sr., Professor of Pathology and Toxicology, has been lauded by her peers for skillfully using her scientific PhD knowledge to think in clinical terms— much to the benefit of Northwestern.

2008 The gothic tower of the Montgomery Ward Memorial proudly stands above the Method Atrium, a bright and airy lobby that links the medical school's research buildings: Morton, Searle and Tarry.

2008 One of the Feinberg School's many partners, Northwestern Memorial Hospital's new Prentice Women's Hospital—as seen through an architectural detail of the Montgomery Ward Memorial—expands the horizons of the entire medical campus. Northwestern Memorial Hospital is the medical school's primary clinical partner.

2008 Medical school seniors eagerly look ahead to bright futures during Northwestern's commencement ceremonies held May 16 in Navy Pier's Grand Ballroom.

2009

2008 The April 21 groundbreaking ceremony for the Ann & Robert H. Lurie Children's Hospital of Chicago (scheduled for completion in 2012) fostered the spirit of "One Northwestern." In attendance were (front row and from left) Henry Bienen, PhD, president, Northwestern University; Dean Harrison, president and CEO, Northwestern Memorial HealthCare; Mary Hendrix, PhD, president and scientific director, Children's Memorial Research Center; and Larry Jameson, MD, PhD, Lewis Landsberg Dean and vice president for medical affairs, Feinberg School of Medicine.

What was the client's directive?
The client's directive was for us to create an annual report that doubled as a celebration piece for the institution's sesquicentennial.

How did you define the problem?
The communications problem paralleled the client's directive in that the piece needed to be multifunctional and successful in both aspects. The annual report needed to capture and convey the year's successes without being overshadowed by celebrating the organization's sesquicentennial year and vice versa.

What was the approach?
The approach was to leverage a simple but engaging solution: to create a piece with only two sides, one that functioned only as the annual report and one that functioned only as a celebration of the sesquicentennial. The finished accordion-fold piece can be read page by page on the annual report side, or unfolded to stretch nearly two meters as a sesquicentennial timeline on the opposite side.

What disciplines or people helped you with the project?
Historians, researchers, writers and photographers were involved, of course. The printer played a much more important role in this project due to the unique nature of the finished piece. We worked very closely with the printer to find the right structural solution.

How involved was the CEO in your meetings, presentations, etc.?
We worked closely with the school's Vice Dean and COO, as well as other project team related staff.

Were you happy with the result? What could have been better?
We were very pleased with the finished piece (as was the client). There are numerous small things we would change given more time and expanded resources, but that can be said of nearly all of our work. As soon as you think something can't be improved, you're not looking critically enough.

What are clients looking for when it comes to designing an Annual Report?
Hopefully, most clients are looking for an annual report that accurately

capture's the year's achievements and projects those achievements through a lens that is "of" the client's brand. Unless directed otherwise, that's how we approach an annual report.

Do you and the client both view the Annual Report as part of the company's communications strategy? And how important is it within the overall strategy?
Unless there's a good reason to have the annual report fall outside an overall communications strategy, it should be a part of it for sure. In today's increasingly busy communications marketplace, sending consistent signals across channels and across deliverables is more important than ever.

How do you define success in Annual Report design?
If an annual report meets or exceeds the client's stated goals or objectives, we consider it a success. Happily, our solutions most always do.

In which direction do you see Annual Reports moving?
With the increased emphasis on electronic filing, the annual report as analyst tool is waning, and its importance as a brand-building vehicle or outright marketing tool is growing. We see this trend continuing both in printed and interactive annual reports.

How large a role does environmental policy play in the design and production of your Annual Reports?
This particular annual report was printed on recycled paper stock manufactured using Green-e certified electricity generated exclusively by renewable wind power.
We believe environmental policy should play a role in the design and production of everything, including annual reports. As such, by purchasing carbon credits, our agency is a certified CarbonFree™ business. It's one more small contribution.

We believe environmental policy should play a role in the design and production of everything, including annual reports.

2008

Italië

Met ste
selectie
Collect
eeuwse
da Perego
moderne k
door de vo
Coleta, e
uit de
van kr
Willie
Nicolas
stelling

Comm...
Nederl...
€14.776
februari

Dutch Fashion, Amsterdam
Francisco Benthum, Sjaak Hullekes,
Hans Ubbink
€2.585 - €2...
juni 2008

De Du
steun
van Be
Sjaak Hullekes en Ha
zich in
het eerst in Mil...
White/Benthum, zu
hoofdkle...
het accent
Van Benthum
voor vanmin.

Europe...
Amst...
Monti...
€...
Juli -

Kestnergesellschaft, Hannover
Rezi van Lankveld
€2.689 - €36.867
mei - augustus 2008

Kestnergesellschaft ontving een bijdrage voor de deelname van Rezi van Lankveld aan de internationale groepstentoonstelling Back to Black. De organisatie programmeert internationaal, met kunstenaars als Thomas Hirschhorn, Gilbert & George en Per Kirkeby. In tentoonstellingen die soms doorreizen naar andere presentatieplekjes. In Back to Black werd belang gehecht aan de kleur zwart in eigentijdse kunst gestaleerd. De bijdrage van de Mondriaan Stichting deel uit van een serie thematische groepstentoonstellingen, die in 2007 is begonnen met Made in Germany. Naast Rezi van Lankveld namen twintig andere kunstenaars deel, onder wie Pablo Alonso, Udomsak Krisanamis en Neil Weira.

Ludwig Forum for International Art, Aken
Atelier Van Lieshout
€35.000 - €92.900
september - december 2008

Voor de tentoonstelling Paul Hana van Atelier Van Lieshout gaf de Mondriaan Stichting een bijdrage aan het Ludwig Forum. Dit museum, voor hedendaagse kunst behelst de collectie van Peter en Irene Ludwig en ontwikkelt tentoonstellingen met voornamelijk hedendaagse partijen. Ook heeft het vermaarde de tweejaarlijkse Kunstpreis Aachen uitgereikt, die in 2006 werd uitgereikt aan Aernout Mik. Deze tentoonstelling geeft een overzicht van het werk van Atelier Van Lieshout in de jaren tachtig tot heden.

Pinakothek der Moderne, München
Hans Aarsman, Edwin Zwakman
€24.000 - €76.000
oktober 2008 - januari 2009

Pinakothek der Moderne ontving ondersteuning voor de tentoonstelling Nature & Artifice New Dutch Landscape in Photography and Video Art, met deelname van een groot aantal fotografen uit Nederland, van Hans Aarsman tot Edwin Zwakman. De Pinakothek programmeert internationaal en wellicht tamen met belangrijke instellingen over de liefde wereld. Nature as Artifice ging over de manmatige in Nederland geconstrueerde natuur, zoals die is ervaren en gevisualiseerd door vele fotografen. De tentoonstelling zou, ook te zien in het Kröller-Müller Museum eilandelijk en Duitsland door naar het George Eastman House, in de Verenigde Staten. De catalogus verscheen bij kull Uitgevers.

---

6. Beeldende kunst en vormgeving internationaal – **Ondersteunde projecten**

6. Beeldende kunst en vormgeving internationaal – Ondersteunde projecten

---

rts Buddha...
n Korfeu, Bani...
13.50 - €...
september - dec...

East studie
culaar wil deel te nemen aan
soim Boom, Jan jager
voor de verg...
door kunstenaars.
t Kitgpie. Hup
kunstinitief wilde kennis
aken met de
produceren in de openbare ruimte
onder mobiliteit...
articipatie van publiek.
escoland van Boom vertegenwoordigd
de kunstenaars... Bert Kramer,
antas Lesauska en Major. Het was de eerste
emstrale- en present... van Cascoland naar
rngtie, met als doel gezamenlijk een
ascolandproject te begekelen.

KHOJ International Artists Association, New Delhi, India
Els Reijnders, Gmy Van, Friso Witteveen
€3.500 - €84.461
november - december 2008

KHOJ International Artists' Association kreeg binnen het Arts Collaboratory-programma een bijdrage voor de deelname van curator Els Reijnders en kunstenaars Gmy Van en Friso Witteveen aan het internationaal KHOJ project in Witteveen. KHOJ werd in 2007 opgericht en is gelegen aan de Triangle Arts Trust, de programmering van een workshops en residencies is internationaal, met het accent op Zuid-Azië voor het ontwikkelen van een regionaal netwerk. 48 C Public Art Ecology was een van de eerste hedendaagse kunstfestivals in Delhi, het was gericht op ecologie en milieuvraagstukken en speelde zich af in de openbare ruimte.

...A, Centro de Experimentação e Informação ...Arte, Belo Horizon Brazilië
Abraz, Nena Heij...
2.599 - €27920
- augustus 2009

a kreeg een bijdrage voor de deelname van Rose
zras, Nena Heijnan, Dirk Jan Jager, Elke Veltman
zitelle Valder aan de tweede editie van de
antfestival. Het project was het tweede effect van de
ntrum werd opgericht als doorstap van de Performance, Het
eding van de van de Rijksakademie, en ontwikkelt onder
er Paulo Rolla-producties, doorgaans binnen
t Rain Artists Initiatives Netwerk en vaste met
zin uit Nederland. De selectie van kunstenaars
npuaren waar MFR kwam tot stand met
stellingen aan de Rijksakademie. MF12 werd onder...
pracy aan de Rijksakademie, Metz werd onder...
und binnen het Arts Collaboratory-programma.

MAMA, Rotterdam, Nederland
Reis- en verblijfkosten Douala, Casablanca,
Johannesburg
€1.450 - €4.950
februari 2008

Showroom MAMA organiseerde de Project(or) Art Fair, een concept voor actuele kunstpodia. Vijf dagen lang presenteerden 28 voortstrevende kunstpodia uit binnen- en buitenland zich met werk van meer dan honderd kunstenaars in het voormalig casino in Rotterdam. Podia zoals Artur Gallery uit Berlijn, maar ook Kop uit Breda en Tag uit Den Haag, presenteerden zich zelden op topniveau. Door het Arts Collaboratory-programma, varierend van een performance tot een beurshow. De Mondriaan Stichting droeg bij in de reis- en verblijfskosten van Doual/Art (Douala), La Source de Lion (Casablanca) en xArts Emerging (Johannesburg).

Trans Artists, Amsterdam, Nederland
Artists in-Dialogue
€10.000 - €70.000
oktober 2008

Trans Artists organiseerde van 9 tot 12 oktober de Res Artist General Meeting 2008 in Amsterdam en maakte het daarmee mogelijk dat de contacten tussen Nederlandse en buitenlandse hedendaagse kunstinstellingen verbeterden. Een belangrijk onderwerp van de conferentie was gastvrijheid: dit ligt de Mondriaan Stichting na aan het hart en sluit aan bij de ambitie die zij eerder, met een groot aantal conferentiepartners zoals nivos en en Stichting norm, heeft gevraagd voor het gastverspreid beleid. Tijdens de conferentie werd het Arts Collaboratory-programma toegelicht aan het internationaal publiek.

Centre Soleil d'Afrique, Bamako, Mali
ost van Haaften, Harald Schole
0.000 - €21.600

de deelname van Joost van Haaften en Harald
hole aan het project Station Mali Gate Mali
weg Soleil d'Afrique een bijdrage. Soleil d'Afrique
ma Goro, de kunstinitiatief onder leiding van
ademe beide Nederland en wijlt aan de Rijks-
tuen. Het bereik van het initiatief is groot aan
ntion Mali namen niet alleen kunstenaars uit
ali deel, maar ook uit landen als Benin, Joost/opt
Togo. Het project was gericht op het inter-
tionaal uitwisselen van ideeën en het scheppen
o voorwaarden voor creative industries in Mali
o werkbezoek vond plaats binnen het samen-
rkingsverband Arts Collaboratory.

Mondriaan Stichting Jaarverslag

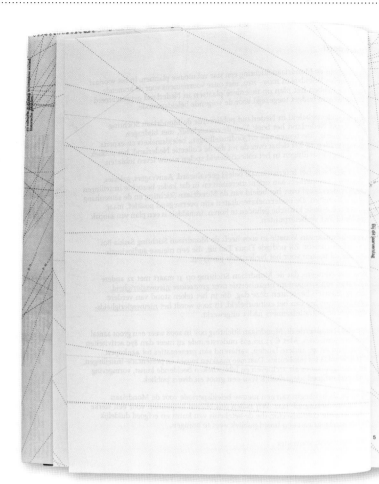

Bij dit jaarverslag

Om de nationale en internationale publieke belangstelling voor en afname van beeldende kunst, vormgeving en cultureel erfgoed te bevorderen heeft de Mondriaan Stichting in 2008 in totaal 1572 aanvragen ontvangen. Met € 23.110.498 ondersteunde zij 877 activiteiten, waarvan 406 voor internationale presentaties in 46 landen, variërend van presentaties tot aankopen, van programma's tot publicaties. Het grootste deel van dit budget is, als onderdeel van de Cultuurnota, afkomstig van het ministerie van Onderwijs, Cultuur en Wetenschap. Voor de internationale activiteiten ontvangt de Mondriaan Stichting gedelegeerd budget uit de Hgis-Cultuurmiddelen van de ministeries van ocw en Buitenlandse Zaken.

Met het jaarverslag verantwoordt de Mondriaan Stichting zich voor de manier waarop zij de beschikbare middelen heeft aangewend. Centraal in het verslag staan de projecten en activiteiten die in 2008 zijn ondersteund. In 2008 werden meer aanvragen ingediend dan in 2007 doordat er weer een aanvraagronde van de KunstKoop plaatsvond. Het toekenningspercentage was relatief laag. Als gevolg van de stijgende druk op het budget, onder meer doordat projecten steeds duurder worden, heeft de Mondriaan Stichting streng moeten selecteren. Om versnippering te voorkomen ondersteunt zij projecten bovendien zoveel mogelijk op een reëel niveau.

Het ontwerp van dit jaarverslag maakt zichtbaar wat normaal gesproken in gedrukte vorm niet gezien wordt. De hiërarchische structuur van het boek wordt opgeheven door een lijst trefwoorden en hun synoniemen die als hyperlinks met elkaar verbonden worden. Er ontvouwt zich een alternatieve representatie van gegevens. Deze toont de complexiteit en biedt tegelijkertijd nieuwe perspectieven die bijdragen tot inzicht en transparantie. Het jaarverslag als 'data cloud' waarin de sporen van verschillende netwerkstructuren zichtbaar zijn.

Het jaarverslag wordt verzonden naar relaties van de Mondriaan Stichting, inclusief alle instellingen die in 2008 aanvraag deden. Tot die relaties behoren behalve musea en kunstinstellingen ook het ministerie van ocw, de Raad voor Cultuur, de pers en belangenorganisaties. Verder is het verslag bestemd voor iedereen die geïnteresseerd is in het werk van de Mondriaan Stichting.

Doordat het jaarverslag een uitvoerige verantwoording bevat van het werk van de Mondriaan Stichting, is het ook geschikt voor instellingen die nog geen aanvraag hebben ingediend, maar overwegen dat te doen. Uit het verslag kunnen zij een indruk krijgen van de activiteiten die de Mondriaan Stichting ondersteunt en de doelen, prioriteiten en criteria die daarvoor het kader vormen.

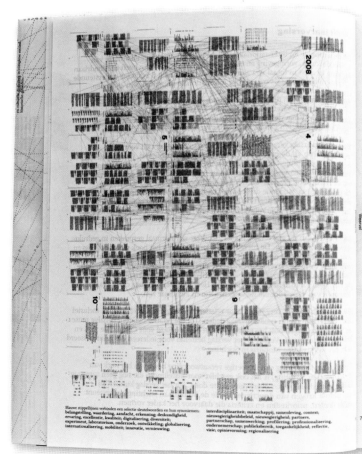

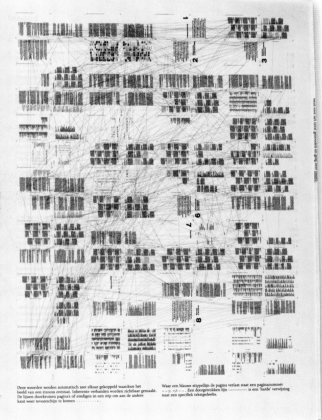

Category: Non-Profit | **Location:** Netherlands | **Creative Director:** Niels Schrader | **Paper Type:** CCP ondervel blauw 54 grs | **Print Producer:** Robstolk | **Print Run:** 2,200 | **Printer:** Robstolk | **Programmer:** Marcel van der Drift

Mondriaan Stichting

1

De Mondriaan Stichting is het (inter)nationale stimuleringsfonds voor beeldende kunst, vormgeving en cultureel erfgoed. Zij zet zich in voor een sterke en professionele cultuursector, die de betekenis van kunst, vormgeving en erfgoed duidelijk onder de aandacht van een breed publiek weet te brengen.

Toezeggingen 2008

	Aantal aanvragen*	Aantal gehonoreerd	Percentage gehonoreerd	Bijdrage MI x 1.000	Percentage totaal bedrag
Beeldende kunst en vormgeving					
Projecten miv Hgis-C	165	63	38,2%	2.804	12,1%
Projecten Antillen en Aruba	4	3	75,0%	255	1,1%
Kinderboeken	23	23	100,0%	53	0,2%
Kunstprojecten onderwijs	6	2	33,3%	98	0,4%
Publicaties	22	14	63,6%	267	1,2%
Programma's	39	17	43,6%	2.662	11,7%
Tijdschriften	9	6	66,7%	253	1,1%
KunstKoop	141	123	87,2%	874	3,8%
Overige projecten en flexibel budget	6	4	66,7%	100	0,4%
Subtotaal	415	255		7.365	32,3%
Cultureel erfgoed					
(Digitale) publieksactiviteiten en zichtbaarheid	98	50	51,0%	2.744	12,0%
Cultureel erfgoed minderheden	22	18	81,8%	678	3,0%
Antillen en Aruba	0	0	0,0%	0	0,0%
Ontwikkel- en overnamekosten	16	16	100,0%	507	2,2%
Vormgevingserfgoed	2	2	100,0%	273	1,2%
Structurele aankopen	18	16	88,9%	3.918	17,2%
Incidentele aankopen	8	6	100,0%	236	1,0%
Volkenkundige aankopen	2	2	100,0%	113	0,5%
Kunsthistorisch onderzoek	4	2	100,0%	236	1,0%
Wet behoud cultuurbezit	2	2	100,0%	43	0,2%
Erfgoed veiligheidszorg	21	25	100,0%	393	1,7%
Gemeenschappelijk cultureel erfgoed	2	1	100,0%	119	0,5%
Overige projecten en flexibel budget	12	10	83,3%	390	1,7%
Subtotaal	207	148		9.450	41,4%
Interdisciplinaire activiteiten					
Cultuureducatie	96	41	42,7%	1.457	6,4%
Interregeling	60	26	43,3%	1.366	6,0%
De Verbeelding	1	1	100,0%	300	1,3%
Subtotaal	157	68		3.124	13,7%
Internationale activiteiten					
Presentaties miv Hgis-C	334	241	72,2%	2.315	10,1%
Kunstbeurzen galeries	71	69	97,2%	328	1,4%
Lofts	87	87	100,0%	80	0,4%
Satelliite biennales	2	2	100,0%	87	0,4%
Overige projecten en flexibel budget	7	7	100,0%	88	0,4%
Subtotaal	501	406		2.899	12,7%
Totaal	1280	877		22.837	100,0%

* Het aantal aanvragen is exclusief de niet in behandeling genomen aanvragen.

Ontwikkelingen 2004 – 2008

	2004		2005		2006		2007		2008	
	Aantal	Bijdrage x 1.000	Aantal	Bijdrage x 1.000	Aantal	Bijdrage x 1.000	Aantal	Bijdrage x 1.000	Aantal	Bijdrage x 1.000
Beeldende kunst en vormgeving										
Projecten miv Hgis-C	67	2.168	75	2.066	59	1.981	54	1.959	63	2.804
Projecten Antillen en Aruba			3	66	4	100	2	109	3	255
Kinderboeken	35	1.169	11	21	4	8	22	41	23	53
Kunstprojecten onderwijs	15	947	7	379	9	380	7	401	2	98
Publicaties	12	116	17	223	9	155	11	181	14	267
Programma's	21	2.513	19	1.940	8	1.187	12	1.855	17	2.662
Tijdschriften	9	521	3	101	3	204	4	263	6	253
KunstKoop									123	874
Overige projecten en flexibel budget			1	25	1	50	13	306	4	100
Subtotaal	159	7.434	136	4.821	97	4.065	125	5.115	255	7.365
Cultureel erfgoed										
(Digitale) publieksactiviteiten en zichtbaarheid	66	2.819	67	2.891	51	2.594	51	2.568	50	2.744
Cultureel erfgoed minderheden	19	465	16	526	17	624	21	718	18	678
Antillen en Aruba									1	35
Ontwikkel- en overnamekosten					1	30	1	300	0	0
Vormgevingserfgoed							8	393	16	507
Structurele aankopen	2	325	9	921	6	800	19	2.175	2	273
Incidentele aankopen	7	5.283	18	9.075	10	2.832	21	5.785	16	3.918
Volkenkundige aankopen	6	99	3	83	9	219	3	47	6	236
Kunsthistorisch onderzoek	2	120	1	111	1	113	2	149	1	113
Wet behoud cultuurbezit	7	351			1	96	3	68	2	43
Erfgoed veiligheidszorg					26	385	38	423	25	393
Gemeenschappelijk cultureel erfgoed			1	37	3	107	2	126	1	119
Overige projecten en flexibel budget			6	105	2	30	2	65	10	390
Subtotaal	109	9.462	121	13.749	127	7.830	171	12.817	148	9.450
Interdisciplinaire activiteiten										
Cultuureducatie			21	601	63	2.183	41	1.457		
Interregeling					12	499	26	1.366		
De Verbeelding							1	300		
Subtotaal			21	601	75	2.682	68	3.124		
Internationale activiteiten										
Presentaties miv Hgis-C	226	2.002	178	1.712	191	2.002	229	2.282	241	2.315
Kunstbeurzen galeries	62	341	70	290	74	294	68	306	69	328
Lofts									87	80
Statelijke biennales			3	634	3	435	2	844	2	87
Overige projecten en flexibel budget			9	11	3	69	3	94	7	88
Subtotaal	288	2.343	260	2.647	271	2.800	302	3.526	406	2.899
Totaal	556	19.239	517	21.217	516	15.296	673	24.140	877	22.837

What was the client's directive?
The annual report reviews the Mondriaan Foundation's international activities in the year 2008.

How did you define the problem?
A detailed visualization of its large cultural network has been lacking in previous editions of the Mondriaan Foundation's annual reports.

What was the approach?
The 2008 annual report makes visible the structures and connections of related content and should be considered as a digital data cloud pressed into the physical embodiments of a book.

What disciplines or people helped you with the project?
The project was developed in collaboration with a programmer.

Were you happy with the result? What could have been better?
Of course we are very pleased with the final result, but during the design process some time was lacking to elaborate further some technical details.

What was the client's response?
The client and the audience responded both very well.

What are clients looking for when it comes to designing an Annual Report?
For an individual design solution.

Do you and the client both view the Annual Report as part of the company's communications strategy? And how important is it within the overall strategy?
Except the company's logo on the last page, the annual report does not consider any corporate design strategy.

How do you define success in Annual Report design?
It cannot be generalized and depends on the individual design approaches.

In which direction do you see Annual Reports moving?
In future years, annual reports hopefully will be considered to be something more than just an array of colourful pie charts.

How large a role does environmental policy play in the design and production of your Annual Reports?
This could play an important role, for example, during paper choice.

In future years, annual reports hopefully will be considered to be something more than just an array of colourful pie charts.

SD

2008
Report on Sustainable
Development

Cascades
GREEN BY NATURE

Category: Paper Companies | **Location:** Quebec, Canada | **Account Director:** Jean Doyon | **Creative Director:** Louis Gagnon | **Design Director:** Sébastien Bisson | **Paper Type:** Cover on Cascades InverKote; Text on Cascades 100% PC | **Print Producer:** Transcontinental Litho Acme | **Printer:** Transcontinental Litho Acme

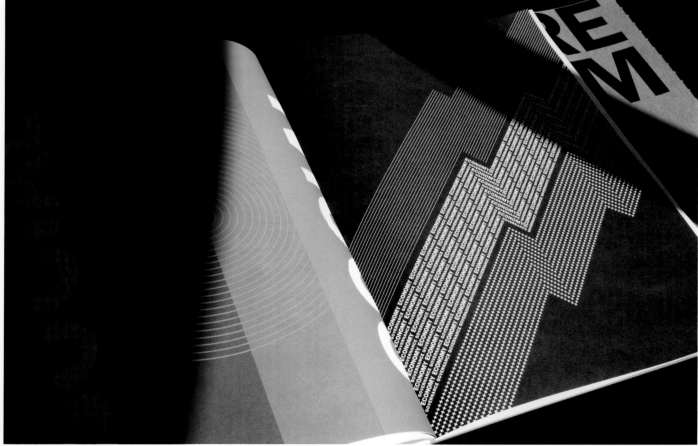

What was the client's directive?

Reusing resources has been a basic Cascades business practice since its founding in 1964. Our mandate was to create the graphic equivalent of the Cascades commitment to a smaller ecological footprint. In order to do so, we had to use paper that was manufactured by Cascades. Far from being a constraint, this allowed us to highlight their line of papers made from recycled fibre in all its diversity.

How did you define the problem?

The Report on Sustainable Development, which is distributed to shareholders, business partners, environmental sector and to employees, should reflect their commitment in its design as strongly as in its published content.

What was the approach?

Various devices were employed to summarize and organize information. We emphasized human capital with examples of everyday employee commitments, conveying their achievements in a document that was easy to consult and where each section had a strong personality of its own.

What disciplines or people helped you with the project?

With our client and our printer, Transcontinental Litho Acme, we tested an experimental environmental paper that has been certified EcoLogo. It will be marketed later this year.

How involved was the CEO in your meetings, presentations, etc.?

He was involved in the briefing and all throughout the creative and decision process.

What was the client's response?

Reception has been outstanding. In fact, the CEO has been kind enough to forward us the many emails of congratulations he had received.

Do you and the client both view the Annual Report as part of the company's communications strategy? And how important is it within the overall strategy?

Even before sustainable development become a buzzword, Cascades was a pioneer on recycling. So it's their most important piece. The Report on Sustainable Development could be seen as how their code of ethics and their environmental mission has been fulfilled.

In which direction do you see Annual Reports moving?

It's still a prestigious tool to seduce investors and partners, to do headhunting. It has to be useful, to communicate with effectiveness and efficiency and to move people.

How large a role does environmental policy play in the design and production of your Annual Reports?

For that report, a huge one. Sustainable development is part of the DNA of that company. So we had to design a communication tool with more than environmentally friendly materials (vegetable inks, papers with post-consumer fibres, no varnish, etc.). Functionality and waste reducing were important (for exemple, we reduce the use of paper with a cardboard cover that allow to ship it without extra wrapping).

The Annual Report is still a prestigious tool to seduce investors and partners, to do headhunting.

SL GREEN
REALTY CORP.

ANNUAL
REPORT 2008

SL GREEN LEADERSHIP

2008 HIGHLIGHTS

LEASING

RENEWED VIACOM FOR OVER 1 MILLION SQUARE FEET

LEASED OVER 3.5 MILLION SQUARE FEET
THROUGHOUT ENTIRE PORTFOLIO

ACHIEVED AVERAGE MARK-TO-MARKET ON NEW LEASES
SIGNED OF MORE THAN 30% (NYC ONLY)

REDUCED 2009–2010 LEASE ROLLOVER BY
1.6 MILLION SQUARE FEET (NYC ONLY)

OPERATIONS

COMPLETED $70 MILLION REDEVELOPMENT OF
100 PARK AVE. AND COMMENCED $40 MILLION
REFURBISHMENT OF 1515 BROADWAY

RECEIVED BOMA PINNACLE AWARDS FOR NEW YORK CITY'S
RENOVATED BUILDING OF THE YEAR
FOR 485 LEXINGTON AVE. AND OPERATING OFFICE BUILDING
OF THE YEAR FOR 120 WEST 45TH ST.

AWARDED BOMA MIDDLE ATLANTIC REGIONAL
BUILDING OF THE YEAR IN THE RENOVATED BUILDING
CATEGORY FOR 100 PARK AVE.

REAL ESTATE INVESTMENT

HARVESTED 4 ASSETS FOR $792* GROSS SALES PROCEEDS
GENERATING $442 MILLION OF GAINS

SOLD $110 MILLION OF STRUCTURED FINANCE INVESTMENTS

REALIZED PROMOTES IN EXCESS OF $25 MILLION

LIMITED NEW INVESTMENT ACTIVITY BY DESIGN

*SALES PRICE REPRESENTS COMBINED OWNERSHIP INTERESTS

FINANCE

ACHIEVED RECORD HIGH FFO OF $6.19 PER SHARE (DILUTED)

EXTINGUISHED $262 MILLION OF DEBT
VIA NEW BOND REPURCHASE PROGRAM RECOGNIZING GAINS
IN EXCESS OF $88 MILLION

YIELDED NET PROCEEDS OF $160 MILLION THROUGH
STRATEGIC ASSET FINANCING

FINISHED OFF YEAR WITH $726 MILLION CASH ON HAND

Category: Real Estate | **Location:** New York, United States | **Design Director:** Jason Miller | **Designer:** Jason Miller | **Illustrator:** Bryan Christie | **Paper Type** | Uncoated - Finch Opaque Bright White Smooth | **Photographer:** Jason Schmidt | **Print Producer:** Georgiann Baran | **Print Run:** 7,000 copies | **Printer:** Earth Thebault | **Project Manager:** Michelle Steg Faranda

THE SL GREEN PLATFORM HAS A STRONG FOUNDATION AND IS WELL POSITIONED TO WEATHER THE CHALLENGES OF THIS MARKET

SL Green Realty Corp. 2008 Annual Report

If an annual report communicates a big idea in an interesting fashion, and it's a book that someone would actually want to keep, then it's probably a success.

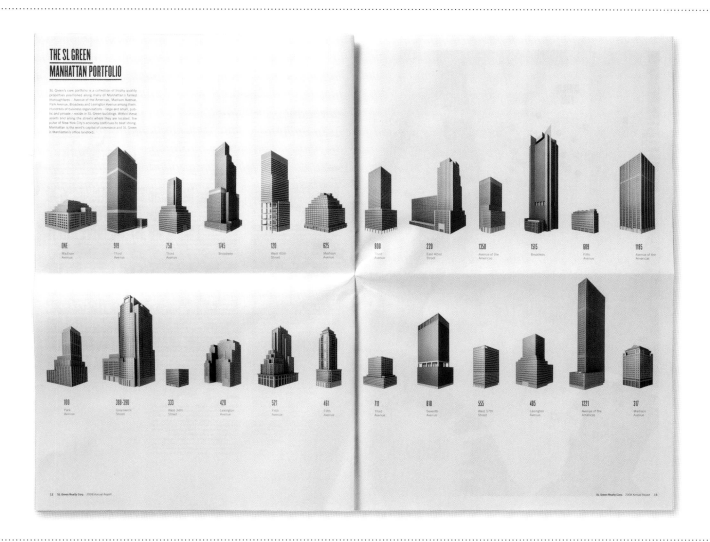

Q&A with Addison

What was the client's directive?
SL Green is a commercial real estate investment trust that is primarily focused on the Manhattan market. To invest in SL Green is to own "a piece of New York City." Our charge this year was to communicate the company's focus on fundamental real estate strategy.

How did you define the problem?
We needed to create a piece that is bold and confident, without being at all flashy or pretentious, which also expresses the scale and drama of real estate in Manhattan.

What was the approach?
We designed an unbound, tabloid-sized piece, and printed it on lightweight paper that very much evoked the spirit of a newspaper—a document at once both grand and humble. We developed a strong yet straightforward typographic voice that punctuates and drives the book, and then integrated property, contextual and executive photography into one grand image that ran very large.

What disciplines or people helped you with the project?
Jason Schmidt photographed the large format executive photo and Bryan Chrisite worked with us on the property illustrations.

Do you and the client both view the Annual Report as part of the company's communications strategy? And how important is it within the overall strategy?
Yes, the annual report is this client's primary marketing vehicle, and is used throughout the year for multiple uses.

How do you define success in Annual Report design?
If it communicates a big idea in an interesting (or even surprising) fashion, and if it's a book that someone would actually want to keep (or steal), then it's probably a success.

In which direction do you see Annual Reports moving?
Companies that value high quality communication will continue to produce Annual Reports in some form.
Companies that don't will continue to not.

2005
2006
2007
iStar Financial Annual Report > 2008
2009

To our valued Investors,

The Panic of 2008. The year the financial system imploded, the pillars of our economic system were shaken and years of prosperity were destroyed. Now, tectonic changes in our country are taking place and a new foundation must be built.

So, our message this year is simple:

Don't Give Up.
Don't give up on the United States.
Don't give up on Real Estate.
Don't give up on iStar.

Don't give up on the United States
All Men and Women are Created Equal. Freedom of Speech. Freedom of Religion. Rule of Law. Belief in the Individual. These are the hallmarks of our great nation and as long as we stand by them, the nation will once again prosper. Sacrifices will need to be made, but none of the above can be sacrificed in the name of expediency.

Don't give up on Real Estate
Values overshot. Leverage got ridiculous. Values will decline. But commercial real estate is not going away and as values reset, real estate will once again be a desirable asset class, representing tangible, "hard" assets that are often difficult to replace, cash-flowing and inflation-protected. Good commercial real estate will be a solid long-term investment and should, from reset levels, generate strong risk-adjusted returns.

Don't give up on iStar
We have been hit hard. Our strengths have been tested. But we have held together as a team and we continue to work to protect value wherever we can. We have honest and hard-working people working diligently every day to preserve value. I have always believed that honesty and hard work lead to the right outcomes and still believe that today.

Recovering won't be easy, but we have made progress. Our unfunded commitments are down materially year-over-year and should be substantially reduced by the beginning of 2010. Our loan portfolio continues to steadily pay off, though many borrowers have been unable to pay us as planned and we have had to negotiate, extend or foreclose on many more loans than we had expected. Our reserves against future losses have been bulked up materially without hurting our book value per share, primarily through offsetting gains realized from sales in our timber, triple net lease and loan portfolios, and through judicious retirement of debt and equity at discounted prices.

2009 will continue to challenge us. We will continue to pare down the portfolio, taking losses where necessary and working to offset their impact with value creation strategies as we restructure our balance sheet and look to utilize our large, intact investment platform whenever and wherever possible. None of this will be easy, but we have the ability, the ambition and the conviction to recover. We're not giving up.

Jay Sugarman
Chairman and Chief Executive Officer

Note: We decided to make our annual report short and sweet this year and focus on delivering results first and talking about them later. No amount of words, explanations or pretty pictures can change the disappointment of 2008's results. Now is the time for actions, not words.

Words can not undo the reality of 2008...

Category: Real Estate | **Location:** New York, United States | **Creative Director:** Richard Colbourne | **Paper Type:** Uncoated - Mohawk Via Pure White Vellum | **Print Producer:** Nicole Anello, Georgiann Baran | **Print Run:** 65,000 copies | **Printer:** Innovation Printing | **Project Manager:** Renee Marmer | **Senior Designer:** Darien Birks

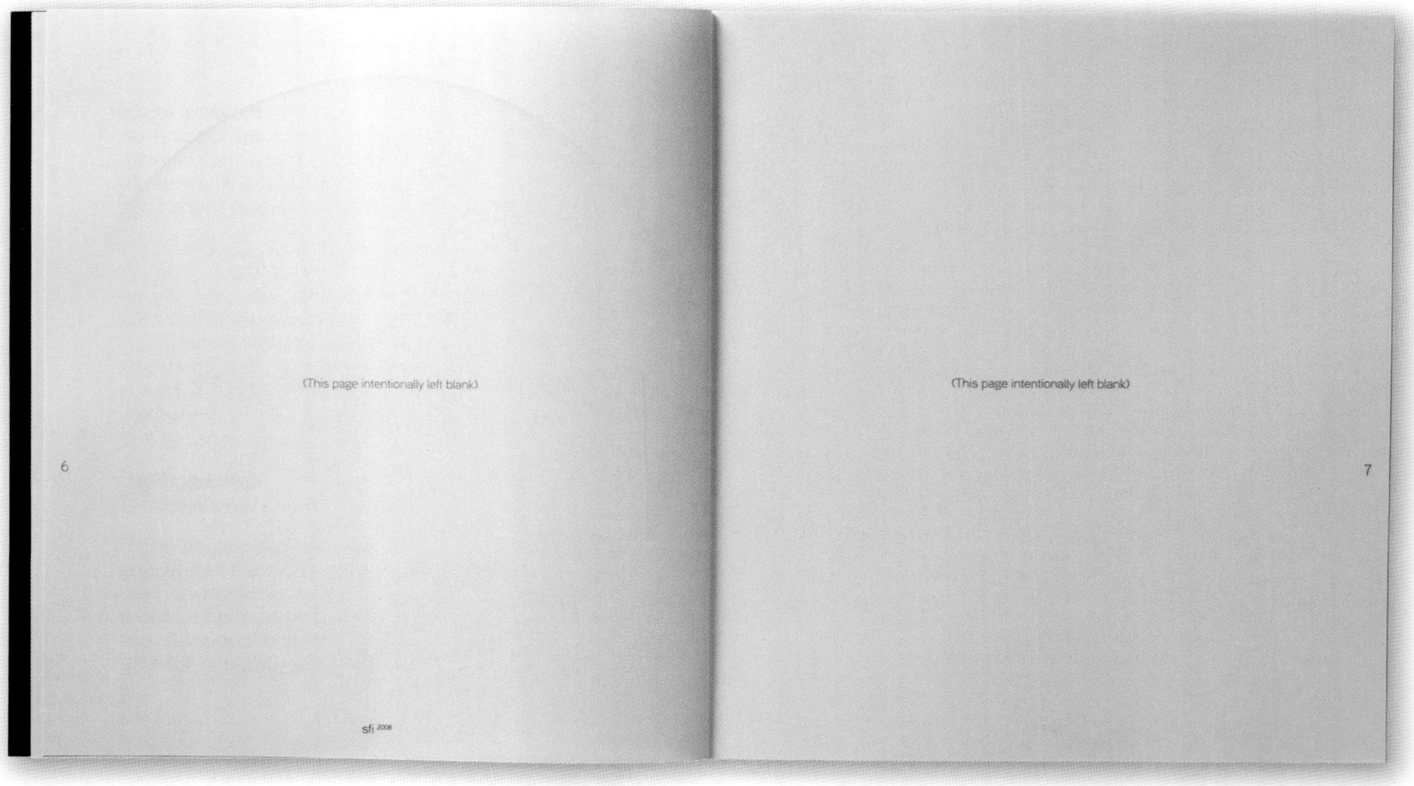
(This page intentionally left blank)
6
sfi 2008
(This page intentionally left blank)
7

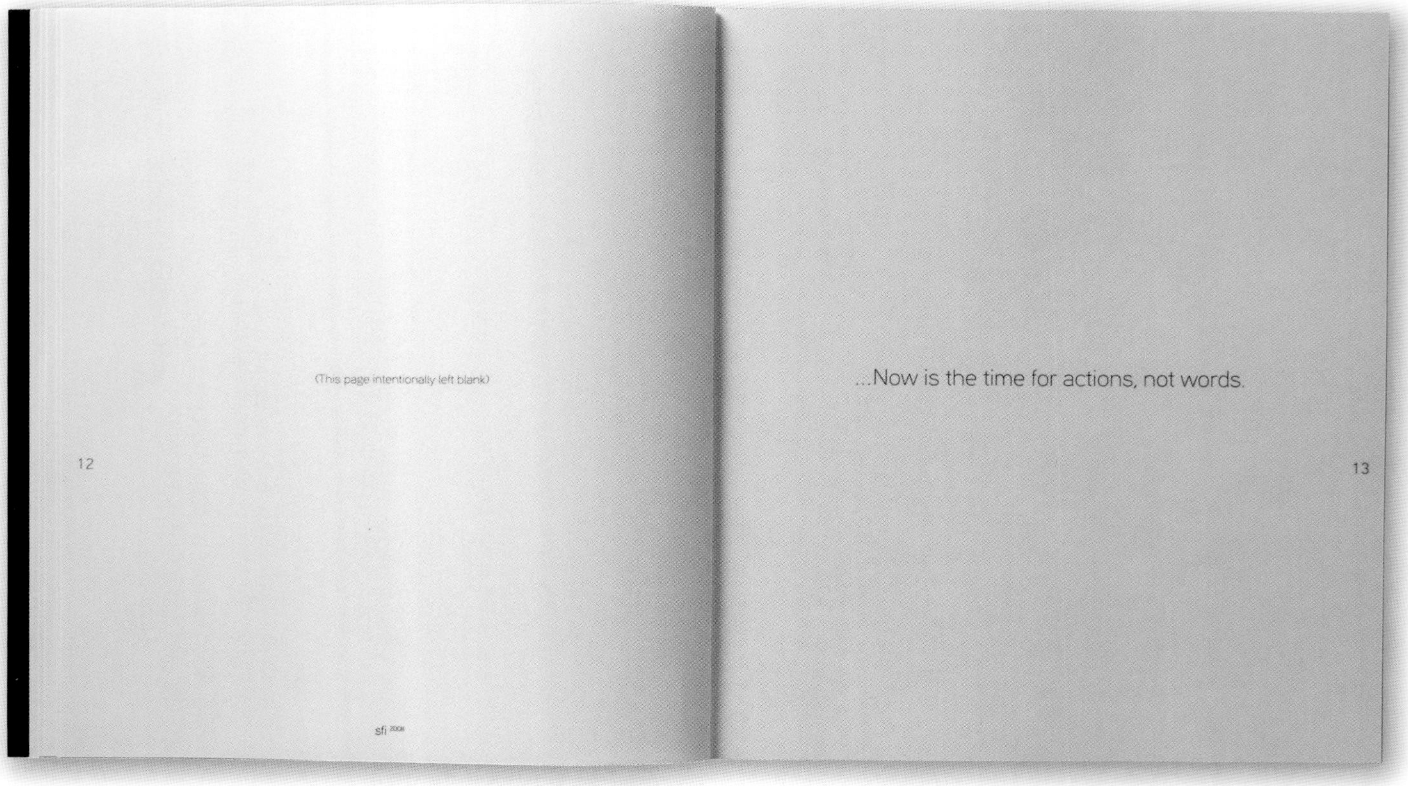
(This page intentionally left blank)
12
sfi 2008
...Now is the time for actions, not words.
13

What was the client's directive?

iStar Financial is a finance company that is focused on the commercial real estate industry. The problem: In a time of great turbulence and a share price that has dropped by 80% what do you say to shareholders? Our challenge was to create an effective and relevant articulation of a very challenging year.

How did you define the problem?

Be honest. Admit your shortfalls and do not try and cover it over with business platitudes. Any other approach would be insulting to the shareholder. The report needed to feel austere and serious, yet also preserve the high level of sophistication for the brand.

What was the approach?

Less is more than more.... Historically, the report has had a colorful, highly impactful section. This year, we replaced that with a simple powerful statement: eight pages of silence. No sales pitch. No bullshit. Just the statement "Words cannot undo the realities of 2008" followed by eight pages of "This page intentionally left blank." We communicated the unique financial situation facing iStar with an immediate and unquestionable acknowledgement of the challenging times, signifying that this is a time of action, not empty words.

How involved was the CEO in your meetings, presentations, etc.?

We benefited greatly by having access to and input from the CEO. He was involved in all critical presentations and decisions.

Were you happy with the result?

Never before, in an annual report, has white space made such a powerful and frank statement. Addison managed to turn a lack of appetite for spending money on the annual report into an opportunity for creativity and strong messaging.

What was the client's response?

Very positive.

What are clients looking for when it comes to designing an Annual Report?

Smart ideas and creative execution.

Do you and the client both view the Annual Report as part of the company's communications strategy? And how important is it within the overall strategy?

The annual report is iStar's flagship document and primary ambassador of their brand. This annual report is in fact part of a multi-year communications effort: it's fourth in a series of five, designed as a continuum for the others: all use the same typeface, and the final illustration in each report serves as the cover of the next.

Never before, in an annual report, has white space made such a powerful and frank statement.

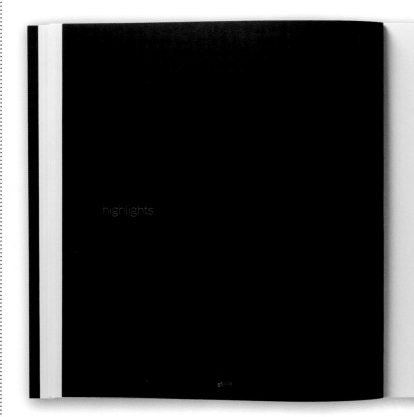

highlights

sfi

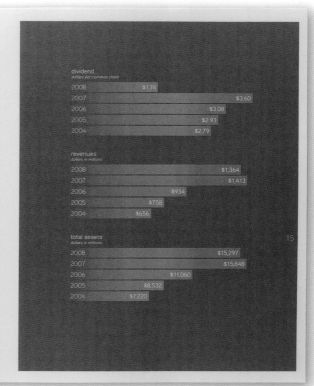

dividend
dollars per common share

2008	$1.74
2007	$3.60
2006	$3.08
2005	$2.93
2004	$2.79

revenues
dollars in millions

2008	$1,364
2007	$1,413
2006	$934
2005	$758
2004	$656

total assets
dollars in millions

2008	$15,297
2007	$15,848
2006	$11,060
2005	$8,532
2004	$7,220

15

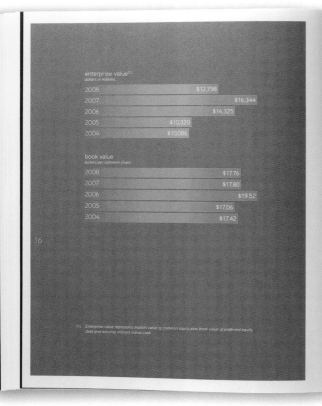

enterprise value[1]
dollars in millions

2008	$12,798
2007	$16,344
2006	$14,325
2005	$10,320
2004	$10,086

book value
dollars per common share

2008	$17.76
2007	$17.80
2006	$19.52
2005	$17.06
2004	$17.42

16

(1) Enterprise value represents market value of common equity plus book value of preferred equity, debt and minority interest minus cash.

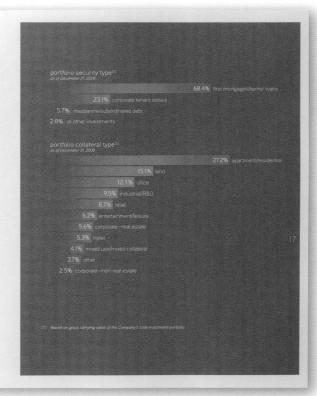

portfolio security type[1]
as of December 31, 2008

68.4% first mortgages/senior loans
23.1% corporate tenant leases
5.7% mezzanine/subordinated debt
2.8% all other investments

portfolio collateral type[1]
as of December 31, 2008

27.2% apartment/residential
15.1% land
12.1% office
9.5% industrial/R&D
8.7% retail
6.2% entertainment/leisure
5.6% corporate—real estate
5.3% hotel
4.1% mixed use/mixed collateral
3.7% other
2.5% corporate—non-real estate

17

(1) Based on gross carrying value of the Company's total investment portfolio.

results

SELECTED FINANCIAL DATA

The following table sets forth selected financial data on a consolidated historical basis for the Company. This information should be read in conjunction with the discussions set forth in "Management's Discussion and Analysis of Financial Condition and Results of Operations." Certain prior year amounts have been reclassified to conform to the 2008 presentation.

For the Years Ended December 31,		2008	2007	2006	2005	2004
(In thousands, except per share data and ratios)						
Operating Data:						
Interest income		$ 947,661	$ 998,008	$ 575,598	$ 406,668	$ 353,799
Operating lease income		318,600	314,740	293,934	270,948	248,091
Other income		97,851	99,938	64,220	80,370	53,886
Total revenue		1,364,112	1,412,686	933,752	757,986	655,776
Interest expense		660,284	627,720	429,609	312,806	231,585
Operating costs – corporate tenant lease assets		23,575	28,926	23,125	21,675	20,780
Depreciation and amortization		97,368	86,223	68,691	63,928	56,524
General and administrative		159,096	165,128	96,332	63,751	157,588
Provision for loan losses		1,029,322	185,000	14,000	2,250	9,000
Impairment of goodwill		39,092				
Impairment of other assets		295,738	144,184	5,683	–	–
Other expense		22,040	333	–	–	–
Total costs and expenses		2,326,515	1,237,514	637,440	464,410	475,477
Income (loss) before earnings from equity method investments, minority interest and other items		(962,403)	175,172	296,312	293,576	180,299
Gain (loss) on early extinguishment of debt		392,943	225	–	(46,004)	(13,091)
Gain on sale of joint venture interest, net of minority interest		261,659	–	–	–	–
Earnings from equity method investments		6,535	29,626	12,391	3,016	2,909
Minority interest in consolidated entities		991	816	(1,207)	(980)	(716)
Income (loss) from continuing operations		(300,275)	205,839	307,496	249,608	169,401
Income from discontinued operations		15,715	25,287	43,104	31,951	47,671
Gain from discontinued operations, net of minority interest		87,769	7,832	24,227	6,354	43,375
Net income (loss)		(196,791)	238,958	374,827	287,913	260,447
Preferred dividend requirements		(42,320)	(42,320)	(42,320)	(42,320)	(51,340)
Net income (loss) allocable to common shareholders and HPU holders[1]		$ (239,111)	$ 196,638	$ 332,507	$ 245,593	$ 209,107
Per common share data [2]						
Income (loss) from continuing operations per common share:	Basic	$ (2.56)	$ 1.26	$ 2.24	$ 1.79	$ 1.05
	Diluted[3]	$ (2.56)	$ 1.26	$ 2.23	$ 1.79	$ 1.03
Net income (loss) per common share:	Basic	$ (1.78)	$ 1.52	$ 2.82	$ 2.13	$ 1.87
	Diluted[3]	$ (1.78)	$ 1.51	$ 2.79	$ 2.11	$ 1.83
Per HPU share data [2]						
Income (loss) from continuing operations per HPU share:	Basic	$ (482.46)	$ 239.60	$ 425.73	$ 340.07	$ 184.50
	Diluted[3]	$ (482.46)	$ 237.07	$ 421.61	$ 336.67	$ 186.60
Net income (loss) per HPU share:	Basic	$ (336.33)	$ 287.93	$ 533.80	$ 402.87	$ 337.30
	Diluted[3]	$ (336.33)	$ 285.00	$ 528.67	$ 398.87	$ 330.60
Dividends declared per common share[4]		$ 1.74	$ 3.60	$ 3.08	$ 2.93	$ 2.79
Supplemental Data:						
Adjusted earnings (loss) allocable to common shareholders and HPU holders[5][6]		$ (359,483)	$ 355,707	$ 429,922	$ 391,884	$ 270,946
EBITDA[6][7]		$ 580,704	$ 1,006,943	$ 902,633	$ 684,824	$ 564,762
Ratio of earnings to fixed charges[8]		0.6x	1.4x	1.7x	1.9x	1.8x
Ratio of earnings to fixed charges and preferred stock dividends		0.6x	1.3x	1.6x	1.6x	1.5x
Weighted average common shares outstanding – basic		131,153	126,801	115,023	112,513	110,205
Weighted average common shares outstanding – diluted		131,153	127,792	116,219	113,703	112,464
Weighted average HPU shares outstanding – basic and diluted		15	15	15	15	10
Cash flows from:						
Operating activities		$ 418,529	$ 561,337	$ 431,224	$ 515,919	$ 353,566
Investing activities		(27,943)	(4,745,080)	(2,529,260)	(1,406,121)	(465,636)
Financing activities		1,444	4,182,299	2,088,617	917,150	120,402

For the Years Ended December 31,	2008	2007	2006	2005	2004
(In thousands, except per share data and ratios)					
Balance Sheet Data:					
Loans and other lending investments, net	$10,586,644	$10,949,354	$ 6,799,850	$4,661,915	$3,938,427
Corporate tenant lease assets, net	3,044,811	3,309,866	3,084,794	3,115,361	2,877,042
Total assets	15,296,748	15,848,298	11,059,995	8,532,296	7,220,237
Debt obligations	12,516,023	12,399,558	7,833,437	5,859,592	4,605,674
Minority interest in consolidated entities	36,853	53,948	38,738	33,511	19,246
Total shareholders' equity	2,389,380	2,899,481	2,986,863	2,446,671	2,455,242

Explanatory Notes:

(1) HPU holders are Company employees who purchased high performance common stock units under the Company's High Performance Unit Program.

(2) See Note 13 of the Company's Notes to Consolidated Financial Statements.

(3) For the years ended December 31, 2007, 2006, 2005 and 2004, net income used to calculate earnings per diluted common share and HPU share includes joint venture income of $85, $115, $28 and $3, respectively.

(4) The Company generally declares common and preferred dividends in the month subsequent to the end of the quarter. In December of 2007, the Company declared a special $0.25 dividend due to higher taxable income generated as a result of the Company's acquisition of Fremont CRE. No dividends were declared for the three months ended September 30, 2008 and December 31, 2008.

(5) Adjusted earnings represents net income allocable to common shareholders and HPU holders computed in accordance with GAAP, before depreciation, depletion, amortization, gain from discontinued operations, ineffectiveness on interest rate hedges, impairment of goodwill and intangible assets, extraordinary items and cumulative effect of change in accounting principle. (See "Management's Discussion and Analysis of Financial Condition and Results of Operations," for a reconciliation of adjusted earnings to net income).

(6) Both adjusted earnings and EBITDA should be examined in conjunction with net income as shown in the Company's Consolidated Statements of Operations. Neither adjusted earnings nor EBITDA should be considered as an alternative to net income (determined in accordance with GAAP) as an indicator of the Company's performance, or to cash flows from operating activities (determined in accordance with GAAP) as a measure of the Company's liquidity, nor is either measure indicative of funds available to fund the Company's cash needs or available for distribution to shareholders. Rather, adjusted earnings and EBITDA are additional measures the Company uses to analyze how its business is performing. As a commercial finance company that focuses on real estate lending and corporate tenant leasing, the Company records significant depreciation on its real estate assets and amortization of deferred financing costs associated with its borrowings. It should be noted that the Company's manner of calculating adjusted earnings and EBITDA may differ from the calculations of similarly-titled measures by other companies.

(7) EBITDA is calculated as net income (loss) plus the sum of interest expense, depreciation, depletion and amortization.

For the Years Ended December 31,	2008	2007	2006	2005	2004
Net income (loss)	$(196,791)	$ 238,958	$374,827	$287,913	$260,447
Add: Interest expense[1]	660,284	627,732	429,807	313,053	232,918
Add: Depreciation, depletion and amortization[2]	102,745	99,427	83,058	75,574	67,853
Add: Joint venture depreciation, depletion and amortization	14,466	40,826	14,941	8,284	3,544
EBITDA	$ 580,704	$1,006,943	$902,633	$684,824	$564,762

Explanatory Notes:

(1) For the years ended December 31, 2007, 2006, 2005, and 2004, interest expense includes $12, $198, $247 and $1,333, respectively, of interest expense reclassified to discontinued operations.

(2) For the years ended December 31, 2008, 2007, 2006, 2005, and 2004, depreciation, depletion and amortization includes $4,075, $8,144, $10,134, $9,142 and $8,556, respectively, of depreciation and amortization reclassified to discontinued operations.

(8) This ratio of earnings to fixed charges is calculated in accordance with GAAP. The Company's unsecured revolving credit facilities and unsecured senior notes both have fixed charge coverage covenants; however, each is calculated differently with the terms of the respective agreements. The fixed charge coverage ratios for the unsecured revolving credit facilities and unsecured senior notes were 2.7x and 2.2x, respectively as of December 31, 2008.

Greetings from
LINCOLN
Nebraska

POWER MAGAZINE NAMED THE WALTER SCOTT, JR. ENERGY CENTER UNIT 4 ITS 2007 "PLANT OF THE YEAR." EDITORS CITED THE FACILITY'S FUEL EFFICIENCY AND ADVANCED AIR QUALITY CONTROL SYSTEM.

EACH YEAR, LES EMPLOYEES DONATE THOUSANDS OF HOURS TO WORTHY CAUSES IN OUR COMMUNITY. HERE, JASON SMITH, OPERATIONS DIVISION ENGINEER, IS HELPING JUDGE A LOCAL SCIENCE FAIR. IN 2007, EMPLOYEES ALSO DONATED MORE THAN $78,000 TO LOCAL CHARITABLE CAUSES.

2007 Year in Review

January A December 2006 ice storm that downed transmission lines across Nebraska severely limits energy deliveries to LES from two key, low-cost power plants—the Laramie River Station in Wyoming and the Gerald Gentleman Station in central Nebraska. LES begins to purchase higher-priced replacement power to meet customer needs while the transmission system is repaired, an endeavor that is expected to take five months.

LES crews work 5,637 hours and amass labor costs of more than $300,000 while helping other utilities restore power lost during the December storm. The utilities requesting this assistance reimburse LES for the costs.

Between February and December 2006, LES customers donated $69,298 to Lincoln Cares, a program that enables them to voluntarily contribute one dollar through their monthly LES bill payment for special projects and programs of the City Parks and Recreation department.

February LES holds a public hearing February 20 on staff recommendations regarding the adoption of Amendments to the 1978 Public Utilities Regulatory Policies Act (PURPA). The Act's purpose is to encourage energy conservation by electric utilities, optimal efficiency of electric utility facilities and resources, and equitable rates for consumers. An analysis shows the number of power outages in 2006 was the second lowest in LES' history.

March Faced with more than $7 million in replacement power costs since storm

Sunken Gardens
LINCOLN, NEBRASKA

damage impacted LES' ability to receive electricity from two low-cost power plants, the LES Board on February 16 asks and the Lincoln City Council on February 26 agrees to declare an emergency and approve a 5.5 percent surcharge on electric bills

effective in March. It is expected to generate about $9.4 million—the estimated cost for LES to buy and generate higher-priced electricity while the state's transmission system is repaired. The surcharge is to remain in effect until December 31, 2007.

A $291 million Six-Year Capital Improvement Program is approved by the LES Board and submitted to the City of Lincoln as part of its budget. The Program calls for investment in a regional coal-fired power plant by 2012.

Three percent of the energy LES receives in March comes from its newest resource—Walter Scott, Jr. Energy Center Unit 4. The unit was first fired-up the last week of February and has been undergoing operational tests.

April LES launches a new quarterly television program, *LES Energy Ideas.*

LES pays about $9.8 million to governmental subdivisions as an annual revenue tax payment. The tax is distributed as follows: Lincoln School District, $6,593,000; City of Lincoln, $1,492,000; Lancaster County, $1,428,000; and Waverly, $252,000.

The Nebraska Forest Service presents the Tree Line USA award to LES at its April 3 Community Forestry recognition program. It honors LES' commitment to the management and enhancement of trees.

The City of Lincoln and LES implement the National Arbor Day Foundation's "The Right Tree in the Right Place" program for trees located on City rights-of-way that conflict with overhead power lines.

6

7

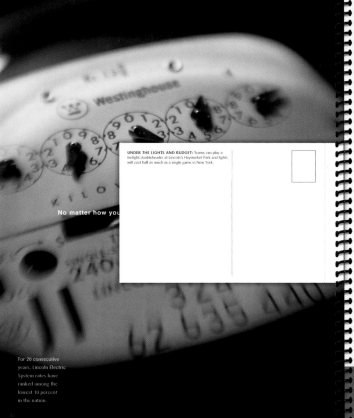

Lower rates. Added value.

UNDER THE LIGHTS AND BUDGET: Teams can play a twilight doubleheader at Lincoln's Haymarket Park and lights will cost half as much as a single game in New York.

No matter how you

For 20 consecutive years, Lincoln Electric System rates have ranked among the lowest 10 percent in the nation.

National surveys and publications have confirmed what our customers already know: there's great value in owning a home or business in the fair City of Lincoln.

We're proud of the fact LES' low rates play a major role in these findings. An article in the August 10, 2007, *USA Today* shows that our customers pay rates that are among the lowest in the country. The article states that the highest rates are found in Hawaii, at 23.36 cents per kilowatt-hour (kWh). And the lowest are in Idaho, at 6.12 cents per kWh—the same average price found here in Lincoln. The article goes on to say that the national average cost of electricity is 10.4 cents per kWh. That's a full 70 percent higher than the average price in Lincoln.

In addition to staying abreast of national surveys, we also like to conduct our own studies to help keep us on track in reaching our management goals. A 2007 study of electric bills paid in 106 U.S. cities revealed LES' bills as the 9th lowest overall. Lincoln residential bills ranked 7th lowest in the nation, while commercial and industrial bills ranked 11th. We're pleased to report that for the past 20 years, our electric rates have been among the lowest 10 percent in the nation.

So how does LES manage to keep rates so affordable? We have our proven business practices to thank. For starters, low operating costs at the plants that provide our electricity account for about 70 percent of the cost of providing service to our customers. By employing a diverse mix of coal, water, oil, gas and renewable resources, we're able to keep costs down and pass the savings on to customers. And since our bonds and commercial notes have received high AA ratings, we're also able to borrow money at lower interest costs.

Better rates and a better quality of life—that's what we provide our current customers. And what we can offer those who may be planning to make Lincoln their new home—or place of business.

OVER THE YEARS, LES HAS FOUND ONE OF THE BEST WAYS TO KEEP RATES DOWN IS TO KEEP OPERATING COSTS DOWN. AND ONE OF THE MOST EFFICIENT WAYS TO ACCOMPLISH THAT IS TO STAY ON TOP OF MAINTENANCE. HERE, LES EMPLOYEES ARE SEEN REPAIRING AN ELECTRICAL OUTLET ON THE EXHAUST STACK OF ROKEBY UNIT #2.

Category: Utilities | **Location:** Nebraska, United States | **Account Director:** Rich Claussen | **Art Director:** Ron Sack | **Creative Director:** Sean Faden | **Designer:** Brandon Oltman | **Photographer:** Scott Dobry | **Printer:** Lincolnland Printing & Specialties Inc | **Writer:** Jim Watson

No matter how you add it up, it doesn't add up as quickly here.

For 20 consecutive years, Lincoln Electric System rates have ranked among the lowest 10 percent in the nation.

Lower rates. Added value.

National surveys and publications have confirmed what our customers already know: there's great value in owning a home or business in the fair City of Lincoln.

We're proud of the fact LES' low rates play a major role in these findings. An article in the August 10, 2007, *USA Today* shows that our customers pay rates that are among the lowest in the country. The article states that the highest rates are found in Hawaii, at 23.36 cents per kilowatt-hour (kWh). And the lowest are in Idaho, at 6.12 cents per kWh—the same average price found here in Lincoln. The article goes on to say that the national average cost of electricity is 10.4 cents per kWh. That's a full 70 percent higher than the average price in Lincoln.

In addition to staying abreast of national surveys, we also like to conduct our own studies to help keep us on track in reaching our management goals. A 2007 study of electric bills paid in 106 U.S. cities revealed LES' bills are the 9th lowest overall. Lincoln residential bills ranked 7th lowest in the nation, while commercial and industrial bills ranked 11th. We're pleased to report that for the past 20 years, our electric rates have been among the lowest 10 percent in the nation.

So how does LES manage to keep rates so affordable? We have our proven business practices to thank. For starters, low operating costs at the plants that provide our electricity account for about 70 percent of the cost of providing service to our customers. By employing a diverse mix of coal, water, oil, gas and renewable resources, we're able to keep costs down and pass the savings on to customers. And since our bonds and commercial notes have received high AA ratings, we're also able to borrow money at lower interest costs.

Better rates and a better quality of life—that's what we provide our current customers. And what we can offer those who may be planning to make Lincoln their new home—or place of business.

Haymarket Park
LINCOLN, NEBRASKA

OVER THE YEARS, LES HAS FOUND ONE OF THE BEST WAYS TO KEEP RATES DOWN IS TO KEEP OPERATING COSTS DOWN. AND ONE OF THE MOST EFFICIENT WAYS TO ACCOMPLISH THAT IS TO STAY ON TOP OF MAINTENANCE. HERE, LES EMPLOYEES ARE SEEN REPAIRING AN ELECTRICAL OUTLET ON THE EXHAUST STACK OF ROKEBY UNIT #2.

If you can make it here, you can make it for a lot less.

"Low power costs, efficient operations and reliable service position LES as one of the best-managed power companies in the nation—of any size."

Terry L. Bundy
Administrator and CEO

Best practices reap rewards.

What can Lincoln, Nebraska, population 235,594, teach the Big Apple about supplying electricity to its residents? Apparently, plenty.

The publicly owned LES has been providing a reliable source of electricity to customers for more than 40 years. New York Con Edison customers felt they had been left in the dark one too many times, after a flurry of mishaps—from numerous blackouts to a steam explosion—left them without power.

So, when a NYC councilman suggested the City take over the troubled company, he got an enthusiastic thumbs-up from Lincoln residents. In an editorial, the *Lincoln Journal Star* praised the councilman and offered LES as an example of public power done right. Not only can residents count on the lights coming on, they also know they'll be charged significantly less than if they were living in New York. In fact, LES' rates are among the lowest in the nation.

But NYC doesn't have to take Lincoln's word for it. A report by the American Public Power Association on utility performance found LES has an extremely effective operation. The study provides ratios based on such indicators as revenue, debt, system costs and system operation.

In it, you'll see that LES' power cost is 33 percent below the national average, proving its long-term decisions have provided resources that are both efficient and economical. LES' non-power production costs for items such as transmission, distribution, accounting, customer service and general expenses are 26 percent below the survey average. The cost to operate the electrical distribution system is 38 percent below average.

The survey also showed LES has one of the best reliability records in the country, with an outage time per customer 67 percent below the national average. With these kinds of statics, it's no wonder New York representatives are being urged to look at the way LES conducts both business and electricity. To that we say, stop by. The lights will be on for you.

International Quilt Study Center
LINCOLN, NEBRASKA

IN ANY WELL-MANAGED OPERATION, IT'S IMPORTANT THAT THE LEFT HAND KNOW WHAT THE RIGHT HAND IS DOING. AND IT BECOMES CRITICAL WHEN OPERATING POTENTIALLY DANGEROUS EQUIPMENT. THAT'S WHY RON PAYTON, CONTROL ROOM OPERATOR AT LES' SALT VALLEY GENERATING STATION, STAYS IN RADIO CONTACT WITH HIS AUXILIARY OPERATOR WHEN FIRING GAS TURBINES.

What was the client's directive?
The client's directive was to tout the fact that Lincoln Electric System (LES) has some of the lowest rates in the nation...thus the line "Wish You Were Here" was used to communicate this message.

How did you define the problem?
We needed to let the consumer know that LES is very responsible to their customers by delivering some of the lowest electric rates in the nation...in a strong, conceptual, memorable way.

What was the approach?
Through the theme line "Wish You Were Here" and a series of post-cards touting low rates, energy savings, and low cost of living, we set up the benefits of living in Lincoln, Nebraska and using LES as your electric provider.

What disciplines or people helped you with the project?
From a client standpoint, their PR, advertising and marketing team. Every discipline from our advertising firm was included: art director, designer, writer, account planner, public relations, and photographer.

How involved was the CEO in your meetings, presentations, etc.?
The CEO led the charge in terms of the tone and messaging. He was involved from the beginning to the very end.

Were you happy with the result? What could have been better?
We're pleased with how the design communicates the message for their 2007 fiscal year. Our budget was very limited from a production stand-point, so certain things had to be cut out of the process (photography, paper stock, etc.).

What was the client's response?
They were very pleased with how well recipients responded to the annual. Everyone loved (and used) the attached postcards.

What are clients looking for when it comes to designing an Annual Report?
Strong conceptual design and relevant messaging.

Do you and the client both view the Annual Report as part of the company's communications strategy? And how important is it within the overall strategy?
It absolutely needs to fit within their brand messaging. Their tag line is "Use LES to save more." That line feels as though it's part of this report from start to finish.

How large a role does environmental policy play in the design and pro-duction of your Annual Reports?
Green is a big thing with them. We used recycled stock. They are very sensitive to making sure they are one with the environment.

They were very pleased with how well recipients responded to the annual. Everyone loved (and used) the attached postcards.

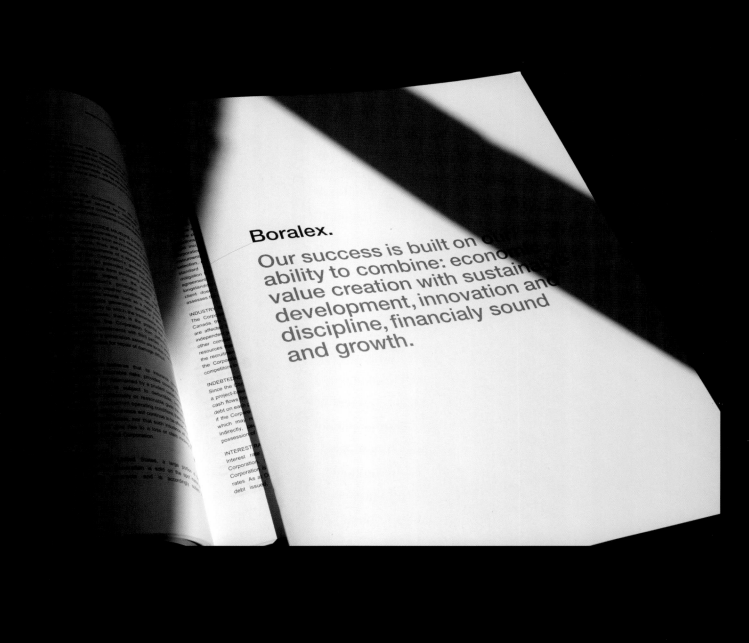

Boralex.

Our success is built on our ability to combine: economic value creation with sustainable development, innovation and discipline, financialy sound and growth.

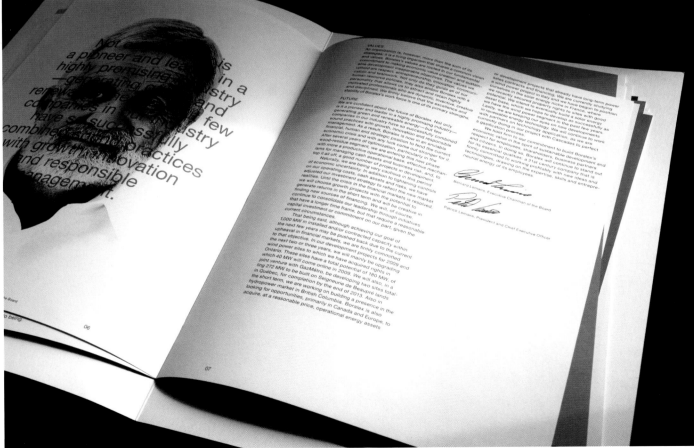

Category: Utilities | **Location:** Quebec, Canada | **Account Director:** Jean Doyon | **Creative Director:** Louis Gagnon | **Design Director:** René Clément | **Paper Type:** Rolland Enviro 100 (Cover 200M and Text 160M) | **Print Producer:** Transcontinental Litho Acme | **Printer:** Transcontinental Litho Acme

The Annual Report is one of the most important vehicles for delivering the client's public relations.

Q&A with Paprika

What was the client's directive?
Boralex is a private electricity producer. The company awarded Paprika the mandate of creating an annual report reflecting their dynamism, expertise in renewable energy (wind, hydroelectric and thermal powers) and potential for development.

How did you define the problem?
With the economic conjuncture, we had to show some sobriety while putting forward their dynamism and their innovative spirit.

What was the approach?
We created a simple black and white grid with a twist : colored pages that are binded in different angles, creating movement and energy.

What disciplines or people helped you with the project?
Monic Richard, a renowned photographer, has been involved in the project. We also work with Transcontinental Litho Acme for the printing and binding.

Were you happy with the result? What could have been better?
Yes, we were happy with it. As the financial statement was a separate document, we would have liked to be more involved in the design process of it. We have created the covers only.

What are clients looking for when it comes to designing an Annual Report?
That we create the graphic equivalent of their ecological and social commitment. That we reflect their dynamism, their position in their branch of industry.

Do you and the client both view the Annual Report as part of the company's communications strategy? And how important is it within the overall strategy?
Yes, we are. It's one of their most important pieces for their public relations. It gives them the opportunity to expose their management philosophy. It materializes their values.

How do you define success in Annual Report design?
When we put in concrete form the values that guides them. When the information is clear and the design is appealing. When the design is renewed year after year.

How large a role does environmental policy play in the design and production of your Annual Reports?
The impact goes beyond the reduced number of copies. We used paper that was manufactured by Cascades, their parent company. Vegetable-based inks were used in printing the project.

A BETTER
TOMORROW

OUR JOURNEY TO BECOME THE LEADING UTILITY STARTS
ANEW EVERY DAY WITH THE QUESTION: WHAT MUST WE
DO TODAY TO BE BETTER THAN WE WERE YESTERDAY?
THIS SIMPLE IDEA IS GUIDING OUR PROGRESS FROM DAY
TO DAY, YEAR TO YEAR, AND GENERATION TO GENERATION.

EASY

Is it possible to love your gas and electric company? Most utilities would think this is a crazy question. We embraced it as a challenge and set a goal to delight our customers. Customers today are busier and more stretched than ever. We know that a smooth and satisfying customer experience is one of the best ways for us to provide them with real value. One of the places we are starting is finding ways to make it easier to do business with PG&E. Accordingly, at virtually every major touch point with customers, we are asking how service can be quicker, clearer, cheaper, cleaner, more convenient, or—ideally—all of the above.

8

SMART

Helping consumers use less energy sounds like a losing business proposition for a utility. We see it differently. Empowering customers with the know-how and technologies to become smarter energy users is an increasingly important source of value. PG&E has the potential to earn $100 million to $200 million in incentives in the next four years if it helps customers successfully achieve aggressive energy-savings targets. This not only saves money, it is also one of the most effective and economic ways to cut greenhouse gases. PG&E's energy efficiency programs over the past 30 years have saved customers $22 billion and kept over 135 million tons of carbon out of the skies, while our company and California's economy have flourished.

16

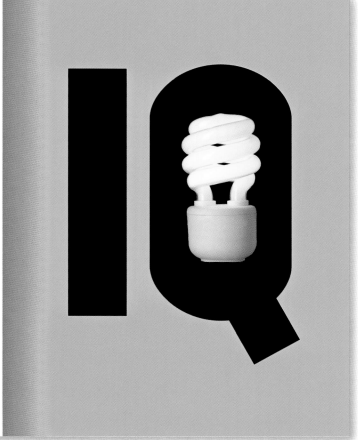

Category: Utilities | **Location:** California, United States | **Creative Director:** Kit Hinrichs | **Photographer:** John Blaustein | **Printer:** Blanchette Press | **Senior Designer:** Belle How

SUSTAINABLE

Finding ways to produce and use energy sustainably may be the single most important global challenge of the next 50 to 100 years. If the best thinking of our leading scientists today is correct, the future of the planet is at stake. Becoming smarter energy users is one essential piece of the solution. But producing clean, cost-effective energy from new sources is undoubtedly another. On average, more than half of the electricity PG&E delivers already comes from carbon-free sources, including our own hydroelectric and nuclear facilities. We are also one of the nation's largest buyers of renewable energy. And we have helped customers connect more solar installations to the grid than any other utility. But even this is only a beginning.

20

CONNECTED

Serving 15 million Californians, PG&E is plugged into hundreds of economically and culturally vibrant communities throughout the state. We are intertwined with life there in a multitude of ways. As the provider of a service that is absolutely essential to everyday living and economic vitality. As a provider of quality jobs. As a solid partner for diverse small and mid-sized businesses that are the lifeblood of local economies. As a giver of volunteer time and charitable dollars to support causes that reflect the values we share as neighbors and fellow Californians. In return, our communities give back to us—by giving us the great privilege to serve them and by being great places for our employees to live and work.

24

What was the client's directive?
To take a forward-looking position on the environment and the role of utilities in the future.

How did you define the problem?
By taking five specific positions about the role utilities will need to play in the future: easy to use, dependable, smart, sustainable, and connected to the world.

What was the approach?
We illustrated each position with an emblematic photograph to provoke the reader into finding out more about those editorial themes.

What disciplines or people helped you with the project?
Design by an associate partner, Belle How; photography by John Blaustein; retouching by David Faulk. In addition, we had an outside typographer set all the financials, and all editorial copy was provided by the client.

How involved was the CEO in your meetings, presentations, etc.?
He was very involved at the beginning, in directing the point of view of the utility, and he gave it a final sign-off at the end.

Were you happy with the result? What could have been better?
I was very happy with the result. The only aspect I question is the length of the financial section, which seems inconsistent with the theme of sustainability. I suspect it will be shorter in future years.

What was the client's response?
It was well received, and they hired us again for the following year.

What are clients looking for when it comes to designing an Annual Report?
As annual reports become less and less relevant within the corporate communications scheme, we find the clients want effective positioning statements on where they're going, not just on where they have been. So in many ways, those that still produce more than 10K wraps are seeking more adventurous, effective annual reports that make a forward-looking statement.

Do you and the client both view the Annual Report as part of the company's communications strategy? And how important is it within the overall strategy?
The clients that hire us for annual reports do consider it an integral part of the communication strategy. That said, their importance in the corporate sector does seem to be diminishing, and for sustainability reasons, many companies are turning away from printed annual reports.

How do you define success in Annual Report design?
We design for two audiences: the one that commissions us and the audience that is ultimately going to read the report. We feel it's important to achieve effective goals for both audiences.

In which direction do you see Annual Reports moving?
In recent years, annual reports are less important within the total communications program of a company. We are finding more involvement with corporations on the digital side of annual reports. They are talking to the same audience with interactive tools online. They're moving more and more into the digital world.

How large a role does environmental policy play in the design and production of your Annual Reports?
We inevitably choose paper stock and print technology that is as environmentally conscious as possible. We advise our clients to follow this model not only on annual reports, but for everything they print. We certainly find that in many cases our clients lead the way in wanting to meet very high environmental standards. They are motivated by symbols they can add to their book to advertise their commitment to sustainability.

We certainly find that in many cases our clients lead the way in wanting to meet very high environmental standards.

SilverWinners

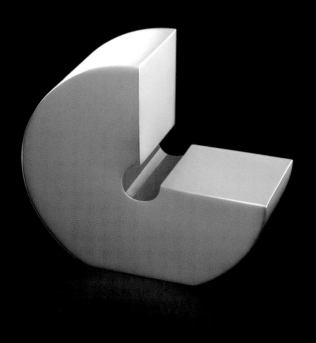

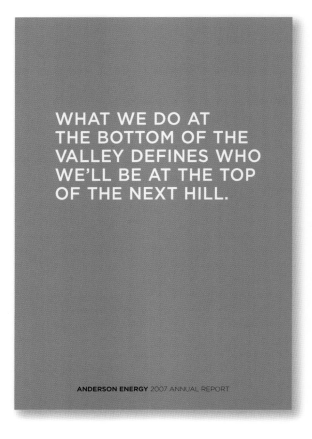

Category: Oil Companies | **Location:** Alberta, Canada | **Art Director:** Jonathan Herman | **Creative Director:** Monique Gamache | **Photographer:** Justen Lacoursiere | **Printer:** Blanchette Press | **Writer:** Sebastien Wilcox

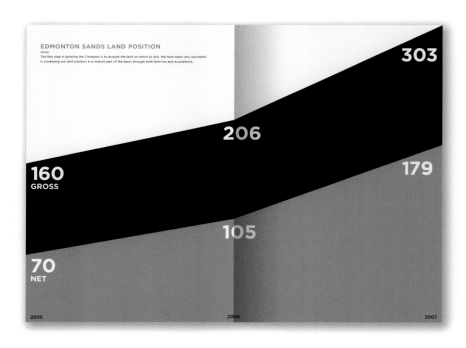

The natural gas industry is going through a very difficult period. Gas prices have been weak in the last couple of years and some competitors are being forced to sell off their assets. Anderson Energy is capitalizing on this down-turn. This annual report confidently highlights the strategic decisions that vAnderson is making as it prepares to become a much stronger company when natural gas prices rebound and the market bounces back.

Category: Corporate | **Location:** British Columbia, Canada | **Account Director:** Christine Marks, Barbara Moreira | **Paper:** Cover - 100lb Centura Dull Cover; Text - 100lb Centura Dull Text; Sleeve - 100lb Centura Dull Cover | **Photographer:** David Duchemin | **Printer:** 3S Printers | **Senior Designer:** Heather Nguyen

Challenge: Develop Canada Place's first annual report with the objective to help secure government support and funding for capital intensive upgrade projects. It needed to have a two-year shelf life and both educate and inspire.

Strategy: Evoke a sense of national pride by calling upon the values we uphold as Canadians. Separate the editorial information from the finan-cials so the report would have a longer shelf life.

Solution: A distinctive white gloss sleeve embossed with Canada Place's tagline, "the experience starts here," neatly packages both the report and financials; the financials can then be updated year-to-year. Through the use of striking photography and inspirational copy, the report documents the vital role Canada Place plays in nurturing the Canadian spirit.

Category: Financial Services | **Location:** British Columbia, Canada | **Account Director:** Maya Dimitrijevic | **Creative Director:** Ian Grais, Chris Staples | **Designer:** Lisa Nakamura | **Photographer:** Hans Sipma | **Print Producer:** Cary Emley | **Typographer:** Miles Linklater | **Writer:** Abeer Verma

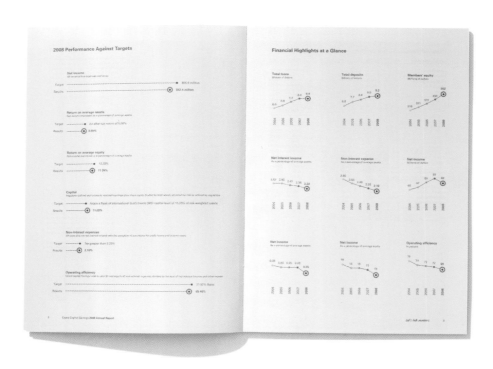

Coast Capital Savings is Canada's second largest credit union with 404,000 members and over 50 branches in British Columbia.This year, their annual report theme was "Let's talk numbers." The idea was to focus purely on the financials. To fit with this theme, a slim, removable calculator was fastened to the cover of the report. It was an appropriate tool for the target audience and it implied transparency and accountability because the reader could double check the numbers themselves.

Category: Government | **Location:** Quebec, Canada | **Acount Director:** Stephen Hards | **Art Director:** Martin Poirier | **Creative Director:** Jean-Luc Denat | **Print Producer:** St. Joseph Communications | **Print Run:** 3,000 copies | **Printer:** St. Joseph Communications | **Project Manager:** Stephen Hards | **Senior Designer:** Martin Poirier | **Writer:** Jennifer McCarthy

The Social Sciences and Humanities Research Council of Canada wanted their 2007-08 Annual Report to reflect the impact that the organizationís support and funding of diverse research activities is having on Canadian society and the way Canadians are living. Kolegram responded by creating an innovative layout that used a unique ëvertical half pageí treatment and info listing format to showcase various research projects undertaken by the Canadian Research Community. Spare use of imagery and more white space combined to create a clean design that exceeded the clientís expectations.

Category: Paper Companies | **Location:** Quebec, Canada | **Account Director:** Jean Doyon | **Creative Director:** Louis Gagnon | **Design Director:** Sébastien Bisson | **Photographer:** Monic Richard | **Paper Type:** Cover on corrugated board; text on Rolland Enviro 100 and some pages on kraft paper | **Print Producer:** Transcontinental Litho Acme, Norampac SPB | **Printer:** Transcontinental Litho Acme

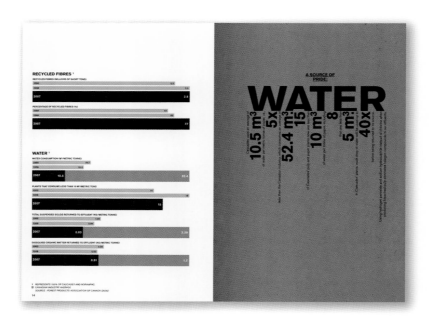

Paprika | Cascades

Cascades, a leader in paper transformation and recycling, publishes yearly a Report on sustainable development, announcing their environmental results. It is, for them, a very important document that has to be conceived in cohesion with Cascades' environmental concerns. We had to respect Cascades' philosophy and ethical concerns about environment. We also had to use only Cascades' papers. As soon as we decided what paper to use, our concept was pretty clear. We wanted the document to be a good representation of Cascades' environmental concerns. We also decided to create a hard cover, with some cardboard that usually isn't made for publication design. At the end it closes itself with a sticker and can be sent directly, without having to put it in a envelope for shipping. This is the environmental equivalent of an annual report; it shows all the progress, stats, decisions that has been made from an ecological point of view. For a company like Cascades, it is a very important document. It is distributed to investors, journalists, partners, employees and different people with ecological concerns.

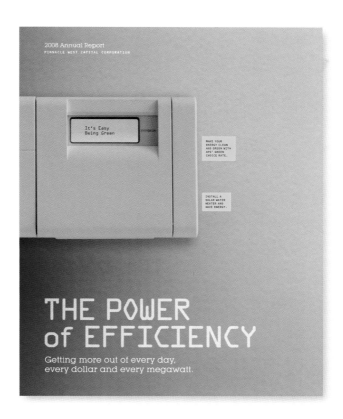

Category: Utilities | **Location:** Arizona, United States | **Art Director:** GG LeMere | **Creative Director:** Greg Fisher | **Designer:** GG LeMere | **Paper Type:** Cover - French construction pure white 80#C; Letter - French lemon drop 70#T; Narrative - French durotone butcher white 80#T | **Print Producer:** Andy Mrozinski | **Print Run:** 85,000 copies | **Writer:** Bill Marks

Pinnacle West Capital Corporation and its subsidiaries generate, sell and deliver electricity and energy-related products and services in the western United States. This year's objective was to focus on efficiency, and with a print run of 85,000 books, CFD had to find a way to address a broad audience. The cover's interactive wheel speaks directly to customers, showcasing simple ways to make their homes and businesses more efficient, while the narrative pages focus on Pinnacle West's corporate efficiencies, featuring specific events from the past year in review. The design itself is also inspired by the efficiency concept. The black type on a bright yellow background suggests energy and light, and immediately engages the reader, making the content the star. Simple, full-bleed imagery showcases the subtle nuances of the butcher-style paper, and the stark contrast of classic Lubalin with technical typography makes the bulleted style information inviting and accessible.

Category: Entertainment | **Location:** California, United States | **Art Director:** Jane Lee | **Creative Director:** Marcie Carson | **Senior Designer:** Nicole Bednarz, Christine Kenney | **Printer:** ColorGraphics

IE Design + Communications partnered with the Academy of Motion Picture Arts & Sciences, the world's preeminent professional motion pictures organization, to create their annual report. Best known for its annual Oscar telecast, the piece highlights the Academy's involvement in a wide array of education, outreach, preservation and research activities. Infused with Hollywood prestige and red-carpet glamour, the piece utilizes a visual approach to design with captivating images and unique typographic styles and elements. The annual showcases golden moments of achievement with personal member testimonials. An organization that touches people, the annual report reinforces the Academy's legacy, community impact and global reach.

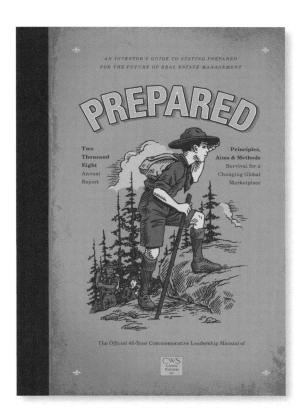

Category: Real Estate | **Location:** California, United States | **Account Director:** Lauretta Anderson | **Creative Director:** Michael Stinson |
Designer: Claire De Leon | **Illustrator:** Greg Copeland | **Project Manager:** Marcus Lam | **Writer:** CWS Capital Partners & Ramp Creative+Design |
Print Producer: Blanchette Press | **Print Run:** 1,000 copies | **Printer:** Blanchette Press

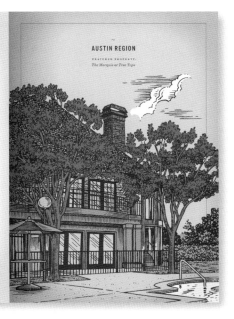

As a fully-integrated residential real estate investment management company providing homes for people in the US and Canada, CWS Capital Partners really knows how to excel in a turbulent economy. "Prepared" was designed to help guide the investor with CWS' company values, opportunities and expertise for their investor communications report. The annual report is a survival guide with CWS Capital as the leader in the field of investments.

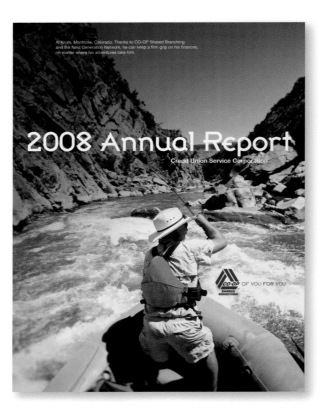

Category: Financial Services | Location: California, United States | Account Director: Dave Robinson | Account Executive: Katia Wu | Account Supervisor: Katie Krum | Copywriter: Matt McNelis | Designer: Mike Miyamura | Director of Print Production: Carol Knaeps | Executive Creative Director: Deidre McQuaide | Photographer: Getty Images, iStock | Printer: Primary Color | Print Producer: Bridget Rodriguez | Project Manager: Priscilla Meza | Studio Manager: Carol Isago | Writer: Matt McNelis

CO-OP Financial Services is the nation's largest credit union-owned electronic financial transaction network and processor. Built on the cooperative spirit and strength of the credit union industry, CO-OP continuously strives to empower its members with the latest products, knowledge and support. This annual report is for CO-OP's Shared Branching service, which connects members to thousands of credit union branches around the world, using the most dependable and fraud-resistant technology available. Previous annual reports have looked very corporate, filled with bland headshots and cold graphics. For this annual report, the focus was put on the value of membership, CO-OP's history of innovation, and CO-OP's leadership position as the only credit union provider that's of the credit unions, and for the credit unions. The annual report not only reflects back to CO-OP's financial affairs, but it is also a depiction of the CO-OP personality. Throughout the annual report, stories about members and how the Shared Branching service has improved their lives add an element of warmth not typically found in an annual report for a service like this. Which further showcases CO-OP Financial Services as both innovative and approachable.

Category: Architecture | **Location:** California, United States | **Creative Director:** Mark Coleman | **Designer:** Peiti Chia, Mark Jones, Tiffany Ricardo | **Editor:** John Parman | **Printer:** Hemlock Printers, Ltd.

Gensler's annual report provides an overview of the firm's year, noting exemplary design and community service accomplishments, along with firm and practice area developments. This annual report is distributed to all Gensler staff, clients, consultants and friends to celebrate the firm's annual achievements in building communities.

Category: Technology | **Location:** California, United States | **Art Director:** Earl Gee | **Creative Director:** Earl Gee | **Designer:** Fani Chung, Earl Gee | **Illustrator:** Earl Gee | **Paper Type:** Sundance Felt 100# Cover, Centura Dull 80# Cover | **Photographer:** Geoffrey Nelson | **Print Run:** 1,000 copies | **Printer:** Fong & Fong Printers and Lithographers | **Typographer:** Earl Gee

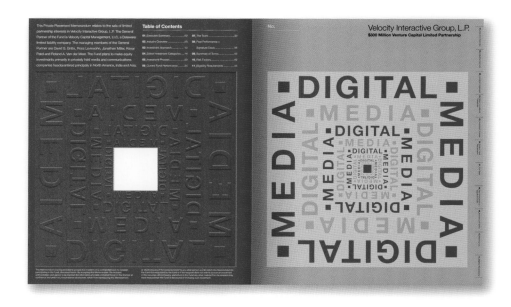

Objective: To create an offering memorandum for a venture capital firm who invests in the Digital Media opportunities created by the global convergence of media, communications and the Internet. **Solution:** The black, embossed die-cut cover suggests a window of opportunity for investment in Digital Media, opening to a colorful title page. Bold divider pages employ an unusual Op Art approach representing the company's expertise in distinguishing signal from noise, and seeking out successful strategies for growth. The typographic compositions incorporate the companyis content as a metaphor for examining Digital Media investments in a new way: the more you look, the more you see, and the more intriguing the opportunity becomes. Brightly colored orange tabs aid navigation throughout the book.

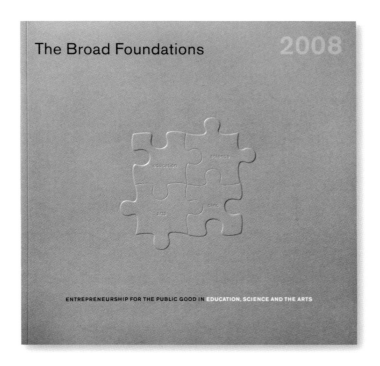

Category: Non-Profit | Location: California, United States | Account Director: Tracey Shiffman | Art Director: Tracey Shiffman | Creative Director: Tracey Shiffman | Design Director: Tracey Shiffman | Designer: Tracey Shiffman | Executive Creative Strategist: Karen Denne | General Director: Eli Broad | Paper Type: Cover: 130# Mohawk Options Crystal White Smooth Cover; Interior: 100# McCoy Matte Silk Book | Photographer: Mark Hanauer | Photographer's Assistant: Naj Jamai | Print Run: 6,000 copies | Printer: ColorGraphics | Strategy Director: Rachel Smookler

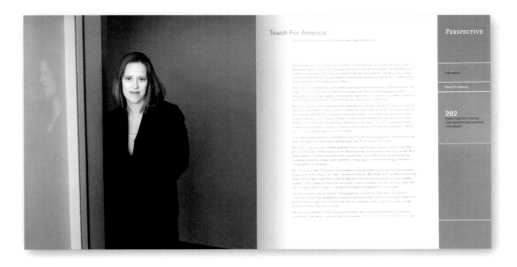

The Broad Foundations were established by entrepreneur and philanthropist Eli Broad to advance entrepreneurship for the public good in education, science and the arts.

The Eli and Edythe Broad foundation's education work is focused on dramatically improving urban K-12 public education through better governance, management, labor relations and competition. The foundation's scientific and medical research investments are in the areas of human genomics, stem cell research and inflammatory bowel disease. The Broad Art Foundation was established in 1984 to foster public appreciation of contemporary art by increasing access for audiences worldwide. Operated as an active lending library, the Santa Monica, Calif.-based foundation has provided more than 3,000 loans of artwork to more than 400 museums and university galleries worldwide. The Broad Foundations, which include The Eli and Edythe Broad Foundation and The Broad Art Foundation, have assets of $2.1 billion.

The Broad Foundations' Internet address is www.broadfoundation.org.

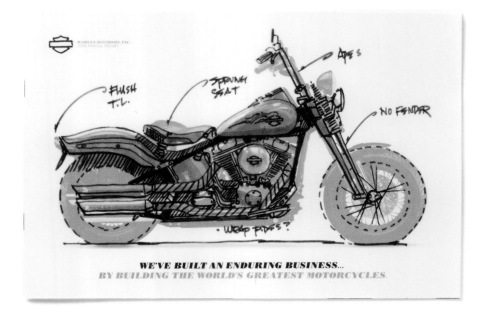

Category: Corporate | **Location:** Illinois, United States | **Account Director:** Melissa Schwister | **Associate Partner:** Melissa Schwister | **Creative Director:** Dana Arnett | **Design Director:** Luke Galambos | **Designer:** Conor McFerran, Jarrod Ryhal | **Writer:** Andy Blankenburg - VSA Partners, Rebecca Bortner - Harley Davidson | **Printer:** ColorGraphics

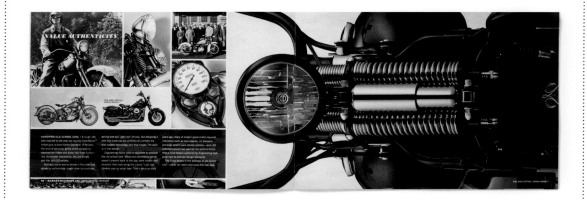

Harley-Davidson, Inc. is a global leader in fulfilling dreams and providing extraordinary customer experiences through mutually beneficial relationships with our stakeholders.

The 2008 Annual Report exemplifies this vision. As the Report's cover statement reads: We've built an enduring business by building the world's greatest motorcycles.

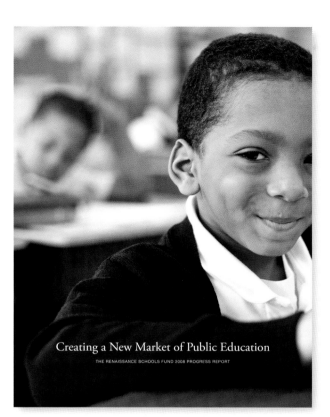

Creating a New Market of Public Education

THE RENAISSANCE SCHOOLS FUND 2008 PROGRESS REPORT

Category: Education | **Location:** Illinois, United States | **Creative Director:** Kym Abrams | **Designer:** Jess Weida | **Photographer:** Roark Johnson - Tony Armour Photography | **Printer:** Active Graphics

In America, one high school student drops out every 26 seconds.

Renaissance Schools Fund works on creating new schools in economi- cally challenged communities. In an effort to gain fundraising and estab- lish new partnerships, this report makes the case for the success of the program and promise of this free market approach to education.

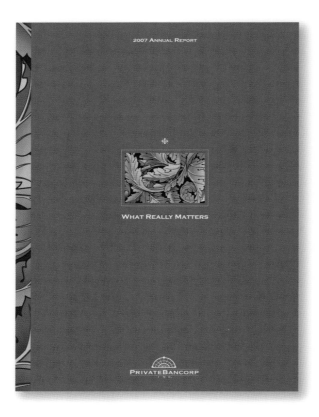

Category: Financial Services | **Location:** Illinois, United States | **Creative Director:** Jeffrey Heidekat | **Design Director:** Jan Gulley Gerdin | **Designer:** Jan Gulley Gerdin, Jeffrey Heidekat, Mary Rintz | **Photographer:** Jeff Corwin, Andy Goodwin | **Printer:** Lake County Press | **Typographer:** Mary Rintz

The PrivateBancorp philosophy is to know what really matters to each client, so Managing Directors can do what it takes to support their needs.

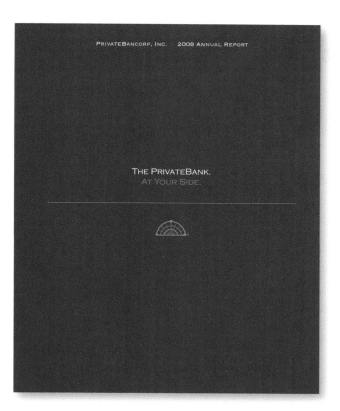

Category: Financial Services | **Location:** Illinois, United States | **Design Director:** Jan Gerdin, Jef Heidekat | **Designer:** Mary Rintz | **Photographer:** Andrew Young | **Printer:** Lake County Press

The people of The PrivateBank believe strong relationships with clients and with each other give the power to deliver and the strength to stand apart in the market.

In these times of uncertainty and change, The Bank wants clients, communities and shareholders to know they are The PrivateBank. And they are "At Your Side."

Category: Manufacturing | **Location:** Illinois, United States | **Design Director:** Fred Biliter | **Printer:** Lake County Press

Meta4 Design, Inc. | The Manitowoc Company, Inc.

The Manitowoc Company has long been a business in three segments with few common threads among their Marine, Food Service and Crane segments. This year's theme for Manitowoc's annual report "Changing the Balance" has a double meaning relating to a major acquisition in Food Service, the sale of the Marine segment, as well as their long-term strategy for growth based on new product development and acquisitions. For years the Crane Segment (a full line of cranes for all lifting applications) was the greater portion of the overall business. Food Service (cold side products only, including ice machines, walk-in/reach-in coolers and freezers and beverage dispensing equipment for restaurants etc.) was second, followed by Marine. The acquisition of Enodis has moved the company into the hot side of Food Service (high tech ovens, fryers, stoves, grills etc) and has given Manitowoc the ability to completely outfit major restaurant kitchens in both cold and hot side equipment, thus balancing Food Service in the same way the Crane Segment is balanced based on lifting capacity. The front and back covers reflect the new balanced segments as well.

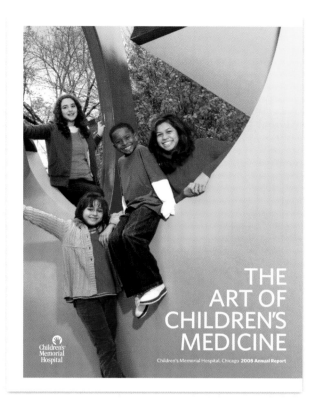

Category: Non-Profit | Location: Illinois, United States | Associate Creative Director: Liz Haldeman | Creative Director: Brock Haldeman | Designer: Melissa Abadie, Maggie Traidman

This Annual Report carried the theme "The Art of Children's Medicine," juxtaposing the artist and the scientist, as they share compelling gifts and work from a palette of innovation and inspiration. Targeted to the donor base, staff, peer institutions and the community at large, our solution utilizes compelling artwork from around the city of Chicago to showcase the visionary pursuits and creative thinking behind this inspiring institution. Large, portrait photography shot in distinct locations throughout the city add emphasis and emotional impact.

Category: Corporate | **Location:** Illinois, United States | **Art Director:** Pamela Lee | **Designer:** Pamela Lee, Lisa Toy | **Illustrator:** Leif Peng, Adrien van Viersen | **Photographer:** James LaBounty | **Printer:** Hemlock Printers, Ltd. | **Writer:** Stephen Forgacs, Winnie Tam, Tara Turner

BC Children's Hospital Foundation raises over $50 million annually to support BC Children's Hospital, Sunny Hill Health Centre for Children and the Child & Family Research Institute in Vancouver, BC. In 2008, the foundation launched a $200 million capital campaign to support the construction of a new hospital. The annual report had to perform all of its usual functions, donor recognition and stewardship, provision of financial information, etc., but also had to reflect the dynamic theme of The Campaign for BC Children, which called on people to "Be A Superhero" for the province's children.

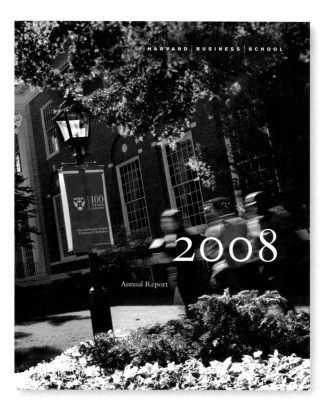

Category: Education | **Location:** Massachusetts, United States | **Creative Director:** Robert Krivicich | **Senior Designer:** Gary Pikovsky |
Paper Type: Monadnock Astrolite PC 100 80C/80T, Finch Casablanca 60T | **Photographer:** Tim Llewellyn, Gary Pikovsky, Mike Weymouth |
Print Producer: Dynagraf, Inc. | **Print Run:** 11,500 copies | **Printer:** Dynagraf, Inc. | **Writer:** Susan Geib

Harvard Business School, as a participant in the global economy, has embraced its responsibility to educate leaders who make a difference in the world. This yearís Annual Report focuses on four main stories: the Centennial Global Business Summit, the HBS Science-Based Business Initiative, the new HBS office in Shanghai, and the schoolís efforts to broaden their applicant pool. The design of the annual echoes the professionalism and organization of the school itself, while directing readers to further content online.

Category: Financial Services | **Location:** Minnesota, United States | **Account Director:** Melinda Church | **Creative Director:** Mike Haug | **Designer:** Bill Pflipsen, Michelle Solie | **Print Producer:** Pam Borgman | **Printer:** Bolger | **Project Manager:** Amy Ambrose | **Writer:** John Andreini, Gwyneth Dwyer

The goal of this annual report was to confirm to agents and stakeholders the enduring nature of Old Republic Title based on its strong history and dedication to the bottom line.

To accomplish this, we took a bold and irreverent approach ó directly acknowledging market difficulties and describing how the company's business practices have kept them from being seriously affected by such extremes. This bright, simple, and direct approach reflects Old Republic Title's ongoing strength and reliability.

THE KRESGE FOUNDATION 2007 Annual Report

Category: Non-Profit | **Location:** Minnesota, United States | **Creative Director:** Linda Henneman | **Designer:** Linda Henneman | **Paper Type:** Neenah ENVIRONMENT | **Photographer:** Douglas Schaible Photography, Jack Alterman, Don Hamerman, Lars Hansen, Greg Staffidi | **Printer:** University Lithoprinters | **Writer:** Jonathan Wiese, Claudia Capos

In the field: Priming the entrepreneurial pump in Detroit.

A 12-block research and technology park in the heart of Detroit's New Center area may well hold the key to unlocking Michigan's entrepreneurial talent and driving the commercialization of research discoveries that one day will generate new high-wage jobs and greater prosperity for the city and surrounding region.

Since its launch in 2000, TechTown has worked diligently to prime the entrepreneurial pump in Detroit. Over the past eight years, the fledgling organization has gained traction and established itself as fertile ground for new-venture creation. A strong triumvirate of institutional, community and corporate support, anchored by founder Wayne State University, in collaboration with the city of Detroit, General Motors and the Henry Ford Health System, has helped to build organizational capacity and expertise.

Today, TechTown operates the central city's only technology-business incubator and accelerator, TechOne. The facility houses 39 tenant companies employing more than 350 people in a historic building. These micro-businesses, many of them funded through a city of Detroit initiative, are pursuing promising start-up and early-stage ventures in biotechnology, information technology and advanced engineering.

TechTown's proximity to major educational and medical institutions, including Wayne State University, Detroit Medical Center, Henry Ford Hospital and Karmanos Cancer Institute, provides virtually limitless opportunities for harnessing cutting-edge research and spinning out new companies. NextEnergy's $15 million headquarters across the street from TechOne has brought additional prospects for developing technologies and business models that can advance alternative energy in Michigan.

The Kresge Foundation awarded TechTown a $1.5 million grant — $500,000 in growth capital to advance its role as a business accelerator and $1 million to assist with the build-out of committed lease space in the TechOne facility. This represents an investment in the present and the future.

Description: The objective this year was to communicate the foundation's new and evolving approach to grantmaking; an exciting new approach instituted to allow The Kresge Foundation to be more flexible and adaptable to the ever-changing needs of the nonprofit community. It was critical that the foundationís current and potential grantee organizations become aware of, and familiar with, Kresgeís new grantmaking tools. Our challenge was describing this new approach to grantmaking, which was still evolving and a work in progress.
Our visual direction: The Dotted Line. When something is just starting to take form, we delineate it with dotted lines. Dotted lines show us where to fold, to drive our carsó giving us direction without dictating our path. Dotted lines make the connections between people and ideas. Best of all, dotted lines are not rigid (thatís why theyíre dotted).
The notion of the dotted line giving shape, providing direction and creating connections was our visual direction. We used laser-cut dotted images to exemplify the foundationís new direction, and its willingness to be less rigid in grantmaking and more flexible and adaptable to changing community needs.

Category: Education | **Location:** New York, United States | **Art Director:** Michael J. Walsh | **Creative Director:** Anthony P. Rhodes | **Designer:** Patrick Tobin | **Printer:** The Thomas Group

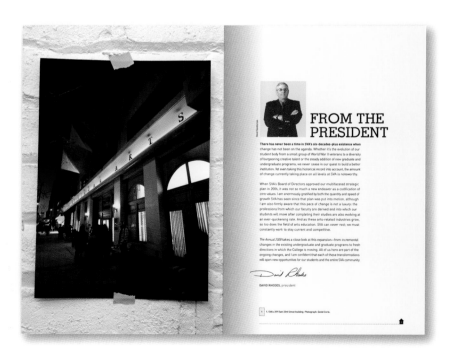

The Annual is a publication that is created to speak to the School of Visual Arts community—students, parents, alumni, faculty and staff. Its objective is to restate the mission of the College and give an overview of the happenings of the last year. This 2008 edition was themed "Things Change." This was to highlight a year of particularly rapid transformation at the College— from the incremental modifications in the undergraduate and graduate pro-grams, to the expansions and fresh directions in which the College is moving. These changes are highlighted throughout, alongside selected student and alumni artwork, along with images of the campus. Additionally, important facts about the College are included—such as student demographics and a brief budget overview. The client is the Communications Department at SVA, but ultimately its intended audience is the SVA community at large.

Category: Financial Services | **Location:** New York, United States | **Creative Director:** Richard Colbourne | **Paper Type:** Uncoated - Neenah Environment Ultra Bright White Smooth | **Photographer:** Markku Lahdesmaki | **Print Producer:** Georgiann Baran | **Print Run:** 50,000 copies | **Printer:** Earth Thebault | **Project Manager:** Mark Reilly | **Senior Designer:** Aidan Giuttari | **Writer:** Edward Nebb

Blackstone's second annual report builds on its strong brand identity, firmly positioning this elite investment firm as a visionary leader in today's economy. Using striking typography on the cover and opening pages, the report boldly addresses the past year's economic downturn head on. The report reiterates Blackstone's confidence in its investment strategy despite steep market declines, and speaks to the opportunities available to the firm. Bold assertions and important data are emphasized typo-graphically, backed up by key points.

Dramatic photography visually articulates the massive resources and assets that Blackstone has available. Dynamic charts help stakeholders visualize the scale of the opportunity presented by current market conditions. Elegantly simple, clean visuals and text are used throughout the Blackstone annual report. This combination of look, feel and tone rein-forces Blackstone's brand identity.

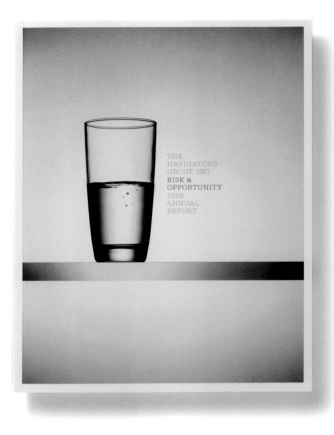

Category: Insurance | Location: New York, United States | Creative Director: Richard Colbourne | Paper Type: Uncoated - Coronado SST Bright White Vellum | Photographer: Dan Saelinger | Print Producer: Georgiann Baran | Print Run: 10,000 copies | Printer: Digital Color Concepts | Project Manager: Mark Reilly | Senior Designer: Adam Dines

Addison | **The Navigators Group, Inc**

In an economic environment filled with risk and uncertainty, the Navigators Group had distinguished itself from its peers through proven experience, prudent underwriting methods and a unique perspective. For their 2008 Annual Report, we employed a classic water glass metaphor to highlight the company's unique perspective while alluding to their primary focus and background in Marine insurance.

By maintaining simple and striking still life photography, we were able to communicate Navigators' intangible qualities through concise metaphor and symbolism. The overall theme of "Risk & Opportunity" is first established by dramatic front cover imagery of a water glass half-full, and is then further supported throughout the narrative: an inverted glass captures Navigators' culture of seeing, understanding and managing risk; a dynamic flow of water between two glasses celebrates expertise being brought to new markets; a drinking straw exemplifies an ability to deliver product innovations which meet customer needs; and multiple glasses of water convey growing opportunities through operational streamlining, enabling the firm to continue offering high quality service while keeping costs low.

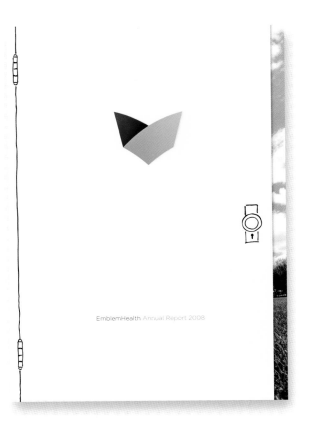

EmblemHealth Annual Report 2008

Category: Insurance | **Location:** New York, United States | **Art Director:** Hershell George | **Paper Type:** McCoy Matt 100# cover, McCoy Matt 100# text |
Print Run: 10,000 copies | **Printer:** Tana Seybert | **Senior Designer:** Rafi Bernstein | **Writer:** Shelley Mazor

making it easier for people

OPERATIONS & CUSTOMER SERVICE

A plan that works is a plan that makes health care coverage as easy as possible so that members can go about their lives, brokers can go about their business, and providers can spend more time taking care of patients and less time managing their practices. To achieve this, we are working to improve the customer experience at every point of contact . . . by using plain English to make our communications easy to understand . . . by providing the online tools that members need to manage their health care and that providers, brokers and administrators need to do business with us . . . and by getting the fundamentals right, with fast and accurate claims processing and phone inquiries answered promptly, courteously and effectively. In 2008, we did our best to create a customer experience that is distinctively EmblemHealth: respectful of the time, money and intelligence of the individuals who are behind every member ID number.

In the fall of 2008 EmblemHealth was launched with a media saturation campaign in the NY Metropolitan area featuring distinctive line illustration. This book, their first AR since the launch, uses the same illustration style on the cover to literally be a "door" to a "fresh take on health coverage." The brand relies on simple, straight messages and images as exemplified in the section dividers: "making it easy…" "helping people…" etc.

Category: Manufacturing | Location: New York, United States | Account Director: Michelle Steg Faranda | Creative Director: David Kohler | Design Director: Rick Slusher | Designer: Rick Slusher | Photographer: Lorne Bridgman | Print Producer: Georgiann Baran | Printer: Earth Thebault | Writer: Stephen Starbuck

Client's Challenge: Following a large, significant acquisition, Vulcan Materials Company posted record results despite difficult market conditions. The construction aggregates company wanted to reinforce to investors that the merger was another strategic move by a resilient organization that always focuses on growth over the long term. / Our Approach: Addison's solution was to boil Vulcan's position down to it's three core descriptors: "strategic, stable, growing." We underscored—literally—the company's assets with a dramatic showcase of Vulcan's new operations and projects in strategic locations. We then emphasized the company's solid fundamentals supported by key market metrics. The design's bold yet clean modern aesthetic lets Vulcan's assets and numbers speak for themselves, and enhances the annual report's net takeaway: a company of strength, consistency, and execution.

Category: Utilities | Location: New York, United States | Design Director: Rick Slusher | Designer: Rick Slusher | Paper Type: Uncoated - Mohawk Superfine Softwhite Smooth | Photographer: Lorne Bridgman | Print Producer: Nicole Anello, Georgiann Baran | Print Run: 30,000 copies | Printer: Earth Thebault | Project Manager: Michelle Steg Faranda | Writer: Stephen Starbuck

Client's Challenge: Vulcan Materials Company provides the basic materials for transportation infrastructure and industrial development. As such, the company wanted its annual report to present Vulcan as uniquely essential to the country's economic recovery.

Our Approach: Our solution remains true to both Vulcan's brand as well as to the serious economic climate the company faces. Right from the cover's theme of "Well-positioned," the report takes a plainspoken, austere approach to the company's communication. The company's message is boiled down to its essence for maximum impact and efficiency, and the design presents this simple three-part message superimposed on imagery of Vulcan's core markets. The clean, modern aesthetic offers multiple "points of entry" for the reader. The various elements combine to leave the reader with a pure impression of a company that is "essential to infrastructure, integral to development, and primed for the recovery."

Category: Non-Profit | **Location:** New York, United States | **Art Director:** Jen Lopardo | **Executive Creative Director:** John Paolini | **Paper Type:** Finch Opaque | **Print Run:** 4,000 copies | **Printer:** ColbyCo Graphics | **Project Manager:** Tina Citron

Many people know that Human Rights Watch (HRW) is one of the world's leading independent organizations dedicated to defending and protecting human rights. What most people do not know is that HRW is literally changing the world. Founded by journalists and lawyers, the work they do is at a policy level, not grass roots—they fight with meticulously researched facts. The reports they create and the evidence they uncover is powerful, and what they do with the information is culturally transformative—from getting Charles Taylor on trial for crimes against humanity to being the first organization reporting on both sides of the Georgian conflict. HRW's past communications failed to capture the impact of their work and who they are, oftentimes taking the form of dense text documents or photojournalistic essays only focusing on the victims. After an extensive repositioning assignment, the annual report became the opportunity to reintroduce HRW to a new generation of donors. Our answer was to create a document that stays true to their fact-based heritage but delivers the information in a bold, evocative way. By displaying and humanizing telegraphic information without melodrama, it provides context and meaning to the evidence and impact HRW has made. In brief, the report visualized impact, progress, and evidence, by truly bringing to life the new positioning "Tyranny Has A Witness." According to Michelle Leisure, Director of Development, not only has the new positioning and design work helped them surpass their donor goals—in a challenging economic environment—their donors are actually taking ownership of the information and using the new, approachable format to spread the word.

Category: Utilities | **Location:** New York, United States | **Art Director:** Lynda Decker | **Designer:** Lynda Decker, Carrie Leuci | **Photographer:** John Madere | **Printer:** Digital Color Concepts | **Writer:** Katharine Anderson, Michael Kinney

New Jersey Resources is a regional energy company that is committed to conservation. As a leading voice for energy independence, NJR has integrated an innovative business model in conjunction with the state of New Jersey. The program stipulates compensation based on reaching energy conservation goals. This year's annual report focuses on the shore environment of the service territories to communicate a commitment to preserving the future and the environment that customers and investors call home.

Mangos | **Harbor Point**

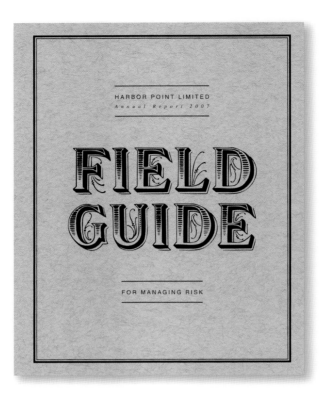

Category: Financial Services | **Location:** Philadelphia, United States | **Account Director:** Patti Monaco | **Art Director:** Bradley Gast | **Creative Director:** Joanne de Menna | **Executive Creative Director:** Bradley Gast | **Paper Type:** Domtar Proterra | **Print Producer:** Susan Trickel | **Print Run:** 2,000 copies | **Printer:** Brilliant Graphics | **Writer:** Joanne de Menna

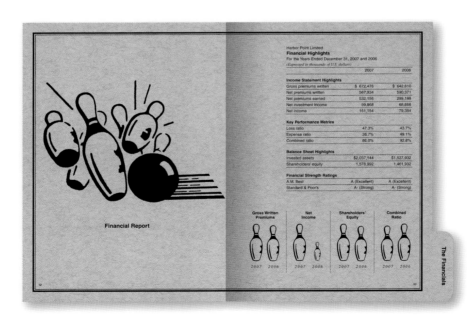

Harbor Point is a reinsurance company that adheres to a core set of business principles. In the 2007 Annual Report, we "repackaged" these ideas into Harbor Point's "Field Guide for Managing Risk"—a slightly tongue-in-cheek look at the importance of sticking to the rules.

Category: Government | **Location:** Philadelphia, United States | **Account Director:** Dan Giroux | **Chief Creative Officer:** Darryl Cilli | **Creative Director:** Jim Walls | **Designer:** Greg Ash, Adam Flanagan | **Photographer:** Matthew Bednarik, Joshua Dalsimer | **Printer:** George H. Dean Co. | **Writer:** Brendan Quinn

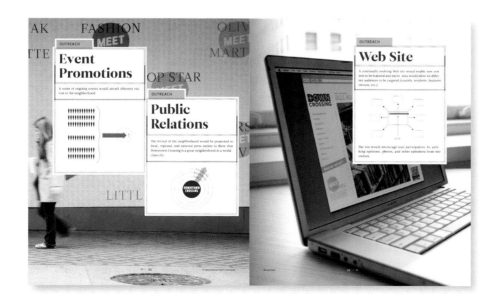

The Boston Redevelopment Authority assembled an international team to survey the Downtown Crossing neighborhood to make recommendations on how to bring this once vital shopping district into the 21st century. This executive summary presents a condensed version of our findings in a breezy, consumer-friendly format typically foreign to official municipal documents.

Category: Non-Profit | Location: Texas, United States | Account Director: Dana Opar | Art Director: Kevin Polonofsky | Chief Creative Director: John Brady | Production Specialist: Alice Benninger, Dan Yazvac | Project Manager: Christie Moeller

Brady worked with the Boy Scouts of America - Greater Pittsburgh Council to create an annual report that not only summarized BSA's accomplishments for the 2007 year, but also informed readers about the advantageous life-developing qualities that scouting offers to young people. Brady first identified a theme to be carried out throughout the entire report: "Molding Young People into Successful Adults." Using this theme, a report was created that included letters from individuals who have participated in scouting. The letters depicted each person's appreciation for the scouting program and the impact that scouting has made on their lives. Each letter was accompanied by a montage of personal and professional memorabilia to give readers a glimpse into each person's life. Scouting assets were included as visuals throughout the report to support the related copy. And to bring the theme full-circle, an envelope was included in the back of the report with a request for readers to submit their scouting story to the council.

Category: Education | Location: Texas, United States | Art Director: Scott Herron | Author: Kathy Anthony | Creative Director: Neely Ashmun |
Illustrator: Michelle Dewey | Photographer: David Omer Photography | Printer: Ginny's Printing | Project Manager: Asad Rahbar

The Urban Advantage is the Austin Independent School District's annual report. This report focuses on the high quality educational experience derived from this premier urban school district and how that experience shapes the students lives and inspires them to make positive contributions to society.

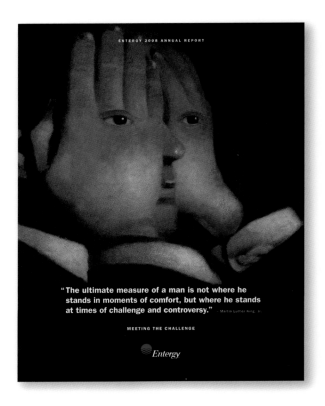

Category: Utilities | Location: Texas, United States | Art Director: Dennis Benoit, Jay Guiles | Creative Director: Dennis Benoit | Design Director: Dennis Benoit | Financials: Billie Cox - Sir Speedy Printing | Illustrator: Brad Holland | Narrative: Benoit Design | Senior Designer: Jay Guiles | Paper Type: 80# Environmental PC100 White | Print Run: 175,000 copies | Printer: Williamson Printing | Writer: Barbara Kieker

In 2008 the challenges came fast and furious. Entergy entered the year with an ambitious agenda that include achieving the spin of their non-utility nuclear assets and the formation of a nuclear services joint venture, continuing the transformation of their utilitiesí generation portfolio and pursuing constructive regulatory outcomes at the local, state and federal levels. Then extraordinary challenges emerged including a crisis in global financial markets, unusually high volatility in commodity markets and back-to-back, record-setting hurricanes. Entergy tackled these challenges with the same hard work, determination and focus that they bring to every element of their business. These essentials—along with their point-of-view-driven business model and adaptable employees—enabled them to respond quickly and effectively. In their annual report they offer quotes from great thinkers and inspirational leaders. Reflected in their words—and the accompanying illustrations—are the fundamental values, beliefs and spirit of Entergy Corporation.

Category: Non-Profit | **Location:** Virginia, United States | **Creative Director:** Gary Bloom | **Print Producer:** Mike Kalyan | **Printer:** Linemarc Printing |
Programmer: Daniel Chen - Ranzenhaus.com, Genevieve Konecnik - demadesign | **Project Manager:** Laura Berry, Barbara Michelman |
Senior Designer: Reece Quiñones, Greer Wymond

ASCD is a non-profit education association celebrating 65 years of service. We felt it was appropriate to create a digital annual report and include an interactive timeline to show how far we have progressed over the years. Rather than divide the timeline by dates, however, it was more appropriate to present our history through the major themes in education that helped shape our policies.

Category: Non-Profit | **Location:** Virginia, United States | **Chief Creative Officer:** Gregg Glaviano | **Print Producer:** Heath Dwiggins, Regina Esposito | **Printer:** Mofaic Printing | **Senior Designer:** Milagros Arrisueño | **Writer:** Meredith Light

Grafik | **Volunteers of America**

Our main objective for the 2008 Volunteers of America annual report was to convey the legacy of change and accomplishment that the organization has achieved during its more than a century commitment to serving the nationsí neediest individuals through actions and giving. We set out to demonstrate how this concept is present at all levels of the organization from the overarching strategic direction to the supportive programs and services offered, and through the individual lives that Volunteers of America has touched.

We used captivating portraits and a simple visual number device to tell their stories in a more intriguing manner. The over-sized format is intended to be more engaging and the crisp, black and white photography gave the piece an impact-full, editorial feel.

Category: Food & Beverage | **Location:** Washington, United States | **Account Director:** Anne Traver | **Creative Director:** Dale Hart | **Designer:** Regina Baerwalde, Goretti Kao, Albert Treskin | **Illustrator:** Sean Mosher-Smith | **Photographer:** David Hawxhurst, Audra Melton, Judith Pishnery, Michael Pugh, Gui von Schmidt, Walter Smith | **Print Producer:** Harry Wirth | **Project Manager:** Reeve Washburn | **Senior Designer:** Goretti Kao | **Strategy Director:** Anne Traver | **Writer:** Corporate Reporting, The Coca-Cola Company, Serena Levy

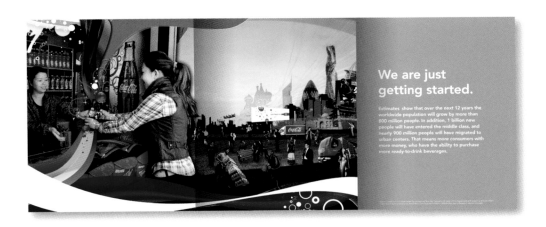

Even though it is a financial document, The Coca-Cola Company's Annual Review needs to live up to the iconic brand. Clear and simple messages, an energetic voice, bright colors, and dynamic page layouts contribute to the Review's optimistic tone.

The Review's audience—employees, bottling partners, investors and communities—all have a stake in the continued success of the company, so keeping the brand alive with them is just as important as it is with consumers. Readers should recognize the spirit and optimism of The Coca-Cola Company and feel confident that The Coca-Cola Company is well positioned for the future.

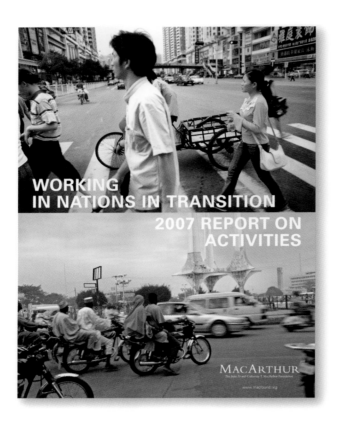

Category: Non-Profit | **Location:** Washington, United States | **Account Director:** Anne Traver | **Creative Director:** Dale Hart | **Designer:** Minh Nguyen | **Print Producer:** Derek Sullivan | **Project Manager:** Erina Malarkey

The MacArthur Foundation supports creative people and effective institutions committed to building a more just, verdant and peaceful world. In addition to selecting the MacArthur Fellows, the Foundation works to defend human rights, advance global conservation and security, make cities better places, and understand how technology is affecting children and society. The goal of the Foundation's annual Report on Activities is to communicate about the Foundation—its work, its values and characteristics—in a transparent way. The report draws attention to the key fields in which the Foundation and its grantees work (especially related to the themes of justice, sustainability and peace), and it is intended to inspire and engage key audiences. Readers should also walk away with an understanding of the seriousness and impact of the Foundation's work.

Category: Corporate | Location: Washington, United States | Account Director: Andrea Jonas, Sally Siegel | Art Director: Kristel Cornell |
Creative Director: Jason Reimer | Designer: Eric Wicks | Photographer: Brad Rochford | Printer: Tru Line Lithographing | Writer: Marc Glazer

Johnson Outdoors has a long history as advocates for outdoor activities and the environment. For this year's annual report we wanted to create a piece that celebrates these ideals as well as the people who make up the company. The theme "Be Here" is both an anthem for those who dream of traveling to idyllic places as well a symbol of pride to those who work for this forward-thinking organization.

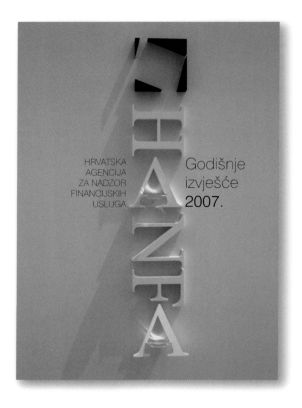

Category: Financial Services | Location: Croatia | Account Director: Ante Samodol | Art Director: Boris Ljubicic | Artist: Boris Ljubicic |
Associate Creative Director: Boris Ljubicic | Author: Boris Ljubicic | Chief Creative Director: Boris Ljubicic | Creative Director: Boris Ljubicic |
Creative Strategist: Ozana Basic | Design Director: Boris Ljubicic | Designer: Boris Ljubicic | Editor: HANFA | Executive Creative Director: Igor Ljubicic |
General Director: Ante Samodol | Illustrator: Igor Ljubicic | Print Producer: AKD | Printer: AKD d.o.o. | Typographer: Boris Ljubicic | Writer: HANFA

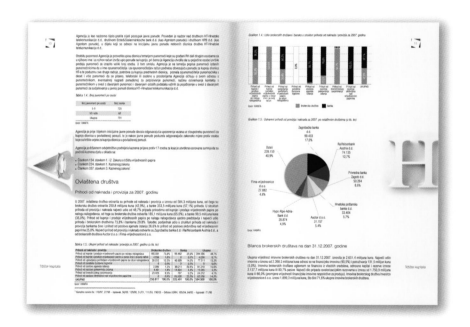

HANFA
Croatian Financial Services Supervisory Agency / Annual Report 2007. New HANFA logo in 3D is main motif of this project. Two "A" letters are rotated and shaped to look like eye (watching) because Agency monitor financial services in Republic Croatia. Logo "travel" through yearbook because, on every page, in the middle by edge is placed one letter, creating word HANFA in chain. Graphic refraining and pastel colours are creating impression of impartiality and intimacy in communication with the user. That is the main characteristic of this design: simplicity and clarity of text and graphic informations for public usage.

Category: Financial Services | **Location:** Croatia | **Account Director:** Helena Rosandic | **Art Director:** Mirel Hadzijusufovic, Imelda Ramovic |
Creative Director: Davor Bruketa, Moe Minkara, Nikola Zinic | **Designer:** Mirel Hadzijusufovic, Imelda Ramovic | **Print Producer:** Kratis | **Printer:** Kratis

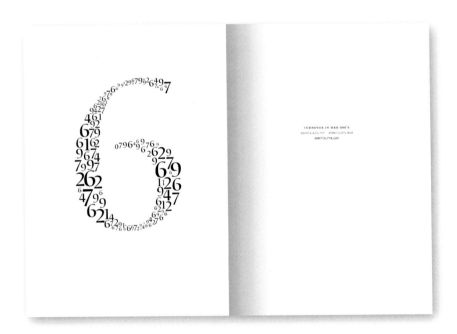

Faces is the 2007 annual report for Adris Group, an investment company from Croatia, with 3000 different covers, each bearing the face of one of its three thousand employees. The year 2007 was a very successful one for Adris Group, not only regarding their profit and competitiveness, but also concerning their relation to the community. They wanted to accentuate this success and all the people behind it in their 2007 annual report with the basic message Acts tell more than words. The creative idea was carried out like this: Imagine what we could achieve if we turned words into actions and numbers into people! The people are the greatest value and the foundation of every successful company. Well-educated, industrious and loyal people are the face of change. And so every copy of the Adris Annual Report bears the face of our three thousand employees and friends. It is to them we dedicate this yearís report. If you get to know them, youíll get to know Adris.

Category: Corporate | **Location:** Germany | **Account Director:** Dr. Martina Berger | **Chief Creative Officer:** Claus Koch | **Creative Director:** Michael Mehler, Dirk Thieme | **Designer:** Laura Gaebert, Daniel Koval | **Photographer:** Markus Meuthen, Katrin Moritz | **Project Manager:** Tatjana Flöthmann | **Printer:** Druckerei Schotte GmbH & Co. KG | **Writer:** Franz Haniel & Cie.

Retail. The annual report focuses on the various aspects of how Haniel conducts business. The strategic realignment of the portfolio has shifted the Group's concentration to the business areas of Retail and Services. At the same time, Haniel has not abandoned its commitment to diversification. The report speaks to the diversity and sustainability of the retail industry. The design concept reflects the exciting and progressive tone of this sector. Retail channels and product distribution methods are illustrated in a striking way. In-depth reports and unusual graphics provide concrete documentation of the business. The clarity of the report demonstrates the profile and enterprising spirit of this international corporation.

Category: Entertainment | **Location:** Germany | **Art Director:** Justus Oehler | **Designer:** Justus Oehler, Christiane Weismüller | **Printer:** Imprimerie Centrale s.a.

The Philharmonie Luxembourg was opened in June 2005. In 2009 they decided to publish the first ever annual report. This annual report was designed to be the major communication tool, corporate brochure, history book and financial report of the organization.

This trilingual, 140 page strong brochure has an unusual landscape format (200 mm high, 300 mm wide) and combines, strong, reportage-style black and white photography with vivid and impactful colour gradations.

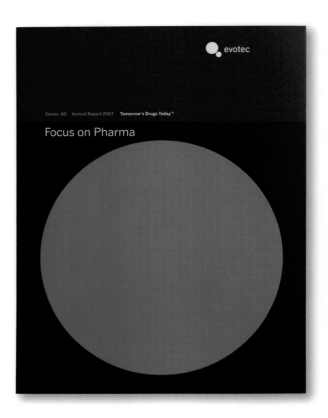

Category: Healthcare | **Location:** Germany | **Account Director:** Eva-Maria Schleip | **Art Director:** Atli Hilmarsson | **Creative Director:** Knut Maierhofer | **Creative Strategist:** Àxel Sanjosé | **Design Director:** Helena Frühauf | **Designer:** Michael Reinhardt | **Printer:** F-Media Druck GmbH | **Project Manager:** Manuela Liebertz

The 2007 Annual Report of Evotec AG is focused on communicating the strategic development of the company, which took the step from a provider of technology, screening, and testing services for preclinical drug research to an independent developer of drug candidates. Evotec is one of Germanyís most successful biotechnology companies. Following its beginnings as a partner and service provider for the pharmaceutical industry in the area of preclinical studies, Evotec over the years steadily expanded its own development of drugs as the company grew in experience and competence. 2007 marked the final strategic step in shifting the business focus to its own drug candidates. The task was to communicate this clearly in the Annual Report. The radical simplicity of the cover signals Evotecís decisive attitude. It is the result of a continuous development; and accordingly the colors and graphical elements are visibly derived from the corporate design.

Category: Non-Profit | **Location:** Germany | **Account Director:** Sandra Ehm | **Creative Director:** Knut Maierhofer | **Creative Strategist:** Knut Maierhofer | **Design Director:** Patrick Märki | **Designer:** Claire Chiquet, May Kato | **Photographer:** Diana Obinja | **Print Producer:** Matthias Karpf | **Printer:** Druckerei Vogl GmbH & Co. KG

Background: Diakonie is the charity association of the Protestant churches and one of the leading social institutions in Germany With over 27,000 member organisations and over 800,000 staff, Diakonie is the biggest employer in the entire country. In order to communicate its attitudes and values professionally and transparently both to members of subordinated organisations as well as beyond the association itself to partners and other interested parties, a new annual report was to be produced as a serious medium to convey issues and values.

Objectives: Engaging content alongside facts and figures: the idea of the new annual report was to provide a visible structure for the emotional presentation of the associationís professional work without deviating from the clear, objective form of a report. As a representative, informative document it was to clearly show the position of Diakonie as well as generate transparency and trust. The presentation of content is illustratively enhanced each year by an artist: another aim of this draft was to provide a design basis using the existing corporate design which could be successively implemented in subsequent years.

Idea and implementation: Based on the breakdown of the Diakonie logo, the cross is adapted to become the basic element of the design grid of the annual report. In this way, a single page is divided into four quadrants, creating four columns over a double page as a basis for the navigation system. The sections thus created provide space for four topic areas, thereby structuring the content of the annual report: introduction, artistic enhancement of the main idea, Diakonie topics and figures section. A colour coding at the upper edge of the type area made up of the mixed colours of the corporate design allows the reader to attribute the relevant section swiftly and simply. An entire column is highlighted in colour to mark the beginning of a new section.

Conclusion: The modular design system allows an extension of Diakonieís visual presentation, providing a flexible basis for future annual reports as well as fulfilling the function of conveying both information and image. The new annual report increases perception of Diakonie within the wide range of charity organisations by creating a visible structure in both content and design.

Category: Utilities | Location: Netherlands | Art Director: Jari Versteegen | Creative Director: Jeroen van Erp | Designer: Martijn Maas, Nils Mengedoht, Joana Muhlenbrock | Illustrator: Robin Nas (ZenkOne) | Photographer: Anton Corbijn | Printer: Thieme Amsterdam | Project Manager: Wouter Dirks (overall), Dim Veldhuisen (technical) | Writer: David Brown

TNT is in the business of transferring documents, packets, parcels and freight worldwide. Through two divisions, Mail and Express, they pick up, transport, sort, handle and store packages in over 200 countries—and they employ around 163,000 people, to enable them to meet TNT's customers' needs. This year's theme for TNT's reports, "Sure we can," shows us how far TNT is willing to go for its clients. In the Corporate Brochure this is highlighted by focussing on the drivers of twelve employees, both visually and in text, aided by Anton Corbijn's photography. As everyone knows, the secret to a company's success lays in the motivation of its employees. To fulfill this year's theme, we have continuously looked for smarter and better ways to make the reports. Ranging from an easy way to find the most important chapter in the Annual Report; a lasered cover of the Corporate Brochure; to the illustrations inside the Corporate Responsibility Report.

Category: Financial Services | **Location:** Norway | **Account Director:** Pål Hjort Berge | **Art Director:** Håvard Dybvig, Trond Fernblad, Elin Minde | **Creative Director:** Håvard Dybvig, Trond Fernblad, Elin Minde | **Design Director:** Trond Fernblad | **Designer:** Trond Fernblad | **General Director:** Katrine Bakka | **Illustrator:** Trond Fernblad | **Paper Type:** Highland Offset 250/135/100 gr. | **Print Producer:** Spesialtrykk | **Print Run:** 4,000 copies | **Printer:** Spesialtrykk | **Project Manager:** Siri Furuheim | **Senior Designer:** Trond Fernblad | **Writer:** Håvard Dybvig

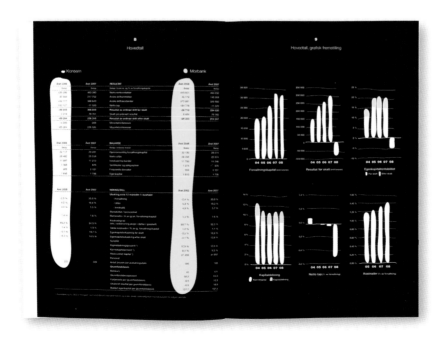

Things come in waves. Sometimes they hit hard and long. 2008 was a year unlike any others. Crisis, negative growth and disaster metaphors have dominated the news picture every day. The situation right now is neither perspicuous nor particularly merry, but it is important to not paint oneself into a gloomy corner either, as one Westerner put it in the Dag og Tid periodical. Sandnes Sparebank conducts most of its business in the Stavanger region. Right now that is a significant advantage. The economic base is decisively tied to the petroleum industry. The oil service industry is big and stable, regardless of whether the oil price is high or low. Investment plans are still extensive, and will only be reversed due to low oil price or financial crisis. The Stavanger region is Europe's "Easy Street." Consequently, we believe that this region will weather the ongoing crisis rather well.

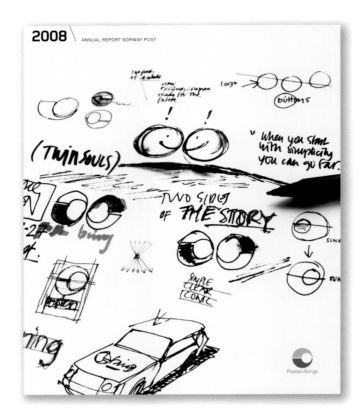

Category: Government | **Location:** Norway | **Account Director:** Elisabeth Hegg Gjølme | **Art Director:** Petter Herming | **Creative Director:** Petter Herming | **Designer:** Tale Frisak, Øivind Winge, Petter Herming | **Editor:** Tina Flem, Elisabeth Hegg Gjølme | **Paper Type:** Artic Volume High White | **Photographer:** Pierre Björk, Erik Burås, Daniel Lindh, Åke E:son Lindman, Søren Nilsen, Mangus Osth | **Print Run:** 5,000 copies | **Printer:** RK Grafisk | **Stylist:** Cato Geertsen

Norway Post LDT have been the national postal company for more than 360 years. The Norwegian parliament converted Norway Post into a limited company in 2002. The Group made considerable investments in order to improve its competitiveness in a market characterised by steadily increasing competition. A new brand (Bring) was launched in 2008 to achieve greater strength and visibility in the market and to show the link between the Norwegian and Nordic postal and logistics operations. Posten and Bring are really two sides of the same coin. The red Posten is there for the Norwegian people. The new brand Bring shows the entire range of the Norway Post Group's products and services for companies in the Nordic region. The new image has also been important for modernising Norway Post while building further on its position in the Norwegian market. The launch of Bring, renewal of Posten's logo, new uniforms and the rebranding of cars, signs and facades cost a total of NOK 221 million in 2008. The annual report 2008 was made totally "in-house" by the Design department, and all text written by our journalist and the financial department. Also all peoaple shown in the photos are employees in the group. The directive for this year's report was to tell about our new brand and redesign. We chose to make the concept more like a magazine, text written as interviews, and presented with editorial look. Norway Post decided to focus on a printed report rather than digital. This document has more value in paper form for the owners (The Norwegian parliament), and it's the only document used as a presentation of the group.

Category: Technology | **Location:** Norway | **Account Director:** Pål Hjorth Berge | **Creative Director:** Marit Mollnes | **Design Director:** Marit Mollnes | **Illustrator:** Marit Mollnes | **Paper Type:** MultiArt Silk (150/250 g) | **Photographer:** Emile Ashley | **Print Producer:** Gunnarshaug | **Print Run:** 1,000 copies | **Printer:** Gunnarshaug | **Project Manager:** Per Olav Haarr | **Senior Designer:** Marit Mollnes

The company: Roxar is an international technology company to the upstream oil & gas industry. Head office is in Stavanger, Norway. / Purpose: Appear as a fresh thinking and innovative company, and at the same time serious. Describe the company's activity in a plain and simple way, using graphics and logical navigation. / Focus areas: Technology – 7 stages / Flagship products: IRAP RMS Multiphase meter

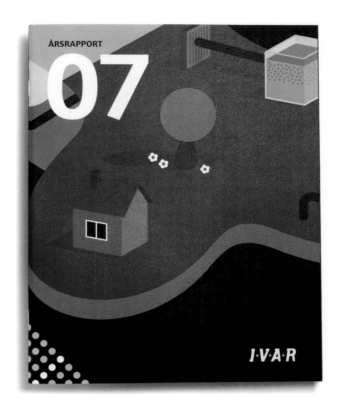

Category: Utilities | Location: Norway | Account Director: Pål Hjorth Berge | Creative Director: Marit Mollnes | Design Director: Marit Mollnes | Illustrator: Marit Mollnes | Paper Type: Highland Offset (135/190 g) | Photographer: Emile Ashley, page 5 and 6 | Print Producer: Spesialtrykk | Print Run: 1,000 copies | Printer: Spesialtrykk | Project Manager: Siri Furuheim | Senior Designer: Marit Mollnes | Writer: Borghild Eldøen, Birgit Høiland Gudmestad

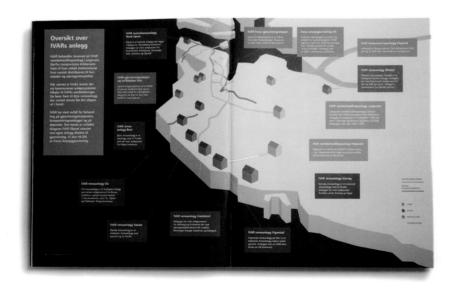

The company: IVAR is a Norwegian company that deals with water, sewage and waste treatment.
Target audience: The target group is mainly local politicians in the districtis municipalities/councils, which donít necessarily understand the whole complexity of IVAR's business.
Purpose – Emphasize that IVAR: (1) is one of the region's leading environmental companies. (2) is a high-tech company. (3) cleans drinking water and sewage in a responsible manner, and also ensures good waste treatment.
Solution: Visualize the cleaning processes etc in a simple way, by the use of clear and pedagogical illustrations. Playful design to soften up an 'unsexy' theme. / Chapters – The three chapters (water, sewage and waste treatment) consist of two parts: (A) Technical illustrations of the WWTP (cleaning system for drinking water and sewage), and waste management. (B) Case-studies in the same illustrative/playful style.

Category: Non-Profit | **Location:** South Africa | **Creative Director:** Lauren Robertson | **Designer:** Lauren Robertson | **Paper Type:** Calendar: Sponsored by Antalis (from their discontinued stock - NOVATECH SATIN); Backing board: Papersmith & Son | **Print Producer:** Ultra Litho | **Print Run:** 1,700 copies | **Printer:** Ultra Litho | **Project Manager:** Karin Boshoff

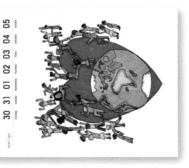

Cotlands is a long-serving South African "non-profit" agency that continues to meet the ever-changing needs of children impacted by HIV/AIDS. Every year they produce an annual report for their stakeholders as well as being used as a marketing tool to obtain sponsors etc. The 2008 annual report was designed with a dual purpose, the annual report figures and editorial featured, but it could also be used as a desk calendar for 2008/2009. A request was sent out for the staff, volunteers, shareholders and public at large to submit artwork (drawings, paintings, poems etc) that portrayed the theme "Hope for our children." There were incredible responses—ages ranging from 4 years old to 68 years old, business to individuals. The best artwork was selected and complied into an A5 desk calendar. The editorial portion of the annual report featured on the left hand pages in a horizontal format, and the desk calendar portion (weekly calendar) on the right hand pages in a portrait format. The desk calendar stands vertically on a desk with each week perforated in order to be torn off. This unique annual report meant that it was used for a longer period of time and remained top of mind as it sat in a prominent position on the recipient's desk. The final product is a beautiful and unique piece of artwork that contains over 60 pieces of illustration, drawings, poems, graphics and messages, all portraying "hope to our children."

Gottschalk+Ash Int'l | Barry Callebaut

Category: Food & Beverage | **Location:** Switzerland | **Account Director:** Rahel Furrer, Gaby Tschofen | **Art Director:** Fritz Gottschalk | **Designer:** Michael Kahn | **Photographer:** Jonas Kuhn | **Print Producer:** Linkgroup | **Printer:** Linkgroup

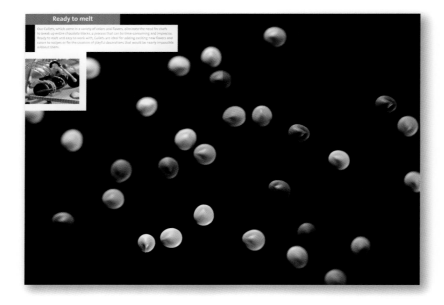

Barry Callebaut is the world's leading manufacturer of high-quality co-coa and chocolate products and one of the preferred solutions provid-ers throughout the food industry. Present in 26 countries, Barry Callebaut operates around 40 production facilities, employs more than 7,000 people and generated sales of more than CHF 4.8 billion in fiscal year 2007/2008. "It's all about quality, first-class and ready-to-use chocolate products. How can we communicate this message in a distinct yet appetizing way?"

A straightforward briefing from the client. The solution depicts various details and macro-photographs of semi- and final products laid out on six spreads in the operating review. Showing the inspiring beauty of choco-late in its various production stages.
A typographically designed cover contrasts the photographic approach with large letters and interspersed key messages. Lead by the maxim "Ready to..."

Category: Manufacturing | **Location:** Switzerland | **Account Director:** Karin Marti | **Art Director:** Fritz Gottschalk | **Designer:** Michael Kahn |
Photographer: Luxwerk | **Print Producer:** Neidhart+Schön AG | **Printer:** Neidhart+Schoen AG

Forbo is a leading producer of flooring systems, adhesives, as well as power transmission and conveyor belt solutions. The company employs some 6,500 people and has an international network of 44 sites with production and distribution as well as 51 pure sales organizations in a total of 35 countries worldwide. Forbo is headquartered in Baar in the canton of Zug, Switzerland. Forbo holds three divisions: Flooring Systems, Bonding Systems and Movement Systems. The client wanted the reader to be visually led by these three divisions. A series of photographs show semi-finished products on the cover and day-to-day applications inside the report. All photographs have been taken from unusual perspectives. To accompany these abstract and technical aspects and to show the people behind the scene, portraits of self-confident employees illustrate the corporate governance chapter.

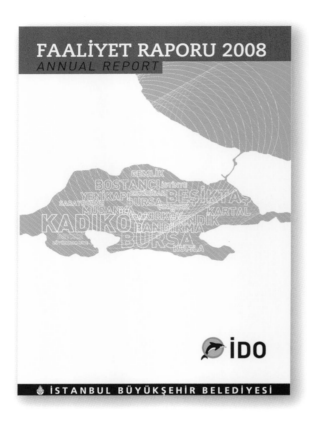

Category: Transportation | Location: Turkey | Creative Director: Zeynep Tasci | Photographer: Serdar Sarihasanoglu | Project Manager: Fatih Özgüzelbas | Printer: EUROMAT | Print Producer: Adem Yamali | Print Run: 3,000 copies | Writer: Selçuk Ergenç

The cover of the 2008 Annual Report designed for IDO (Istanbul Fast Ferries) featured a die-cut illustration of the Marmara Sea where IDO operates. IDO, is the world's leader maritime transportation company with 102 million passengers per year, a huge fleet of 101 boats and the number of lines it serves.

The inner pages decorated with pictures of Istanbul shows the modern structure and dynamism of the organization which was reflected through the use of bright colours and typographic choices.

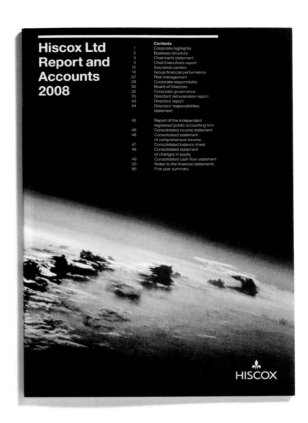

Category: Insurance | **Location:** United Kingdom | **Account Director:** Kendra Futcher | **Creative Director:** Jonathan Ellery | **Editor:** Kylie O'Connor |
Paper Type: Revive 100 Offset | **Photographer:** John Ross | **Print Producer:** Westerham Press | **Print Run:** 13,000 copies | **Senior Designer:** Claire Warner

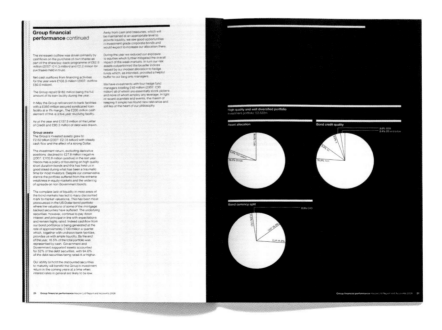

This years R&A for Hiscox demonstrates the client's continued mission to produce an annual report which makes a timely statement about their business. The bold graphic language has been pared back further resulting in a one-colour report. Despite the economic and environmental considerations it was key that the document would still cut a sophisticated figure within the world of corporate reporting.

Category: Insurance | **Location:** United Kingdom | **Account Director:** Maryam Meddin | **Creative Director:** Elen Swetman | **Paper Type:** Challenger Offset | **Print Run:** 1,000 copies | **Printer:** Darwin Press

This Report is produced by the International Tennis Federation in the months following each Olympic event. The ITF is the world governing body for tennis, whose objective is to promote and develop the sport at all levels, from grass roots to the elite professional ranks. Its post Olympic Report serves as a review of the operations, successes and shortcomings of the tennis federation's activities at the Olympics and consequently also serves as a 'guideline' by the organisers of the next Olympic event, four years on. Creatively, the publication is required to strike a balance between reflecting the dynamism of the sport and the thematic aspects of the location (in this case Beijing), whilst still remaining an appropriate vehicle for a sober report on all aspects of the event, behind and in front of the scenes.

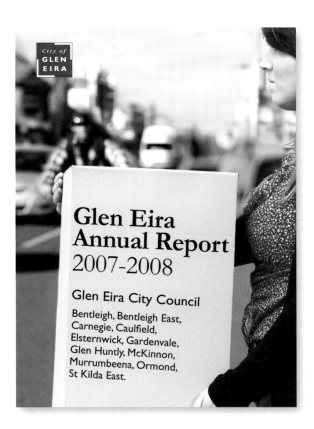

Category: Government | **Location:** Australia | **Creative Director:** Miguel Valenzuela | **Designer:** Andrea Taylor | **Paper Type:** Cover: ecoStar - 100% recycled post consumer waste fibre and is process chlorine free; Internals: Sumo Offset Laser - element chlorine free and is made from well-managed forest pulp. Both are environmentally responsible papers coming from FSC certified mills. | **Printer:** McLaren Press | **Project Manager:** Nancy Bugeja

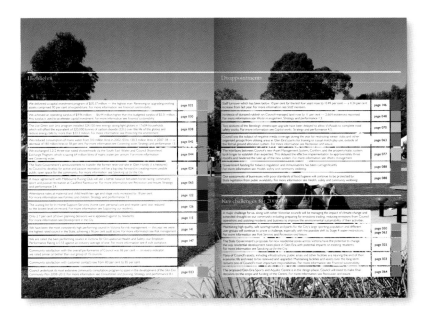

The concept behind the Glen Eira Annual Report 2007-08 was to incorporate the unique voices of the Glen Eira community, the recycled elements and of course the key data. The 280-page report was printed on environmentally friendly paper with vegetable based inks and was printed by a FSC Certified printer. The report also includes a 6-page fold out cover entailing key points and the overall navigation of the report.

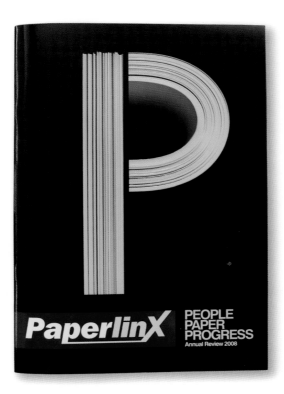

Category: Paper Companies | Location: Australia | Account Director: Mark Bentley | Creative Director: Amanda Roach | Design Director: Amanda Roach | Paper Type: Impress Gloss 300gsm and Hello Silk 130gsm | Print Run: 50,000 copies | Printer: Finsbury Green Printing | Project Manager: Mark Bentley

PaperlinX: Annual Review 2008. When PaperlinX publishes any sort of review, it's really putting its money where its mouth is—as one of the world's largest fine paper merchants, paper is their business. Exactly the kind of challenge we love. The 2008 Annual Review theme was People, Paper, Progress. Running with the alliterative possibilities, we developed a multi-level, embossed 'P' graphic for the cover, which carried through as an 'S' design for the sustainability report. The Chairman's and CEO's review expanded the theme, highlighting in particular PaperlinX's investment in its people. The company is built on its dedicated employees across 27 countries. Through their efforts, PaperlinX continues to be a model of progress in the paper industry. And through ours, their reports—both printed and online—continue to be models of effective corporate communication.

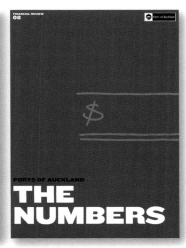

Category: Shipping | **Location:** New Zealand | **Account Director:** Paul Saris | **Design Director:** Katie Rebairo | **Designer:** Katie Rebairo | **Photographer:** Mark Smith | **Typographer:** Katie Rebairo

The Ports of Auckland (POAL) reports to its stakeholders on an annual basis. The main purpose for this initiative is to:
- get important reputation messages out
- communicate POALs mid to long-term strategies
- ensure that POALs objectives and deliverables are clearly understood
Previously POAL produced a great variety of reports each targeted at a select audience. Whilst there's a desire to publish a range of documents again this time we've established that the range should nevertheless be limited. The reality is that a proliferation of POALs messages across a greater range of documents has proven to be challenging to manage, and may lead to stakeholder confusion.

The reporting theme conveys POAL's unique position as a leading port to benefit Auckland and New Zealand. An organisation that is highly aware of international developments, the needs of its client and its responsibilities as the major supply-chain gateway to and from NZ.
Its commitment and investments in resources across its plant, technology and environment are comprehensive (e.g. harbour channel, community initiatives, only port to have completed a CO2 footprint assessment).
The strength of its leadership team (collaborative based on respect, savvy, and is results driven), combined with the qualities of the workforce (e.g. demonstrate pride, loyalty, highly competitive spirit) sets it apart, in other words makes it a highly distinctive organisation in Australasia.

Category: Transportation | **Location:** New Zealand | **Account Director:** Paul Saris | **Design Director:** Katie Rebairo | **Designer:** Michael Hourigan, Katie Rebairo, Bettina Way | **Photographer:** Alistair Guthrie

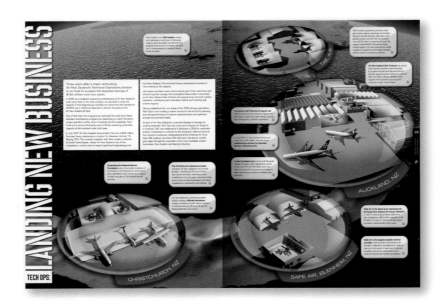

Air New Zealand reports to its investors and stakeholders every six months. The reports include a financial overview (legislative) and a separate document called the Shareholder Review 2009.
The information in the Shareholder Review covers:
- Important reputation messages
- Air New Zealand's mid to long-term strategies
- Air New Zealand's objectives and deliverables

- In addition, a summary overview of top-line financial performance
The reporting theme conveys the airline's unique position as New Zealand's most distinctive airline, championing and promoting New Zealand and its people, culture and business at home and overseas. Air New Zealand's own unique culture is a major contributor to their competitive advantage, empowered by the creativity and innovation of their people. This culture provides the undercurrent for how information is delivered throughout the report.

Category: Healthcare | **Location:** Singapore | **Creative Director:** Edmund Wee | **Designer:** Foo Siewhuey | **Photographer:** Nicholas Leong | **Printer:** Colourscan Co (Pte) Ltd. | **Project Manager:** Connie Lee | **Senior Designer:** Caslyn Ong | **Writer:** Edmund Wee, Roger Hiew

SingHealth is a public healthcare institution in Singapore. Its members include three hospitals, five National Specialty Centres and a network of primary healthcare clinics. Each year, SingHealth institutions attend to over three million patients. Aptly, their motto is: Patients. At the heart of all we do. The title for the 2007 AR -- The Patient, The Whole Patient and Nothing But The Patient -- is based on Singhealth motto. The annual report lives up to the title by having only full portraitures of patients, and only patients. No board members, no nurses, no doctors. Just patients talking about their recoveries. The takeaway message for anyone reading this annual report is unequivocal: At Singhealth, it is all about patients.

Category: Non-Profit | **Location:** Singapore | **Account Director:** Yong Yau Goh | **Art Director:** Eng Teck Tan | **Creative Director:** Lwin Mun Tin Thein |
Designer: Eng Teck Tan | **Editor:** Yong Yau Goh | **Photographer:** Carolyn Strover | **Printer:** Xpoprint Pte Ltd | **Writer:** Laura Reid, Yong Yau Goh

Coal Creative Consultants Pte Ltd | **Singapore Sports Council**

The aim of the annual report is to highlight Singapore's phenomenal ac-complishments in the global sports arena, as well as the effort taken by the Singapore Sports Council and the local sports fraternity to put Singapore on the map that year. The worldis first Formula One night race and Youth Olympic Games are some of the said achievements. To embody the efforts of Singapore and the Council, water was used as a theme, portraying sweat, effort and passion. Marrying this with stylised black-and-white photographs, we captured the greatness that lies in athletes, reflecting the year's immense achievements. In addition, the cover of the annual report hints at the water-based theme at first glance, but it folds out to reveal a picture embodying the spirit of the Council. To reinforce the identities of Singapore and the Council, a vital part of the section divider pictures within the annual report was coloured red - the official colour of both the country and the organisation. The section divider pictures were also treated with a layer of gloss to bring out their distinct nature.

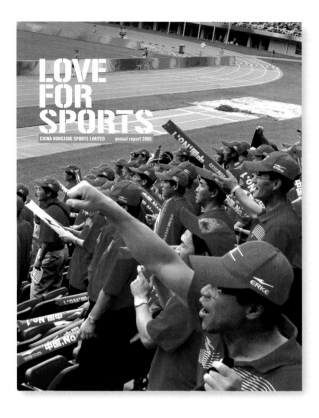

Category: Sports | Location: Singapore | Account Director: Karen Chow | Creative Director: Dillon J. Devan | Paper Type: 300gsm Fine Print, 120gsm Innotech | Photographer: Eng Kwang Chua | Print Run: 14,000 copies | Printer: Grenadier Press Pte Ltd | Senior Designer: Lisar Sng

The primary message of the report was to reinforce that China Hongxing is the leading sportswear enterprise in the PRC and played a role in China's historic hosting of the 2008 Olympic Games. The Company's wide spectrum of sports apparel and accessories are made by people who love sports, for people who are true sports fans. This was the central point in which the design strategy was built around and communicated in the report.

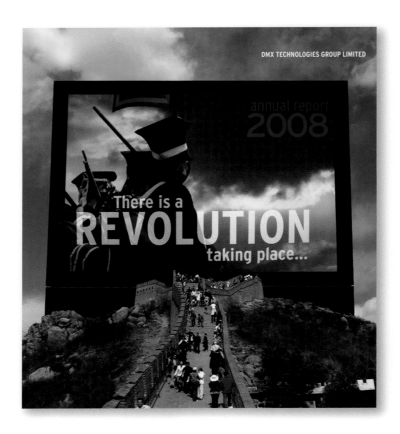

Category: Technology | Location: Singapore | Account Director: Karen Chow | Art Director: Mark Sidwell | Creative Director: Dillon J. Devan | Design Director: Anne Gan | Paper Type: 270gsm Fine Print, 130gsm Innotech, 100gsm Simili | Print Run: 4,000 copies | Photographer: Eng Kwang Chua | Photographer's Assistant: Rafi | Printer: Grenadier Press Pte Ltd

Amidst the financial crisis our client DMX wanted to re-assure its sharehold-ers that there's still a huge market and growth potential in China for Digiti-sation across multiple media platforms. As China plans to go fully digital by 2015, this revolution will only gather pace, as will DMX growth opportunities.

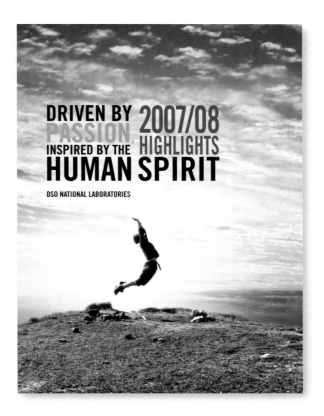

Category: Technology | Location: Singapore | Account Director: Karen Chow | Creative Director: Dillon J. Devan | Paper Type: 300gsm Board wrapped with 120gsm Magno Satin, 120gsm Innotech | Photographer: Charles Chua | Print Run: 2,000 copies | Printer: Grenadier Press Pte Ltd | Project Manager: Gabriel Eng | Senior Designer: Lisar Sng | Writer: Dillon J. Devan

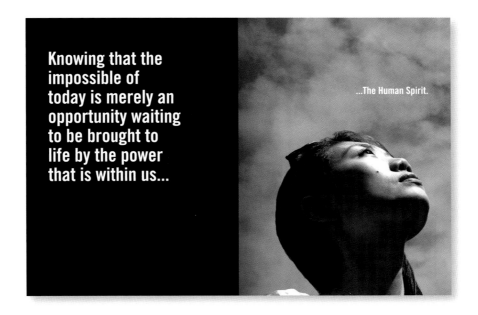

DSO is responsible for the research and development of tecnological solutions to Singapore's national security. In this report our Client wanted to highlight the indomitable spirit and passion of its staff who are behind the breakthroughs that provide the cutting edge to the security of Singapore. DSO wanted to play up this drive that's within their researchers and scientists which guides them in their quest to make the seemingly impossible, possible.

This year, Graphis Inc. honors the Neenah Paper Company Annual Report for its Excellence in Print Production. The Award is presented to Lake County Press in Waukegan, Illinois, www.lakecountypress.com. This outstanding Annual Report was designed and produced by Addison in New York City, www.addison.com, who has also earned a Graphis Platinum Award for its Design.

See pages 54-59 for full presentation of this Annual Report

This Annual Report clearly excelled, and is a great example of outstanding craft in printing.

B. Martin Pedersen, *President & CEO of Graphis, Inc.*

Category: Paper Companies | **Location:** New York, United States | **Creative Director:** Richard Colbourne | **Design Director:** Jason Miller | **Designer:** Jason Miller | **Illustrator:** Ilovedust, Raymond Biesinger, Mario Hugo, Faiyaz Jafri | **Paper Type:** Various Neenah stocks | **Photographer:** Dean Kaufman, Aakash Nihalani, Horacio Salinas, Corriette Schoenaerts | **Print Producer:** Nicole Anello, Georgiann Baran | **Print Run:** 19,000 copies | **Printer:** Lake County Press | **Project Manager:** Michelle Steg Faranda | **Set Designer & Props:** Sarah Illenberger | **Writer:** Edward Nebb

Designers

DesignFirms

DesignDirectors

Clients

WinnersDirectory

160over90 www.160over90.com
1 South Broad Street, Floor 10
Philadelphia, PA 19107, United States
Tel 215 732 3200

Addison www.addison.com
20 Exchange Place, 9th Floor
New York, NY 10005, United States
Tel 212 229 5076 | Fax 212 929 3010

Amanda Roach Design
www.amandaroach.com.au
129 High Street, Prahran, Victoria 3181, Australia
Tel +61 3 9521 1602 | Fax +61 3 9521 1636

And Partners NY www.andpartnersny.com
158 West 27th Street 7th Floor
New York, NY 10001, United States
Tel 212 414 4700 | Fax 212 414 2915

ASCD www.ascd.org
1703 North Beauregard Street | Alexandria, VA
22311, United States | Tel 703 575 5715

BAH! Design www.bahdesign.com
500 E. 53rd Street, Austin, TX 78751, United States
Tel 512 419 9300

Bailey Lauerman www.baileylauerman.com
1248 O Street, Suite 900, Lincoln, NE 68508,
United States | Tel 402 479 0235

Bandy Carroll Hellige www.bch.com
307 W. Muhammad Ali Boulevard | Louisville, KY
40202, United States | Tel 502 589 7711

Benoit Design, Inc. www.benoitdesigninc.com
825 18th Street, Plano, TX 75074, United States
Tel 972 509 7588 | Fax 972 509 7589

Brady Communications
www.bradycommunications.com
Four Gateway Center 16 Floor, Pittsburgh,
PA 15215, United States | Tel 412 288 9300

Browns www.brownsdesign.com
5 Plantain Place, Crosby Row, London SE1 1YN,
United Kingdom | Tel +44 0 20 74 07 9074

Bruketa&Zinic OM www.bruketa-zinic.com
Zavrtnica 17, Zagreb 10 000, Croatia
Tel +385 1 6064 000 | Fax +385 1 6064 001

Campbell Fisher Design www.thinkcfd.com
5013 E. Washington Street, Suite 230
Phoenix, AZ 85034, United States
Tel 602 955 2707

CDT Design Limited www.cdt-design.co.uk
50-52 Wharf Road
London N1 0HQ, United Kingdom
Tel +44 0 20 7242 0992 | Fax +44 0 20 7242 1174

Clarus www.clarus-design.com
31 Chippenham Mews, London W9 2AN,
United Kingdom | Tel +44 0 20 7121 0383

Claus Koch Identity GmbH www.clauskoch.de
Kaistrasse 18, Düesseldorf 40221, Germany
Tel +49 0 211 3010277 | Fax +49 0 211 3010220

Coal Creative Consultants Pte Ltd
www.coal.com.sg
14B Smith Street, 058928, Singapore
Tel +65 6557 0857 | Fax +65 6557 0639

Design Army www.designarmy.com
510 H Street NE, Washington, DC 20002, United
States | Tel 202 797 1018 | Fax 202 478 1807

Epigram www.epigram.com.sg
1008 Toa Payoh North #03-08, 318996, Singapore
Tel +65 62 92 4456 | Fax +65 62 92 4414

Fabrique Communications and Design
www.fabrique.nl
Oude delft 201, Delft 2611 HD, Netherlands
Tel +31 15 219 56 44 | Fax +31 15 219 56 01

Fasett AS www.fasett.no
Lars Hertervigsgate 3, Stavanger 4006, Norway
Tel 47 51844800 or 47 51844815 | Fax 47 51 84 4801

Gee + Chung Design www.geechungdesign.com
38 Bryant Street, Suite 100
San Francisco, CA 94105 United States
Tel 415 543 1192 | Fax 415 543 6088

Gensler www.gensler.com
2 Harrison Street, Suite 400
San Francisco, CA 94105, United States
Tel 415 433 3700 | Fax 415 836 4599

Gottschalk+Ash Int'l www.gplusa.com
Boecklinstrasse 26, Zurich 8032, Switzerland
Tel +41 44 382 18 50 | Fax +41 44 383 1858

GRAFFITI www.graffiti.com.tr
Ethemefendi Cad No:8/3 Babacan Apt
Erenkoy, Istanbul 34718, Turkey
Tel +90 216 302 3022 | Fax +90 216 302 0790

Grafik www.grafik.com
1199 North Fairfax Street, Suite 700
Alexandria, VA 20009, United States
Tel 703 299 4500 | Fax 703 299 5999

h george design www.hgeorgedesign.com
152 Madison Avenue, 24th Floor
New York, NY 10016, United States
Tel 212 696 0177 | Fax 212 696 0422

Hanson Dodge Creative
www.hansondodge.com
220 E. Buffalo Street
Milwaukee, WI 53202, United States
Tel 414 270 8368 | Fax 414 347 0493

HKLM Exchange www.hklm.co.za
Building B, 4 Kikuyu Road Sunninghill
Johannesburg, Gauteng 2157, South Africa
Tel +27114616600 | Fax +27114616606

housemouse www.housemouse.com.au
Level 1, 141 Flinders Lane
Melbourne, Victoria 3000, Australia
Tel +61 3 9650 6866 | Fax +61 3 9650 4966

Howry Design Associates www.howry.com
354 Pine Street, 6th Floor
San Francisco, CA 94104, United States
Tel 415 516 4088 | Fax 415 433 0816

häfelinger+wagner design www.hwdesign.de
Türkenstraße 55-57, München 80799, Germany
Tel +0049 89 20 25 750 | Fax +0049 89 20 23 9696

IE Design + Communications www.iedesign.com
422 Pacific Coast Highway
Hermosa Beach, CA 90254, United States
Tel 310 376 9600 | Fax 310 376 9604

insight creative www.insightcreative.net
Level 1, Old Safrana House, Britmart Precinct,
14 Customs Street East, PO Box 91 576,
Auckland, New Zealand
Tel +0064 9 919 6000 | Fax +0064 9 919 6001

John Madere Photography www.johnmadere.com
303 Park Avenue South, Suite 1083,
New York, NY 10010-3657, United States
Tel 212 966 4136

Kathryn Shagas Design www.kshagasdesign.com
1812 Miller Road, Hunt Valley, MD 21030,
United States | Tel 410 429 0429 | Fax 410 584 9102

KMS TEAM www.kms-team.com
Toelzer Strasse 2c, Munich 81379, Germany
Tel +49 89 490 411 0 | Fax +49 89 490 411 109

Kolegram www.kolegram.com
37 St-Joseph Boulevard
Gatineau, Quebec J8Y3V8, Canada
Tel 819 777 5538 | Fax 819 777 8525

Kym Abrams Design www.kad.com
213 W Institute Place, Suite 608
Chicago, IL 60610, United States
Tel 312 654 1005 | Fax 213 654 0665

Larsen www.larsen.com
7101 York Avenue South, Suite 120
Minneapolis, MN 55435, United States
Tel 952 835 2271 | Fax 952 921 3368

LOWERCASE INC www.lowercaseinc.com
213 West Institute Place, Suite 311
Chicago, IL 60610, United States
Tel 312 247 0652 | Fax 312 274 0659

Mangos www.mangosinc.com
10 Great Valley Parkway, Malvern, PA 19355
United States | Tel 610 296 2555

Mark Hanauer Photography
www.markhanauer.com
2228 21st Street, Santa Monica, CA 90405,
United States | Tel 310 392 0710 | Fax 310 392 8320

Meta4 Design www.meta4design.com
311 W. Superior Street, Suite 504
Chicago, IL 60654, United States
Tel 312 337 4674 | Fax 312 337 3687

Methodologie www.methodologie.com
720 Third Ave, Suite 800
Seattle, WA 98104-1870, United States
Tel 206 623 1044 | Fax 206 625 0154

Mind Design www.minddesign.info
James Cookstraat 46-3,
Amsterdam 1056 SC, Netherlands
Tel +31 0 6 15 43 66 96

Nesnadny + Schwartz www.nsideas.com
10803 Magnolia Drive
Cleveland, OH 44106, United States
Tel 216 791 7721

O'Leary and Partners
www.olearyandpartners.com
5000 Birch Street, Suite 1000
Newport Beach, CA 92660, United States
Tel 949 833 8006 | Fax 949 833 9155

Paprika www.paprika.com
400, Laurier West #610
Montréal (Québec) H2V 2K7, Canada
Tel 514 276 6000 | Fax 514 276 6100

Pentagram, New York www.pentagram.com
204 Fifth Avenue, New York, NY 10010,
United States | Tel 212 802 0225 | Fax 212 532 0181

Pentagram, San Francisco www.pentagram.com
387 Tehama Street
San Francisco, CA 94103, United States
Tel 415 896 0499 | Fax 415 896 0555

Pentagram Design Ltd., Berlin
www.pentagram.com
Leibnizstrasse 60, Berlin 10629, Germany
Tel +49 30 27 87 610 | Fax +49 30 27 87 61 10

pivot design, inc. www.pivotdesign.com
230 W. Huron, 4th Floor
Chicago, IL 60610, United States
Tel 312 87 7707 | Fax 312 787 7737

Porcaro Communications
www.porcarocommunications.com
504-221 West Esplanade
North Vancouver, British Columbia V7M 3J3,
Canada | Tel 604 982 4844 | Fax 604 986 8166

Posten Norge AS www.posten.no
Konsernstaber, Fakturamotak
Mo i Rana 8634, Norway | Tel +4795007672

Q-Plus Design Pte Ltd www.qplus.com.sg
43A Tanjong Pagar Road, 088464, Singapore
Tel +656 227 3064 | Fax +656 227 3405

Ramp Creative+Design www.rampcreative.com
411 S. Main Street, Suite 615 | Los Angeles, CA
90014, United States | Tel 213 623 7267

RBMM www.rbmm.com
8200 Southwestern Boulevard #601
Dallas, TX 75206, United States
Tel 214 987 6500 | Fax 214 987 3662

Rethink www.rethinkcommunications.com
Suite 700-470, Granville Street
Vancouver, British Columbia V6C 1V5, Canada
Tel 604 685 8911 | Fax 604 685 9004

Rovillo + Reitmayer www.rovilloreitmayer.com
5217 McKinney Avenue, Suite 203
Dallas, TX 75205, United States
Tel 214 526 6132 | Fax 214 526 6145

SamataMason www.samatamason.com
101 South First Street
Dundee, IL 60118, United States
Tel 847 428 8600 | Fax 847 428 6564

Savage www.savagebrands.com
4203 Yoakum Boulevard, Fourth Floor
Houston, TX 77006, United States
Tel 713 522 1555 | Fax 713 522 1582

STUDIO INTERNATIONAL
www.studio-international.com
Buconjiceva 43, Zagreb HR-10 000
Croatia (local Name: Hrvatska)
Tel +385 1 37 40 404 | Fax +385 1 37 08 320

Sullivan www.sullivannyc.com
645 Madison Avenue
New York, NY 10022, United States
Tel 212 888 2881 | Fax 212 888 2766

ThinkDesign Group www.thinkdg.com
514 North Third Street, Suite 201
Minneapolis, MN 55401, United States
Tel 612 338 3226 | Fax 612 338 3452

Visual Arts Press, Ltd.
www.schoolofvisualarts.edu/
publishing/index.jsp?sid0=81&sid1=82
220 East 23 Street, Suite 311
New York, NY 10010, United States
Tel 212 592 2380 | Fax 212 696 0552

VSA Partners, Inc www.vsapartners.com
600 W. Chicago Avenue, Suite 250
Chicago, IL 60605, United States
Tel 312 427 6413

WAX www.waxpartnership.com
320 333 24th Avenue SW
Calgary, Alberta T2T 0J5, Canada
Tel 403 262 9323 | Fax 403 262 9399

Weymouth Design
www.weymouthdesign.com
332 Congress Street, Sixth Floor
Boston, MA 02210, United States
Tel 617 259 1442 | Fax 617 451 6233

Visit the new www.**graph**is.com